Studies in Modern Capitalism · Études sur le capitalisme moderne

Past and Present Publications

East-Central Europe in transition
From the fourteenth to the seventeenth century

D0081872

Studies in modern capitalism · Études sur le capitalisme moderne

Editorial board · Comité de rédaction

Maurice Aymard, Maison des Sciences de l'Homme, Paris
Jacques Revel, École des Hautes Études en Sciences Sociales, Paris
Immanuel Wallerstein, Fernand Braudel Center for the Study of Economies,
Historical Systems, and Civilizations, Binghamton, New York

This series is devoted to an attempt to comprehend capitalism as a world-system. It
will include monographs, collections of essays and colloquia around specific themes,
written by historians and social scientists united by a common concern for the study
of large-scale long-term social structure and social change.
　　The series is a joint enterprise of the Maison des Sciences de l'Homme in Paris
and the Fernand Braudel Center for the Study of Economies, Historical Systems,
and Civilizations at the State University of New York at Binghamton.

Other books in the series

Maurice Aymard (ed.): *Dutch capitalism and world capitalism/Capitalisme hollandais et
　　capitalisme mondial*
Iván T. Berend, György Ránki: *The European periphery and industrialization, 1780–1914*
Pierre Bourdieu: *Algeria 1960*
Andre Gunder Frank: *Mexican agriculture 1521–1630: transformation of the mode of
　　production*
Folker Fröbel, Jürgen Heinrichs, Otto Kreye: *The new international division of labour:
　　structural unemployment in industrialized countries and industrialization in developing
　　countries*
Caglar Keyder: *The definition of a peripheral economy: Turkey 1923–1929*
Peter Kriedte, Hans Medick, Jürgen Schlumbohm: *Industrialization before
　　industrialization: rural industry in the genesis of capitalism*
Bruce McGowan: *Economic life in Ottoman Europe: taxation, trade and the struggle for the
　　land, 1660–1800*
Ernest Mandel: *Long waves of capitalist development: the Marxist interpretation*
Michel Morineau: *Ces incroyables gazettes et fabuleux métaux: les retours des trésors
　　américains, d'après les gazettes hollandaises (16e–18e siècles)*
Henri H. Stahl: *Traditional Romanian village communities: the transition from the communal
　　to the capitalist mode of production in the Danube region*
Immanuel Wallerstein: *The capitalist world-economy: essays*
Immanuel Wallerstein: *The politics of the world-economy: the states, the movements and the
　　civilizations*

This book is also published in association with and as part of Past and Present
Publications, which comprise books similar in character to the articles in the journal
Past and Present. Whether the volumes in the series are collections of essays – some
previously published, others new studies – or monographs, they encompass a wide
variety of scholarly and original works primarily concerned with social, economic
and cultural changes and their causes and consequences. They will appeal to both
specialists and non-specialists and will endeavour to communicate the results of
historical and allied research in readable and lively form. This new series continues
and expands in its aims the volumes previously published elsewhere.

For a list of titles in Past and Present Publications, see end of book.

East-Central Europe in transition

From the fourteenth to the seventeenth century

Edited by

ANTONI MĄCZAK, HENRYK SAMSONOWICZ
and PETER BURKE

RETIRED

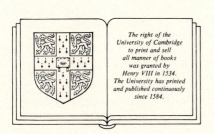

The right of the
University of Cambridge
to print and sell
all manner of books
was granted by
Henry VIII in 1534.
The University has printed
and published continuously
since 1584.

Cambridge University Press

Cambridge

London   New York   New Rochelle   Melbourne   Sydney

& Éditions de la Maison des Sciences de l'Homme

Paris

CARLYLE CAMPBELL LIBRARY
MEREDITH COLLEGE

943
Ea 7

Published by the Press Syndicate of the University of Cambridge
The Pitt Building, Trumpington Street, Cambridge CB2 1RP
32 East 57th Street, New York, NY 10022, USA
10 Stamford Road, Oakleigh, Melbourne 3166, Australia
and
Éditions de la Maison des Sciences de l'Homme
54 Boulevard Raspail, 75270 Paris Cedex 06

© Maison des Sciences de l'Homme and Cambridge University Press 1985

First published 1985

Printed in Great Britain by the University Press, Cambridge

This book is published as part of the joint publishing agreement established in 1977 between the Fondation de la Maison des Sciences de l'Homme and the Press Syndicate of the University of Cambridge. Titles published under this arrangement may appear in any European language or, in the case of volumes of collected essays, in several languages.

New books will apear either as individual titles or in one of the series which the Maison des Sciences de l'Homme and the Cambridge University Press have jointly agreed to publish. All books published jointly by the Maison des Sciences de l'Homme and the Cambridge University Press will be distributed by the Press throughout the world.

Library of Congress catalogue card number: 84-17039

British Library cataloguing in publication data

East-Central Europe in transition: from the fourteenth to the seventeenth century. – (Past and present publications) – (Studies in modern capitalism = Études sur le capitalisme moderne ISSN 0144-2333)
1. Central Europe – History
I. Mączak, Antoni   II. Samsonowicz, Henryk
III. Burke, Peter   IV. Series   V. Series
943   D104

ISBN 0 521 25792 1
ISBN 2 7351 0083 9   (France only)

UP

Contents

v

145307

Illustrations

Introduction: A note on the historiography of East-Central Europe

These studies of early modern Europe have two distinctive features which may require some comment. They are concerned with a region called East-Central Europe and they are written by Polish and Hungarian historians.

The concept of 'East-Central Europe' has established itself in recent years in German (Ostmitteleuropa), Hungarian (Közep-Kelet Europa), Polish, English and other languages, as is testified by the titles of some historical monographs and historical journals published in the last few years.[1] It is not used in exactly the same way by everyone. The western frontier of the region is generally considered to be the River Elbe, while its eastern frontier falls short of Muscovy (if not the USSR). For the editors of the journal *East Central Europe*, it is the area 'presently comprising' Poland, Czechoslovakia, Hungary and the German Democratic Republic, while 'historically' it also includes Estonia, Latvia and Lithuania. For the Hungarian economic historians István Berend and György Ránki, on the other hand, the region also extends south to include the Balkans (but not Greece). Greece is included in another recent study of 'East-Central Europe', but in this case East Germany is omitted.[2] In the present volume, however, the term refers primarily to the three kingdoms of Bohemia, Hungary and Poland.

The region clearly resists attempts at a simple and unequivocal definition. At the same time, there may be said to be a need for the concept 'East-Central Europe' on the grounds that it gets us away from the simple dichotomy between 'Western' and 'Eastern' Europe.

At first sight, even this dichotomy may seem to have much to recommend it. Western Europe has been densely populated since the Middle Ages, while in Eastern Europe the population has been relatively sparse. In Western Europe, Romance and Germanic languages are spoken; in Eastern Europe, Slav languages are dominant. In Eastern Europe the Orthodox Church has long been an important cultural presence. In early modern Europe west of the river Elbe, the export of manufactured articles was increasing, towns were growing, while the peasants were either becoming prosperous smallholders or

1

being reduced to the status of landless labourers. In Eastern Europe, on the other hand, exports were virtually confined to food and raw materials, the towns were in decline, and the peasants were being turned into serfs. For these and other reasons, Western historians have tended to see Eastern Europe not just as different from but even as the inverse of the West.

This contrast between 'Us' and 'Them' is in fact too facile, and the value of the concept of 'East-Central Europe' is primarily that it shatters this dichotomy. It expresses an indigenous point of view, with which anyone who has travelled in Czechoslovakia, Hungary or Poland will be familiar: the sense of living between East and West, or between Russia and Germany, or, in early modern times, between Turks and Habsburgs. It reminds us, as much of this volume will emphasise, of the variations between the different parts of Europe east of the Elbe. Economic and social differences: population density, for example, was considerably greater in Bohemia and in Poland than it was in Russia, or, for that matter, in Scandinavia. Political differences: the power of the elected kings of Poland after 1572 was considerably less than that of, say, the tsar of Russia (even if, as Professor Wyczański argues below, the king of Poland was not as weak as historians have been in the habit of assuming). Cultural differences: the Renaissance made relatively little impact on Russia and the Balkans, while, as Professor Białostocki has shown in this volume and elsewhere, Hungary, Poland and Bohemia all participated actively in that movement. A similar point could be made about the Reformation. Protestantism in various forms was a serious force in Bohemia (where the land of Jan Hus was prepared for it), Poland and Hungary, as it was not in South-East Europe or in Russia.[3] So many reasons for East-Central Europeans to share a sense of identity and to contrast themselves with the 'East'. So many reasons for considering the history of all three kingdoms together in this volume.

Although some of the essays are concerned with political or with cultural history, the emphasis of this collection is on the economic and social history of East-Central Europe. The central problem is that of the place of this region in the general transition from feudalism to capitalism. Such an emphasis reflects the dominance of economic and social approaches to the past among historians currently working in Czechoslovakia, Hungary and Poland (Czech and Slovak historians are unfortunately unrepresented in this volume, but only because those who were invited turned out to be unable to participate).

It is generally assumed in the West that in East-Central Europe an interest in economic and social history is no older than the establishment of regimes professing Marxist principles after the Second World War. In fact, the history of economic and social history goes back considerably further in these parts.

Like Western Europe, East-Central Europe had its medieval chroniclers, such as Jan Długosz and János Thuróczy; its humanist historians, Italian (like Antonio Bonfini, who worked for King Matthias Corvinus), or indigenous (like

Marcin Kromer in Poland or Miklós Istvánffy in Hungary). Like Western Europe, it had its eighteenth-century antiquaries, such as Gelasius Dobner and Matthias Bél. Bél, a Slovak who studied at Halle and wrote, in Latin, on the history of Hungarian agriculture and serfdom (the mixture of languages and cultures was not untypical of the region and the period), might be described as the first economic and social historian of East-Central Europe, provided that we use the terms 'economic' and 'social' in a sufficiently vague, unspecialised sense.[4]

The romantic nationalist historians of the first half of the nineteenth century were also concerned with economic and social history in the sense that they tried to write the history of the people rather than the history of the state. The Poles, for example, had Joachim Lelewel (1786–1861), an intellectual in politics who was one of the leaders of the revolt against Russian domination in 1830, and went into exile, in France and Belgium, after its failure. His *History of Poland* found room for such economic and social topics as the spread of glass windows in the fifteenth century and the decline of industry in the seventeenth.[5] The Czechs had František Palacký (1798–1876), who collected folksongs and took part in politics before writing his famous *History of the Czech People*.[6] During the Revolution of 1848, he was invited to the Frankfurt Parliament and also offered the post of minister of education, but declined both invitations.[7] The Hungarians had Mihály Horváth (1809–78), who was a Catholic bishop and, briefly, minister for cults, before fleeing the country after the suppression of the 1848 revolution. Besides his *History of the Hungarian People*, he wrote a monograph on the development of trade and industry in Hungary.[8]

In the later nineteenth century, despite the dominance of narrative political history on the Ranke model, based on the official documents which were being published in one massive series of *Monumenta Historica* after another, economic and social history remained a minority interest. Some economic documents were published, such as the series on *Poland in the Sixteenth Century* which appeared, from 1883 onwards, under the editorship of the historian–ethnographer Jabłonowski and the historian–archivist Pawiński.[9] In 1894, a *Hungarian Economic History Review* was founded by Károly Tagányi (1858–1924), whose special interest was communal landholding. The journal lasted for only twelve years, but it provided a forum for some important work, notably that by Acsády, Takáts and Kováts.[10] Ignac Acsády (1845–1906) specialised in economic and social history and wrote monographs on both the nobility and the serfs in Hungary. Sándor Takáts (1860–1932) worked on the social history of Hungary under the Turks, while Ferenc Kováts (1873–1956) concentrated on the history of Hungarian towns in the Middle Ages, and held the first chair of economic history in a Hungarian university, the Technical University of Budapest.[11]

The early twentieth century was a time when intellectuals in East-Central Europe, as in Russia and parts of the West, were taking an intense interest in agrarian questions. The Polish writer Stanisław Reymont's famous novel *Peasants* was published between 1902 and 1909. The Hungarian populists flourished a little later; the classic peasant study by the poet Gyula Illyes, *People of the Puszta*, goes back to 1936. As in the case of R. H. Tawney's *Agrarian Problem in the Sixteenth Century*, which was also published at this time, in 1912, current debates stimulated historical research into agrarian questions, and help explain the rise of economic history, especially in Poland. In 1909, Franciszek Bujak was appointed to the first chair of economic history in Poland. In 1914 appeared Ignacy Baranowski's well-known study, *The Countryside and the Manor*.[12] Jan Rutkowski, the most distinguished Polish economic historian of the first half of the twentieth century, was also at work before the First World War. He got his chair at Poznań in 1921 and published in 1927 an important study of the *Agrarian System of Eighteenth-Century Poland*.[13] A sign of the growing success of the subject was the foundation, in 1931, by Bujak and Rutkowski, of a specialist journal, *Annals of Economic and Social History*.

In Czechoslovakia, this was a time when political historians dominated the profession, though local studies in agrarian history were published. The rise of economic history took place after the war, with the work of Klíma, Míka, Petráň and others. Klíma's doctoral thesis at the Charles University, Prague, was in fact supervised by two cultural historians, Chalaupecký and Odložilík.[14] In Hungary, by contrast, several different approaches to what we now call economic and social history were practised between the wars. Besides the surviving members of the *Economic History Review* group, already mentioned, there was Sándor Dománovszky (1877–1955), who held the chair of the 'history of civilisation' at the University of Budapest from 1912 to 1948 and combined interests in cultural and agricultural history. Some of his pupils are still teaching in Hungary today. There was also an 'ethno-historical' group, led by Elemér Mályusz (born 1898), which was concerned with the history of ordinary people, with local history and with ethnic Hungarians beyond the frontiers established in 1919, frontiers which the Hungarians found impossible to accept.[15]

Today, the economic and social historians of East-Central Europe still draw strength from these traditions. Rutkowski and Bujak died soon after the Second World War, in 1949 and 1953 respectively, but by this time they had trained a new generation, including Jerzy Topolski and Marian Małowist, contributors to this volume. To Western European eyes the methods and assumptions of their East-Central European colleagues may appear to be uniform, but a closer examination will reveal both individual and regional variations (such as those between the Poznań, Warsaw and Cracow schools in Poland); considerable interest in the French historians associated with *Annales* (with whom some Polish and Hungarian historians have studied); and lively debates on questions of method, notably the controversy which followed the publication, in 1962, of Witold Kula's brilliant essay *The Economic Theory of the Feudal System*.[16]

Western European readers should find the essays which appear below to be of interest not only for the information they provide – much of it previously inaccessible to anyone unable to read Czech, Hungarian and Polish – but also for the different methods and approaches of their authors.

I should like to thank János Bak, of the University of British Columbia, and Mikuláš Teich, of Robinson College Cambridge, together with a number of historians resident in East-Central Europe, for their help in the preparation of this note.

Editorial note: The volume editors have generally accepted the form of proper names chosen by individual authors.

1 ❧ Feudalism and capitalism: a balance of changes in East-Central Europe

HENRYK SAMSONOWICZ and ANTONI MĄCZAK

What is East-Central Europe? What are its borders? And, above all, how is this concept useful for a historian? The answer to these questions will differ depending not only on specialised research interests but also on the geographical scope. By analysing the territorial range associated with the concept of Central Europe by French, German or Polish historians and by studying the preference shown for either a dichotomic division into East and West or for more complicated divisions, one can also become acquainted with contemporary systems of political and cultural values. The problem of the usefulness of those geographic concepts for examining the past, however, remains.

We believe that dichotomic divisions into West–East as well as centre–periphery oversimplify many historical problems. Poland, Lithuania, Bohemia and Hungary constituted an ensemble of similar tendencies in economic development. Undoubtedly, they consisted of various zones and regions. An analysis of dominant relations in the border areas makes it possible to become better acquainted with the mechanisms of inter-zone connections, while the distinctiveness of a given region as regards economy, politics, culture, etc. is essential to the characterisation of a given period in Europe.[1]

In historical works the term 'Jagiellonian Europe' is frequently used. It undoubtedly includes Lithuania together with its Ruthenian acquisitions, Poland, Bohemia and Hungary from the western Carpathians up to the Dalmatian coast. This is an area difficult to define but, after all, one which constitutes a separate object of historical research. The term 'East-Central Europe' is useful for political history from the beginning of the fifteenth century up to the sixteenth century and for examining the domination of the Jagiellonian dynasty in those countries. This part of Europe was also a cultural unit in the entire process of the development of European culture; it constituted an area incorporated into the Latin world, outside the Ottonian *limes*. From the tenth to the thirteenth century, lands culturally and politically colonised by Western Europe became the cradle of a number of states. Are economic and social contents also concealed here? It can be argued that from the

6

economic point of view these countries were distinctive, between the fourteenth and the sixteenth century, in three ways: their economic backwardness, their incorporation into international trade (beginning in the thirteenth century) as suppliers of raw materials, and favourable terms of trade which led to an acceleration of economic development. An analysis of natural conditions, demography, the structure of property and industrial relations points to this. The same can be said about the analysis of market relations and investment trends. Economic backwardness was accompanied by a backwardness, or perhaps rather a distinctiveness, in the field of social relations. It was also these two factors which characterised the specificity of the four countries under discussion.

By no means were they uniform. Originally, Polish society was the most backward, furthest away from the main centres of both Eastern and Western civilisations. The most powerful demographic, economic and political centres lay to the south of the Carpathian–Sudeten range. This state of affairs changed in the fifteenth century as a result of the Hussite revolution, Turkish expansion into the Balkans and Hungary, and the Polish–Lithuanian Union with its political and social consequences. At the end of the fourteenth century over a half of the inhabitants of these countries was to be found in Bohemia and Hungary, yet only a hundred years later 60 per cent lived in Silesia, Poland, Pomerania and part of Ruthenia and Lithuania.

The countries of East-Central Europe were not uniform geographically either. The north consists of a belt of great post-glacial valleys, in places varied by moraine elevations which in the period under discussion were partly covered by forests and partly cultivated. The south – steppes in the case of the Hungarian plain – is crossed by the ranges of the Carpathians, the Sudeten mountains, Rudawy (Erzgebirge) and Somlo. These areas, convenient for sheep raising, were also a reserve for land cultivation which was utilised for colonisation during the period of demographic increase. Moreover, the deposits of metals such as gold, silver, zinc, copper and lead were richer than anywhere else in Europe. The region comprised, approximately, the Bohemian basin and the area within the Carpathian range enclosed by the Danube and the Drava. Silesia, Little Poland (southern Poland) and at times Moldavia together with Podolia were very closely connected with the Carpathian economy.

Different natural conditions and different stages of development led to the emergence of a variety of economic zones. In the area under examination one can distinguish five such zones: the Baltic zone, which exported grain, timber, furs and, in the case of Sweden, metal ore; the Russian, which supplied furs; the Carpathian–Sudeten, which exported metal ores; the Black Sea with its cattle; and the Balkan which exported metal ores and grain. Of course, other products also played their part – flax, hemp, hides, wool and dyestuffs – but the most important were those first mentioned. These five zones made up a varied region but one characterised by certain common traits, e.g., the domination of raw material and foodstuff exports indispensable for Western Europe, produced and mined by primitive methods which favoured, above all, the landowners: the state, the Church and the gentry.[2] Not only market relations but also socio-political relations between the countryside and the towns could have become established only in a specific way. In Eastern Europe towns developed as intermediaries and, with the cooperation of ethnically foreign entrepreneurs, they controlled the export of raw materials. Here we find Riga, Gdańsk and Wrocław and, from the second half of the fifteenth century, Leipzig, Augsburg and Dubrovnik as well.

The different regions which make up East-Central Europe, so varied politically, ethnically and in religion, were linked not only by common natural resources, opportunities for agriculture and animal husbandry but also by their location practically in the centre of the European continent; the great Baltic lowlands, the Black Sea steppes and the Carpathian mountains bordered on the most important countries along the Naples–London axis.[3]

Let us turn to demography. In the fourteenth century there were three population zones in Europe.[4] The first was an area of a then great population density of more than 20 persons per sq km. It included Italy, western Germany, northern and part of south-eastern France, the Netherlands, England and perhaps southern Germany, i.e., northern Bavaria and Swabia. It also embraced a longitudinal strip, interrupted by the Apennines and the Alps, reaching from Naples and Palermo to Antwerp, Amsterdam and London. On both sides of this area lay lands with a population density of from 8 to approximately 15 inhabitants per sq km. To the west there was southern France, Spain, Portugal – to the east, Denmark, Brandenburg, Mecklenburg, Poland, Bohemia and finally the Turkish possessions in the Balkans. All these had approximately 10 inhabitants per sq km at the beginning of the sixteenth century. There was also Hungary, with 8 inhabitants per sq km. The third range included countries of the lowest demographic density (up to 2 persons per sq km) – Norway, Sweden, Finland, Russia and Lithuania. Thus, East-Central Europe found itself in both the second and in the third range. Regardless of the existence of dense and unequally distributed settlements it seems that those three zones form the necessary starting point for reflections about economic potential, especially considering that in the individual countries development tendencies varied during the course of the centuries under discussion.

Our sources make it clear that this state of affairs went back to the fourteenth century, a period of a great economic crisis in the developed countries. The decline of the income of the feudal class as well as the accompanying political, demographic and social perturbations led to a transfer of estates and people into areas less developed and as a result less affected by the crisis. This process decreased the distance dividing both parts of Europe; on the one hand, it hampered the development of the more prosperous countries and, on the other

Table 1.1. *Growth rates in certain countries from 1300 to 1550 (year 1300 = 100)*[5]

Year	Europe	Italy	England	Germany	France	Russia	Norway	Poland
1300	100	100	100	100	100	100	100	100
1350	70	86	68	63	64	72	50	109
1450	82	80	68	100	82	90	50	181
1500	94	90	81	104	105	100	75	227
1550	106	105	103	116	123	118	75	281

hand, it accelerated the development of the backward countries. During the fourteenth century, attempts at finding a solution to the crisis drew East-Central Europe into the economy of the entire continent.

The results of this situation were extremely significant. The region under discussion became attractive to the developed countries experiencing a crisis of feudal incomes. It created opportunities for favourable capital investment and made possible social advancement for enterprising newcomers. Its raw material resources were a factor which determined the development of industry during the early modern period.

Beginning with the fifteenth century, the economy of all the countries in Eastern Europe (with the possible exception of a part of the Turkish possessions) began to turn towards commodity production, subjugating to this aim the financing of a majority of the investments. The beginnings of the economic division in Europe are connected with an industrial production aimed at a broader circle of buyers. The consequence of this trend was a struggle for new markets and for access to an extensive raw materials supply. The development of European trade, beginning with the close of the fourteenth century, led to specialisation in the production of the different regions which was in turn connected with an improvement in the forms of exchange (money, companies, banks, credit, communications). As a result of these changes, discussed by many historians, the economic integration of the European continent grew.[6] Production in various countries began to be closely dependent upon the supplies of raw materials or semi-products. The early stages of capitalism as it developed in the West demanded large supplies which could be guaranteed by the various areas of Eastern Europe.

This situation created the rapid growth rate so characteristic of East-Central Europe. Table 1.1 suggests comparative rates based on hypothetical or approximate data. A comparison of various parts of Europe immediately shows differences in urban relations. Works on the subject classify medieval towns according to the number of inhabitants, economic or administrative functions, and distinguish from four to seven groups.[7] For East-Central Europe probably five such groups can be identified. Two of the largest towns at the end of the fifteenth century – Prague and Gdańsk, which had over 30,000 inhabitants –

belonged to the great emporia of the continent, the joint number of which did not exceed twenty. Towns in the second category – above 10,000 inhabitants – were not very numerous in the East. Compared to the rest of Europe, they made up only 12 to 16 per cent of all urban centres. On the other hand, regional market centres were already more numerous (approximately 200 in the region examined by us), and approximately 2,000 towns belonged to the last two groups in which the average population did not exceed 1,000 inhabitants. Generally speaking, East-Central Europe was much more rural than the West. In addition, only some of the regions which maintained liveliest contacts with the West, i.e., Bohemia in the fourteenth and a part of Royal Prussia in the fifteenth and sixteenth centuries, had a professional structure similar to that of the Rhineland or Brabant. The remaining regions were inhabited overwhelmingly by a population which supported itself on agriculture and animal husbandry. This does not indicate the dominance of a natural economy. It was precisely in the fourteenth century that varied and broad social groups were first able to join the market economy. This fact was of considerable economic significance and it influenced the emergence of open attitudes towards new opportunities and new trends of civilisation, especially in the fifteenth century.

In summing up these reflections one can say that large-scale economic links between Central, Eastern and Western Europe appeared during the great crisis of the fourteenth century. Contacts made then led throughout the century towards an interdependence of economic development although this development went in opposite directions. The situation altered in the fifteenth century when development trends of both East and West Europe began to run a parallel course. The sixteenth century, or rather its second half, saw increasing disproportion, and the seventeenth century brought the decline of the Polish and Hungarian economy. These developments also made it possible to determine the eastern borderline of the entire region. It reached Russia, the whole of which found itself in the least populated part of Europe. Ruined by the Mongol invasions during the thirteenth century, Russia underwent a different development cycle, i.e., one of gradual economic growth from the close of the fourteenth century onwards, of increasing connections with the West from the second half of the fifteenth century and of an increasingly dynamic development in the sixteenth and seventeenth centuries. However, the development of this region was to a much greater degree autonomous. Even the introduction of harsh serfdom and serf labour occurred against a different background to that of the Polish–Lithuanian 'gentry Commonwealth' or Bohemia after the Thirty Years' War. This led to essential differences between the economy and society of Russia and of the area under discussion.

Transformations in East-Central Europe occurred during a period in which the beginnings of a world economy were being shaped.[8] Hungarian and Ukrainian oxen, Polish and Bohemian grain, Lithuanian furs, and later copper, lead, timber, hops, honey, wax and dyestuffs were products of interest to producers and consumers in the Netherlands, the Rhineland, Westphalia, England and Spain. As a result, the pressure of demand from the developed countries moulded economic relations. It also shaped new forms of production processes and social relations as the world market expanded. In the fifteenth to sixteenth century, specialisation, one-sided as it was, was achieved both on individual gentry estates and in entire branches of production. Still more important, the social structure was changing. The so-called 'second serfdom' which emerged at that time east of the Elbe cannot be understood without analysing the social uniqueness of the region. For example, hamlets of a purely agrarian character were a typical phenomenon. They constituted an extremely important link in both local and foreign trade as markets or as stages upon the great trade routes which cut across Europe. They were, however, generally dependent upon the landowners. Indispensable agrarian products were often obtained by their inhabitants through their own production.[9] These hamlets remained the most characteristic element in the social landscape of East-Central Europe. This state of affairs influenced both the economic structure and socio-political relations in what is known as the 'Estates Monarchy'.

The concept of the estates presupposes both legal and social relations; these can be clearly perceived in Bohemia from the beginning of the Luxembourg dynasty (1310) but not in fifteenth-century Poland. In the latter case, the noble estate began to be defined more precisely only at the turn of the Middle Ages. Membership of it meant economic privileges and political influence, especially at the local level. Following Western models, there were increasingly frequent moves to define other estates – burgher and peasant – although these remained rather fluid, and a variety of legal groups coexisted in the fourteenth and in the first three-quarters of the fifteenth century.

It is, however, safe to assert that the disintegration of the system of ducal (patrimonial) law did not eliminate a situation in which there existed many communities acting on legal or customary principles which regulated duties towards the state and civil as well as criminal jurisdiction. Colonisation based on German law, Ruthenian law (which was subject to various changes) and Valachian and Armenian laws multiplied norms of conduct. Group law did not correspond to the Western system, nor did concepts such as 'burgher' or 'peasant', even after the acceptance of the principles of German law. Not always and not everywhere were knights distinguished by their financial status or place of residence from the wealthier *hospites* of the German law, the heads of hamlets (*sculteti*), or perhaps even a part of the more prosperous rural population which originated from other servile groups. Court records suggest that in the fourteenth and fifteenth centuries the territorial community remained the basic unit in which family, property and territorial connections cut across older group laws. The dominant groups were composed of landowners, who were active not only in agriculture or animal husbandry but also in trade, artisan production and mining. A lack of divisions, or at least of sharp legal divisions, between particular feudal groups remained a characteristic trait. Society, especially the ruling groups, acted in an original way which changed only gradually and was without parallel in Western Europe. At the end of the fifteenth century, as a result of political and religious upheavals, there arose a system which one could call one of 'estates' had there existed representation of other legal groups than those of the gentry.

The close of the Middle Ages was a period of a particularly rapid economic development in East-Central Europe, based not only on favourable commercial situations but also on the very broad social basis of a population beginning to participate in market exchange. Not only did the burghers play a significant role but the gentry, both prosperous and middling, began to show interest in the market economy. The same is true of numerous groups of peasants as well as of landowners of various categories, categories which are not always clear to us today.[10] Independently of goods gained through the payment of feudal dues, the market carried products supplied by peasants and millers – whose number and importance clearly increased – by tavern keepers and the suburban population. Obviously, the gentry still dominated, and this was characteristic of the whole of Eastern Europe. A favourable economic situation in Poland made it possible for various groups of the population, still without precise definitions as estates, to participate in the economic boom.

In the second half of the fifteenth century and especially after the 1480s, a large demand for grain and the consolidation of the gentry estate began to change the entire situation. In Poland and Hungary many individuals played an active part in the economic changes in their own countries which, in turn, became a significant link in the chain of European trade. In Bohemia this process had already occurred a century earlier.

Certain regions of the West developed an industrial production aimed at the mass market and turned out many inexpensive goods of mediocre quality.[11] The need to find new markets led to an increase in production, thanks to the introduction of new methods and techniques into industry and trade (advanced forms of credit, banks and accounting).[12] For the first time growing specialisation enabled a more rapid adjustment to be made to the needs of the market. Such a specialisation was possible only in the conditions of an efficiently functioning exchange. The crisis of the fourteenth century and a search for ways of solving it led to the increasing economic integration of Europe.

Activities aimed at financing Carpathian mining investments, i.e., the construction and exploitation of silver, gold, iron, copper and lead mines, were conducted in an area delineated by Nuremberg, Milan, Venice and the Carpathians.[13] The development of Polish serf-labour estates became connected with the situation in the Netherlands, Spain and Portugal. The great expeditions organised by those countries also changed economic relations in Italy, Flanders and Germany. After 1480 an increasing quantity of cattle, furs and foodstuff was brought out of the East, and the import of Western cloth, spices and metal products also grew considerably. The balance of trade, at least with the West, became a favourable one for East-Central Europe for the next two hundred years.

The sixteenth century as a phase in the economic expansion of Europe initiated new problems for the East-Central regions. According to models proposed both in a highly generalised version by Stein Rokkan and in the detailed interpretation of Immanuel Wallerstein, these regions were peripheries or semi-peripheries.[14] What seems to be important is the fact that the intensification of contacts with the West increased; but there remains the question of the consequences of this intensification for both parts of the sub-continent.

In reference to the 'peripheral' area, one ought to say that it appears uniform only on an extreme macro-scale. Obviously, the historian who concentrates his attention on these lands notices greater differences between them than does his colleague who examines the whole of Europe synthetically; but there remains the unsolved and very important question of what the most appropriate scale in each case would be. For example, from the point of view of the Netherlands it is enough to say that they were connected in a special way with Poland and Lithuania, but the student of the latter two will notice enormous differences in the intensification of trade contacts between particular regions and the 'West' (a geographical concept which is all too frequently interpreted in an over general fashion). In order to understand the mechanism of sea and land exchange as well as the functioning of East-Central Europe as a whole, one ought to concentrate precisely on regional differences in the sixteenth and seventeenth centuries.

In the field of commercial exchange one should delve into the problems of export and import separately and also consider the social and ownership structure. Intensive grain export – a new phenomenon in the sixteenth century – was confined to areas which from this point of view were located particularly conveniently, i.e., those adjacent to navigable rivers and great estates which were able to organise cheap transport.[15] The same, to an even larger degree, is true of the rafting of timber and its by-products; woodlands were found mainly in the royal (grand-ducal) domains or the Church and magnate properties. For technical reasons a considerable part of the Baltic area was still unable to export. In these conditions it was not only possible but it even became the rule that while forests, mainly in the vast expanses of Ruthenia, were exploited only for the needs of the settlers, in the regions which already exported wood in the sixteenth century there was increasing deforestation together with all its consequences.

Although it would be difficult to speak of the technological progress of land transport during this period, the concentration of landed property expanded the exporting region. Thus, the opportunity created, although only for a part of the landowners and burghers, by the export of agricultural and woodland products transformed the general economic conditions and the entire socio-economic structure of the southern part of the Baltic area.

The mechanism of this phenomenon, according to the most likely hypothesis, was as follows.[16] Direct contact with the seaport furnished the supplier from the hinterland with a considerable premium in the forms both of a possibility for wholesale and of favourable prices; another premium consisted of the opportunity to acquire on the spot goods unobtainable further inland or available from merchants at much higher prices. Insufficiently examined credit relations make it impossible to verify the hypothesis that great ports were also attractive because of the supply of credit, unequalled further inland. At any rate, there is no doubt that in the fifteenth century numerous wholesale suppliers of grain, fibres and woodland products were already permanently linked by debt with their buyers in the ports. Under these circumstances, how is one to explain the agitated activity of the agents of the Gdańsk grain merchants who tried to capture contractors rafting goods along the Lower Vistula?[17] Such activity indicates that in the seventeenth century there still existed a rather broad margin of grain suppliers unhampered by debts.

The problem is important, among other reasons, because the gross income from export constituted practically the only source of money for areas exporting grain and woodland products. Since export was dominated, with the exception of Mazovia and Royal Prussia, by great landowners, a major part of the income fell into their hands. The Vistula toll registers of the sixteenth century suggest, for instance, that in the east of Little Poland two magnate families (the Firlejs and the Tarnowskis) had at their disposal practically all the incoming cash. Even if this historical source exaggerates, the scarcity of money during the lean years tipped the balance in favour of the wealthy and enabled them to buy up land from their neighbours who were involved in debts and other payments. We do not know, however, what part of the profits from exported commodities returned in the form of cash, what part was realised in kind or even whether the balance of the trade in Gdańsk v as positive for those magnates or not. On the other hand, even by buying in the port more than he sold, the great landowner was able to win a rapi profit in money by reselling his purchases to his neighbours back in f.e hinterland or by cooperating with the merchants.

The above-mentioned Vistula toll registers in Włocławek, extant for the period 1537–76, inform us only about goods transported by river from Gdańsk and Elbląg, i.e., heavy goods dominated basically by salt and herrings, with no textiles and few spices. Table 1.2 shows the relative increase in the transport of herrings and the division of the trade between merchant and gentry. The gentry was exempt from tolls on goods of its own production or imported for its own needs. In the sixteenth century this was interpreted relatively narrowly; in the following century the gentry, as a rule, transported commodities bought from peasants and neighbours toll-free.

Table 1.2. *The growth in the transport of herrings and the division of the trade*

Periods	Number of years	Growth index	Commodity percentage declared by		
			Merchants	Merchants transporting on gentry-owned ships	Gentry
1537–46	3	100*	92.4	2.7	4.9
1555–8	4	666	63.9	24.1	12.0
1560–9	4	1,564	65.4	15.3	19.3
1572–6	4	3,009	69.0	10.4	20.6

* This is 964.5 barrels; the commercial last equalled 12 barrels.

During the enormous, thirty-fold increase of the herring imports, the original dominance of the merchants receded in the third quarter of the century in favour of a certain stability, within the framework of which one-tenth to one-quarter of this product was transported thanks to the cooperation between the gentry and the burghers. Simultaneously, the scale of cargo *pro usu proprio* increased frequently up to 6 and in one case up to 20 lasts. Both the size of the cargo as well as the appearance of the same persons in a number of cases indicate that business was conducted by magnates and gentry to whom exemption from tolls promised an obvious profit.

This state of affairs continued during a period which did not leave behind similar source material. The considerably less precise Warsaw toll registers (1605–19) indicate that at the time 30 per cent of toll-free herrings were transported mainly to Little Poland and thus primarily by the gentry (exemptions were also enjoyed by certain merchants connected with the king). It is known from other sources that during the seventeenth century transport organised by great landowners for the gentry neighbours and merchants took on a particular importance. The owners of rafts and river boats who also had at their disposal a serf-labour force and qualified sailors as organisers of transport sometimes offered only transport and at other times entered into partnership arrangements, frequently by simply distributing goods imported from afar and in turn buying up grain. All this makes it possible to understand how an industrious landowner was able to make profit even at the time of a passive balance of transactions in Gdańsk–Elbląg. In the inland trade of countries closer to the sale markets, even coercion was unable to bring about such a large concentration of trade in the hands of the magnates.

The group of exporters from the port hinterland was socially and geographically limited but the consumption of goods imported from the West differed considerably – it was more uniform territorially, hierarchically and socially. In all the countries of East-Central Europe imported products constituted status symbols. This is true both of the more durable goods, particularly woollen cloth and silk (the latter came both across the Baltic and by land from Italy and the Orient), and of southern fruit, sugar and especially spices. Here there occurred a price pattern quite different from that in the West. While the prices for local foodstuffs were low, imported products were expensive and, as the English traveller Fynes Moryson noticed, it was sometimes the case that fish was cheaper than the spices used in preparing it.[18]

In woollens there became apparent a characteristic gradation of value in which local products also participated. Quality and price were determined by the place of origin. Flemish (and with time mainly Dutch) as well as English products enjoyed higher prestige than those from Bohemia or Moravia; Silesian and Polish cloth was even less valued. This is clearly shown by the registers and payment tariffs where, as a rule, sums of money were supplemented by a few pieces of cloth, linen or other textiles. On the whole, officials at the level of an estate administrator were entitled to foreign cloth, the manorial manager together with other state officials had to satisfy himself with Bohemian, Moravian or Silesian cloth, and Polish servants settled for local cloth. It was a rule that local cloth was considered to be the most lowly; better cloth was imported, of course. We are not counting the various *panni simplices* (coarse cloths) used for wrapping the more expensive ones, etc. It is significant, however, that in the sixteenth century the usage of imported wool was universal.[19]

One can see this as a symptom of the peripheral character of the economy of East-Central Europe. However, in determining this specific hierarchy of quality, price and prestige connected with the various origins of textiles, we are able to ascertain the gradual character of the phenomenon. The quality of products, as long as they are introduced more broadly onto the market and do not remain only luxury items, is one of the indices of the standard of living. This problem still calls for research and is only rarely posed by historians, but it is precisely the comparative approach which, by examining a number of regions of Europe, should bring us closer to its solution. Hence, the import of consumer articles can be regarded not only as competitive in relation to the local production but also as an expression of the social structure. Although the import of tools (Styrian sickles and scythes) is worthy of attention, it was exceeded by those products which in the importing regions were regarded as luxury items. The output of those textiles and spices (alongside other foreign goods) constituted a stimulus for participating in export even if only by increasing the market surplus of a landed estate; hence the popularity of great urban centres where international exchange took place and the output of goods was particularly broad. Two problems are connected with this – monetary circulation and the inner divisions of the region.

We do not know how monetary circulation changed in the course of the fifteenth and sixteenth centuries; on the one hand commodity circulation increased tremendously and new townships came into being, while on the other hand during the sixteenth century money rents to a significant degree gave way to labour services. Also the process of demographic growth itself must have influenced monetary circulation. However, this increase of circulation undoubtedly varied regionally, as the differences in labour wages and the prices of articles produced and sold locally indicate emphatically, although indirectly.[20]

Wages in Poland were highest in Royal Prussia in the region of Gdańsk, lower in Greater Poland and Little Poland and lowest in the centrally located Mazovia. Volhynia and Red Ruthenia, which in the second half of the sixteenth century were an area of intensive settlement expansion, had salaries higher than any other part of Poland with the exception of Prussia. In this respect Bohemia and Upper Hungary (Slovakia) seem to have outdistanced Poland rather significantly, as was also the case with Silesia. This may be seen both in the levels of prices and wages and in the standard of services, although we are still dealing with very fragmentary source material.

Metal-ore mining, which developed in certain regions of Silesia, Bohemia and Upper Hungary, cannot explain everything. There appear also other factors such as the degree of urbanisation and the spread of money rents in agriculture, since serf labour was a factor hampering money circulation. In this field one can note a significant difference between Poland and her southern neighbours which until now has been examined only slightly and still remains difficult to grasp quantitatively in source materials, although sixteenth- and seventeenth-century travellers found it obvious.

The inner divisions of East-Central Europe will be discussed below on a number of occasions in connection with agricultural production, animal husbandry and the natural environment. Also relevant, however, are international trade and industrial production.

The traditional division of Europe into two parts divided by the Elbe was somewhat disturbed during the period of economic growth in the sixteenth century. If we take serfdom and serf labour as the main criterion for the 'East', then we find Bohemia and the areas of extensive vine cultivation do not fit our model. However, if we were to stress the export of foodstuffs and raw materials from the East as contrasted to the import of industrial products, then the place of Silesia, Bohemia–Moravia and Greater Poland becomes problematic.

In these areas, as well as in Saxony and Lusatia, which we shall not take into consideration at present, there developed an intensive textile production. Linen cloth from Silesia, Saxony (the Electorate) and Bohemia was largely earmarked for export to the West and indirectly for the needs of the Atlantic trade. Sales were organised by Dutch and Upper German firms by developing the credit system in which cloth guilds became intermediaries. On the other hand, the cloth industry in this region, which by and large could be connected with the Upper Odra and Elbe as well as with the River Warta, was expanded to the East. Local textiles cheaper than Western ones were sold either locally or further to the East.[21]

If we were to look at Europe east of the Elbe in more detail, we would notice something like a small West within it. Woollen cloth, which seemed to be drawn in by the flow of industrial goods directed to the East mainly from Upper Germany and the Netherlands, was exported in the same direction and found a market in Lithuania and Muscovy, as well as in Little Poland and Mazovia, whence individual more significant centres also exported cloth. A similar commodity movement can also be noticed south of the Carpathians and towards the Black Sea – partly through Lvov and partly through Hungary. In relation to territories deprived of their own textile centres, Silesia, Greater Poland, Moravia and the like played the role of a sub-centre *sui generis*. The stream of grain flowing towards the North seemed to emphasise this inner boundary running through East-Central Europe.[22]

An additional emphasis is connected with the oxen trade. While the north-east supplied furs, wax, honey and other woodland products, the south-east (the Ukraine, Red Ruthenia, the Hungarian Plain) exported oxen. Within the economic macro-scale one can recognise this to be raw-materials export which passed through the hands of many middlemen and finally underwent improvement at the place of retail sale and consumption. Cattle, tired by the long journey, were fattened near large towns such as Leipzig, Cologne and Frankfurt am Main. It is significant that analogous phenomena can also be found in towns of the region under examination, i.e., Cracow, Prague, Wrocław and Gdańsk, which made use of trade routes and nearby cattle markets (particularly in the case of Wrocław) or (as was the case of Gdańsk) themselves constituted the final stage of the cattle routes.

It is quite difficult to find reliable figures for these transactions. The size of the turnover in oxen has recently been discussed in detail. The production and turnover of textiles remains, in the case of many regions, a true puzzle. The Polish customs registers from the 1580s, which no longer exist but have been published in summary form, make it possible to estimate the annual import of Silesian textiles at 100,000 pieces, Saxon, Bohemian and Moravian at 13,000, while approximately 20,000 pieces arrived by sea from the West.[23] This indicates the great role played by the inner division of East-Central Europe.

The sixteenth century linked together parts of Europe more strongly than ever before; how then did the seventeenth century influence the peripheries and the semi-peripheries? At this stage we should like to avoid involving ourselves in the lively theoretical discussion concerning the 'general crisis of the seventeenth century'. Wallerstein wrote that

...a particularly sober picture may be expected in the peripheral areas of the world-economy. They are the politically weakest areas. It is to be expected that core and semi-peripheral areas will seek to maintain their levels of production and employment at the expense of the peripheral areas. And yet the periphery cannot be dispensed with entirely for many reasons. For one thing, its capitalist cadres wish to remain in the world-economy; they struggle to remain there... For a third thing, the core continues to need *certain* of the products of the periphery...

For the peripheries the phase B of the economic cycle was a 'slowdown of activity, not a stoppage' while the obstructions which entrepreneurs came across and in many cases eliminated, were the reasons why 'the strong not only survived; they frequently thrived'. As a result 'a downturn in the world-economy occasions both involution and evolution, both a seeming decline in the monetarization of economic activity and the emergence of new enterprises ...both a decline in their specialized role in the world-economy and a deepening of it'.[24]

All this can be detected during the seventeenth century in the region under discussion, although among the numerous possible symptoms of a crisis there emerged quite different regional patterns, and the similarity of economic, social and political phenomena was at times rather limited. In the seventeenth century war raged everywhere. Before the crisis of the fourteenth century, the integration of Western and East-Central Europe had occurred mainly through migration and (later) through trade, but they were now brought into close union through political and military events.[25] War was practically endemic in Hungary just as in the Ukraine, threatened by the Crimean Tartars. One can see in this a symptom of the peripheral nature of those regions which were both at the very edge of Christendom (hence the idea of their country as the 'bulwark of Christendom', so significant for the world view of the Polish gentry) and peripheries of the European economic system, i.e., areas of extensive cattle breeding. However, in politics at the close of the sixteenth century, one of the capitals of East-Central Europe, Prague, became the seat of government of the Emperor Rudolf II and, although his brother and successor Matthias restored the former power of Vienna in 1618, the increasing political and religious conflicts were to make Prague more and more central.

At any rate, during the same period both Hungary and Poland were drawn into the conflicts of the rest of the continent. Because the intensification of these problems is impossible to measure, the rather loose periodisation proposed here must remain arbitrary. Up to the end of the sixteenth century the conflicts of Eastern Europe influenced the fate of the West to only a small degree. The defeat of the Teutonic Order in the Battle of Tannenberg (Grunwald 1410) closed only one of the numerous routes which Western knights followed seeking glory and booty. Similarly, the dynastic expansion of the Habsburgs from the Iberian Peninsula up to the Hungarian Plain integrated their opponents to only a slight degree. At the beginning of the sixteenth century attempts at cooperation between Sigismund I of Poland and Francis I of France became more marked; but Vienna found the overtures made by France towards the Ottoman Empire much more important and dangerous. Even in the second

half of that century the dispute concerning the Livonian heritage of the
Teutonic Order remained a local event of a limited geographical range,
although it managed to involve all the Baltic powers.[26]

It would be useful to contrast the Livonian conflict (1557–71) with the later
encounters of the same powers in the seventeenth century. In 1561 the grand
master Gotthard Kettler, threatened by Muscovy, decided to yield Livonia to
Sigismund Augustus, king of Poland and grand duke of Lithuania. Following
the secularisation of the Order, this territory became united with Lithuania
(1566), with the exception of a liege duchy intended for Kettler. Simultaneously,
Sweden, Denmark and Muscovy continued to exert pressure. The Livonian
War (1563–70) placed Sweden and Muscovy on the one side with Poland,
Lithuania, Denmark and Lübeck on the other; during the final year the Swedes
began to liquidate Polish privateers which tried to blockade the sailing routes
between the West and the port of Narva, controlled by the Russians. The
Szczecin Peace Treaty of 1570 ended this conflict on the basis of *uti possidetis*.
Western Europe was interested in its course and outcome in so far as it
influenced trade with Muscovy and thus with central Asia (in the case of
England) as well as the growing trade in bulk in Baltic commodities (England
and the Netherlands). However, interventions into Baltic problems at the time
were still only marginally important.

One could say that in the sixteenth century the political interest shown by
the West in the region under discussion rose whenever the problem of the Turk
appeared. In the endlessly conceived anti-Turkish plans, Hungary and Poland
were for geo-political reasons not to be ignored, and moreover it was precisely
they who initiated a united action against Istanbul. How realistic such action
was is quite another matter. If one were to exclude the Turkish factor, then
sixteenth-century East-Central Europe seems to have been submerged in a
peripheral state.

The Polish–Swedish conflict which followed the election of Sigismund Vasa
to the Polish throne (1587) also seemed to be only a local dynastic dispute.
However, soon afterwards the specific role of Sweden in Europe was to be felt.
As Perry Anderson has recently noticed, Swedish expansionism in the
seventeenth century stimulated a transition to absolutism (Prussia, Russia) and
struck a mighty blow to Poland, which then followed a different trend.[27] The
policy of Gustavus Adolphus, however, became in a broad sense a link between
events in Central and Northern Europe.

French, English and Dutch diplomats actively participated in negotiations
between Poland and Sweden in 1629 which led to an armistice which was to
enable Sweden to carry out an intervention in the empire. In turn, the material
basis for Sweden's action consisted of the armament investments of the
Walloon, Louis de Geer, which made it possible to realise the ingenious
organisational, strategic and tactical conceptions of Gustavus Adolphus. The
intensity and result of struggles at the mouth of the River Vistula or in Livonia

was now of direct importance for the West. Sixteenth-century Baltic trade also became the cause of diplomatic and military undertakings much more vigorous than in the preceding century. In the south, the anti-Habsburg activity of Gábor Bethlen was observed with care in Paris and the Hague, while the election of Frederick the Elector Palatine to the Bohemian throne aptly symbolises the political connections of the whole of Europe.

After the Westphalian treaties, these processes continued and advanced while great projects of international politics, although rarely realised, appeared probable. The England of Oliver Cromwell established contacts with Sweden and the latter, in turn, with Bogdan Chmielnicki, the leader of the Cossacks, and with the Turks. The subsequent stage in the history of international relations in this field was opened by Russia's participation in the Seven Years' War. This short period, which corresponded to the first years of the Thirty Years' War, introduced East-Central Europe into high European politics but, at the same time, it was the last period in which Hungary, Bohemia and Poland still had the opportunity of playing an independent role in international politics.[28] Soon, wedged between Prussian, Russian and Austrian absolutism in new systems of power, they were to become no more than the object of intrigues or the provinces of empires.

All that has been said about international politics can be said *mutatis mutandis* about commodity exchange and particularly about Baltic trade. During the last decade of the sixteenth century a number of consecutive bad harvests brought into the Mediterranean region bountiful supplies of grain imported from Holland, but actually produced by the Baltic countries. The Italians themselves became interested in the possibility of importing grain directly from Poland.[29] Although this Mediterranean demand and price rise turned out to be only temporary, the entire thirty-year period up to 1619–20 witnessed a grain boom and a general increase in commercial activity in the Baltic region.[30]

The decisive years of 1619–21, in which Ruggiero Romano has perceived the beginning of the crisis of the seventeenth century, reveal the nature of the connections between the European East and West, although the essence of the crisis phenomena remains controversial.[31] Disturbances in the Baltic trade caused significant difficulties for the merchants and subsequently for the artisans, leading to unemployment and hunger riots in the production areas. One should, however, note that the Hamburg market which showed similar tendencies was much more important. In the years 1626–9, the Gdańsk outlet was under Swedish blockade. Sales difficulties seemed to cause disturbances in credit and land turnover, but this was not a crisis of agricultural over-production. Perhaps troubles with selling grain and its low prices led to bankruptcy among indebted landowners, but on the whole this could have accelerated the concentration of landed property which had been going on already for a number of decades. 'Some of the lords possess entire provinces; they oppress the husbandmen in order to have greater quantities of corn, which they send to strangers to procure the superfluous demands of luxury', Montesquieu wrote in the next century, adding, 'If Poland had no foreign trade, its inhabitants would be happier.'[32] There are premises which make it possible to agree with this statement as far as the export of grain is concerned and the resulting better supply of the domestic market. Simultaneously, however, the shrinkage of this form of trade weakened the economy and also, although indirectly, the state. The fall in demand from the West, apparent during the seventeenth century and still more obvious in the first half of the next century, was felt much more strongly, although less dramatically, by the Baltic exporters of grain. Previously, especially in the sixteenth century, trade exchange in Europe had been based on a clear division of labour (to which much attention will be devoted in this volume); in the second half of the seventeenth century the West felt itself to be less dependent in those fields which up till then had remained the domain of import. As is known, the cultivation of excellent substitutes for wheat and rye was being developed: rice in north Italy, maize too in Italy and in the Iberian peninsula, while already beginning with the sixteenth century large tracts of land from Italy to England were drained and the agrarian revolution (together with a protectionist policy in the case of England) was already producing results in the Netherlands and in England. Simultaneously, demographic stagnation linked with an increase in production meant that 'only a relatively small decrease in the total demand, and/or a small rise in the total production of corn in Western and Southern Europe, sufficed to produce that radical shrinkage of the corn trade...'[33] For countries which were unable to accommodate themselves, this process signified a deep structural crisis.

To this well-known phenomenon one should add the comment that too little attention has been paid to the economic and social functions of imports from the West. Already the increasing share of wheat as compared to rye (which in the sixteenth century decisively dominated exports) seems to point to the emergence of a purchasing market in the European grain trade; the production of wheat in the river basins of the Dvina, Niemen and even the Vistula encountered serious difficulties. In the seventeenth century additional tension was created by the demand for the attractive Western prestige goods mentioned above, just as in the remaining peripheral or semi-peripheral countries, the attractiveness of imported goods stimulated exchange. This was confirmed by the oriental fashions becoming more widespread in the seventeenth and the first half of the eighteenth century when, regardless of cut, silk for making the national gentry dress came mainly from the West.[34] At the same time, demand for basic industrial articles, which during a period of prosperity were brought from the ports and which as a result the hinterland itself did not produce, remained at the same level. If, and this seems probable although it is difficult to evaluate numerically, great estates and especially a large manor of a wealthy nobleman or magnate bought more of such goods (beginning with copper pots and rope and ending with porcelain and silk) than the lesser property holders, the concentration of landed property led towards an increase of demand for imported goods, by no means only luxury items. The industry of Silesia and Greater Poland was able to exploit this opportunity only partially.

The economy and society of Bohemia developed in diametrically different conditions following the liquidation of the anti-Habsburg opposition, i.e., the local gentry. Miroslav Hroch and Josef Petráň aptly put it that in the sixteenth century and in the first stage of the seventeenth century Bohemia followed Western tendencies: great landed property based upon money rents, hired labour and monopolies developed a large-scale market production, much more varied than in Poland. In the second half of the seventeenth century, Habsburg absolutism in Bohemia and in Upper Hungary was accompanied by the development of serfdom although, as it has been emphasised recently, one should not link together regressive socio-economic changes, the serfdom system and the absolutist strivings of the Habsburgs. The programme of the anti-Habsburg opposition, as long as it was not connected with the political or religious freedom of the estates, did not differ significantly in the social and economic sphere from the programme of their opponents. Already before the Thirty Years' War the great landed-property owner experienced certain difficulties as regards sales; the complicated seventeenth century mercilessly led towards trade monopolies, serfdom and *Cameralism*.

2 ✣ Economic landscapes: historical Hungary from the fourteenth to the seventeenth century

LASZLO MÁKKAI

Historic Hungary extended for a thousand years, up to 1918, over the entire central Danubian basin which is surrounded by the Carpathians, joining the Styrian and Dinaric Alps in a huge semicircle; this region is therefore called the Carpathian basin. It is divided by mountains into three sub-basins: the plain in north-west Hungary, the Great Plain and Transylvania. Although in geological origin and structure the Carpathian basin belongs to the South European system of basins, its vegetation is not of Mediterranean character; the macchia shrub, so typical of Southern Europe, is represented by only a few plants including the domesticated vine and fig. Most of the area is covered by the vegetation of the two other large Eurasian regions, i.e., by mixed forests and grassland. Although Atlantic cyclones and the Asiatic summer monsoon occasionally carry rain here, relatively little falls in the basin because of its distance from seas (over 500 kilometres in every direction) and from the ring of mountains; with its annual rainfall of 400 to 600 mm, the basin is arid in comparison with Western Europe, even tending to drought when the hot Mediterranean air reaches it. The latitude of the basin is the same as that of central France (45°–49°) and the 1,750–2,000 hours of sunshine annually will ripen grapes, but owing to its inland position it has extremes of climate, the temperature varying from an average of 0 °C in winter to $+24$ °C in summer.

These features, together with the uneven distribution of rainfall reaching the maximum in June and October, mean that crops are often menaced by drought and only seldom by excessive moisture. While in Western Europe a rainy autumn presages poor crops, it is indispensable in the Carpathian basin for their survival until the May rains, according to peasant wisdom equivalent to gold – but though much desired these often do not materialise. The agriculture of the Carpathian basin is therefore forced to compensate for the uncertainties of tillage by increased livestock raising.

The Carpathian basin has fewer grasslands suitable for livestock than the Black Sea region, but its rather richer precipitation produces a larger grass crop and this makes transhumance unnecessary. A rotation of winter and summer

24

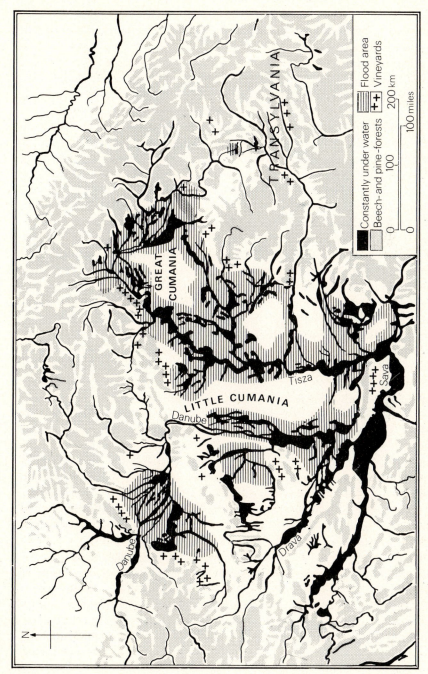

1 Economic landscapes of the Carpathian basin from the fourteenth to the seventeenth century

pastures within relatively small distances is sufficient. But a consequence of more rainfall is that the animals must be kept on dry fodder in winter because the thick snow prevents them getting at the grass. This encouraged the nomads to settle and cultivate the land.

Whether it was Western farming peoples or Eastern livestock-raising peoples that first arrived in the Carpathian basin, each needed to learn from the other to complement their agricultural knowledge. But the peasants of the woodlands and the herdsmen of the steppe had to take into account a third purely local factor and this was a considerable abundance of water despite the dryness of the climate. The difference of altitude between the ring of mountains surrounding the basin and the central plains is 1,500–2,000 metres and the rains become a flood when rushing down the steep slopes. Rain falling abundantly on the wooded mountains – 1,000–1,500 mm annually – flows to the basin through the tributaries of the Danube and the Tisza and so the basin becomes one of Europe's best-watered regions despite its scanty precipitation. The rivers flow slowly in great bends over a plain of very small gradient – not more than 20 cm/km – and deposit their alluvium along their main reaches in the form of gravel and sand banks. The bends were enlarged by every flood, but when the flood receded the entrance of the bends was blocked by alluvium and, if the next flood did not break through these entrances, the water in the bends became stagnant. At the same time new bends were made lower down and the formation of stagnant waters began anew. Willow, alder and poplar gradually established themselves on the sand-banks surrounded by former river channels. Oak woods and wild fruit-trees grew there later, but if the stagnant water was completely cut off from the main course of the river, it became a shallow lake and then a marsh. Thus the rivers built up, destroyed and reshaped their beds for thousands of years and formed a flood area of some 3.5 million hectares that extended over one-third of the plains in the Carpathian basin and was covered by water for the greater part of the year. During the last two centuries, 2.5 million hectares of arable land have been recovered through drainage, an area which is more than Holland, England, the Po and Loire valleys taken together. But prior to this land reclamation the flooded area involved special conditions for farming, just as different forms of farming were required by the sandy and grassy steppes, the hillsides with gallery forests, close beech- and pine-forests, and the alpine fields.

Hence the agro-geographical conditions of the Carpathian basin were not favourable to a farming structure based either predominantly on tillage, or predominantly on animal husbandry; and, since the peoples who had moved here over thousands of years had only specialised farming methods, none of them were able to settle permanently until a people arrived able to utilise all the three types of land in the basin, i.e., the flood areas, the sandy steppes and the gallery-wooded hillsides alike. The Hungarian people had already known the potential of all three types before it moved here in about 900 A.D. A Moslem geography book of the ninth century writes of the Magyars living on the northern coast of the Black Sea that 'they have tents and wander in summer to find grass and vegetation... and in winter they stay by the rivers and engage in fishing... They sow abundantly.' The Magyars adopted from some Bulgarian–Turkish people of the steppe numerous technical terms relating to the breeding of horses, cattle, sheep and pigs, and to tillage (e.g., *eke* = plough, *buza* = wheat, *árpa* = barley, *kender* = hemp, *sarló* = sickle), as well as to wine-growing (e.g., *szőlő* = grape, *bor* = wine, *seprő* = lees), while the basic vocabulary of fishing belongs to their earliest Finno-Ugrian linguistic heritage. The place-names of the Carpathian basin show that the Magyars occupied the grassy steppes, the dry channels of the rivers and the gallery forests, but did not penetrate the 'black' beech- and pine-forests which had no underwood and therefore could not be used as pastures; these they left to the Slavic, German and Romanian settlers for felling. The hilly country and some of the marshy woods of the larger rivers were inhabited by a sparse Slavic population; the plain proper, as a Bavarian chronicler of the end of the ninth century writes, was an unpopulated desert of ten days' journey between the lands of the Moravians and the Bulgarians. The Magyars occupied the desert and the hilly country, assimilated the Slavic population living there, and learned from it everything that was necessary for adjusting their farming methods to local conditions, first of all the drying of fodder of hay and straw required for wintering the livestock, and the cultivation of such plants as rye, oats and flax that had been unknown on the steppe. From their western Slavic neighbours outside the Carpathian basin, the Magyars adopted the heavy plough with which it was possible to till hard ground. This was the beginning of Hungarian agricultural development which has lasted from the thirteenth century practically to our day and which first combined with, and then overtook, the keeping of livestock. In the early centuries, the land fertilised by grazing was broken up and, when exhausted, was replaced by another pasture; this meant that ploughland shifted across the pastures, but from the thirteenth century ploughland was localised and parts of it were alternately cultivated or grazed. Two- or three-course rotation was introduced on the hilly country surrounding the plains.

Before the Magyar conquest, viticulture had been established west of the Danube, in the former Roman province of Pannonia; it survived there and then by the first years of the fourteenth century spread 100 kilometres northward, 300 kilometres north-eastward and 500 kilometres eastward and covered the southern slopes of the hilly country. On the mountains covered by beech- and pine-forests the sparse hunting population, which up to then had paid taxes in wild animal skins, was replaced during the thirteenth century by German, Slovak and Ruthenian settlers who felled forests and engaged in tillage combined with shepherding. In addition to the earlier salt- and silver-mines, gold-mines were opened with the cooperation of German settlers; these mines were the most important in Europe at that time. Furthermore, in

the alpine fields appeared the Romanians who introduced Balkan transhumant
sheep-raising to the region. These shepherds, who drove their flocks of sheep
as far as the Lower Danube and the Dniester every winter, brought the eastern
and south-eastern parts of the Carpathian basin into contact with the
Hungarian kingdom's pattern of life, which was varied both economically and
ethnically and coordinated the potentials of the various types of land and the
particular farming methods of the different peoples.

By the fourteenth century Hungary had reached European standards in
farming technique and had also undergone a social transformation; from
freemen of differing status and from slaves there emerged a feudal stratification
made up of the nobility, the burghers and peasants who had freedom to move
and held their land on hereditary lease, but owed their landlord a labour rent.
A peculiar feature of this structure was that the peasantry free from seigniorial
bonds survived in relatively large numbers, partly as a numerous lesser
nobility, partly as autonomous ethnic groups with their own districts on the
Great Plain: the Transylvanian–Hungarian 'Székely', the German 'Saxons',
the Romanian 'Vlachs' and the Jazygians and Cumanians.[1]

The shaping of economic landscapes in the four hundred years from the
beginning of the fourteenth to the end of the seventeenth century was based
on foundations laid during the previous four centuries. But the various elements
of the same structure developed with different emphasis, and this was the result
of a new situation, namely a steadily increasing connection of the Carpathian
basin's economic life with the whole European economy and the parallel
development of commodity production for both domestic and foreign markets.
The descriptions by occasional foreign travellers from both the beginning and
end of the period discussed here show clearly what was traditional and what
was new.

In 1308 a French Dominican wrote,

The Hungarian Kingdom was formerly called not Hungary, but Moesia and Pannonia.
It was called Moesia after the harvests because this country abounds in rich crops. It
was called Pannonia because of the abundance of bread, obviously because this comes
from abundance of crops. This land abounds in pastures, bread, wine, meat, gold and
silver, and in fish it is richer than any other country with the exception of Norway,
where fish is eaten like bread and instead of bread. The land is on the whole flat with
small hills here and there, but there are very high mountains in some places. Immense
salt-domes rise in the Transylvanian parts from which salt is quarried like stone, and
is carried to all parts of the country and to neighbouring countries.

Hungary is divided into two parts, namely into the Transylvanian and the Danubian
parts. Transylvania is so called because forests of four days' journey extend between
it and the other part. The Danubian part is watered by one of the world's largest rivers
– that renowned river called the Danube – which flows through the middle of this part,
is full of all sorts of fish, and flows eastward...Also the Transylvanian parts are watered
by large, navigable rivers along which salt is shipped in large vessels to the entire
kingdom and to other countries...Most of these rivers bear gold in their sand, and
therefore in Hungary the aristocrats and noblemen who live along the said rivers have

the gold incessantly washed, panned out and collected. Also these rivers abound in fish...There are...in this country many...towns, castles and palaces and innumerable villages, but, despite this, the kingdom owing to its size looks practically empty.[2]

Hungary, prospering in the Middle Ages, was split into three parts after 1541: the north-eastern 'kingdom' under Habsburg rule, the great Plain occupied by the Turks, and the principality of Transylvania, subjected to a Turkish protectorate. The country was practically turned into a constant theatre of war; but the English traveller Edward Browne, who visited this region because of his interest in mines, nevertheless wrote about Hungary in 1673 as follows:

Hungaria...is also the best Rivered Country in *Europe*: nor doth any region thereof afford so many noble and useful Streams...And though the Upper *Hungary* be Hilly, and plentiful in Wood; yet are there large Plains below. I Travelled from *Vienna* to *Belgrade*, about four hundred Miles, upon continued and not interrupted Plains...This plainness of the Country, affordeth an handsome way of Travelling in open Chariots, carrying one or two Men with a Charioter, drawn by two or three, sometimes four Horses of a Breast...

And as this Country excelleth in *Rivers*, so is it very abundant in *Fishes*. The *Tibiscus* or *Teisse*, is esteemed the most Fishy River in *Europe*, if not in the World; insomuch, that they have a common saying, *That it consisteth of two parts of Water, and one of Fish*...As the Waters are also fruitful in Fish, so the Land aboundeth in other *Provisions*; and very eminently in the two supporters of Life, *Bread* and *Wine*: their Bread is hardly exceeded by any in *Europe*; worked up and kneaded with long continued labour; and so made light, wholesome, and well tasted; and at so cheap a rate, that for two pence as much is afforded there, as twelve pence with us in *England*...*Wines* also of a generous and noble sort, the Wines of *Tokay* are highly esteemed; the *Sirmian* Wines are very rich and pleasant...In many other places the Wines are very noble; and some brought unto *Vienna*...And as the ground is not unfruitful in its own nature, so they are not without the practise of *Good-Husbandry*, both in their Arable and Pasture Grounds; especially in *Upper-Hungary*, and parts not subjected to the *Turks*...

...There is also great plenty of *Deer*, *Hares*, all sorts of *Poultrey*, *Partridges* and Pheasants; great store of *Sheep*, which in divers places, have long Spiral Horns and very long curled Wooll. And *Oxen* in great numbers, whereof tis thought they send an hundred thousand yearly into *Italy*, *Germany*, and other parts; and it is commonly said, they have enough, to serve a great part of Europe. They are of a kind of *Mousecolour*...there are *Horses* also in very great number, some large, many but small, yet swift. I saw a Thousand of them belonging to the peasants at *Sone*, *Sene* or *Senia*, a Village upon the *Danube*...[3]

The abundance in rivers and fish is emphasised in both descriptions and great economic importance is ascribed to fishing. Knowing that at that time one-third of the Carpathian basin consisted of flood plains, it follows that fishing was practised as the main occupation by a considerable part of the population. Fish is always mentioned during that period as a due of the landlord, but there are also references to it in a frozen, salted and dried form on the home market, and to a lesser extent even as an export commodity. Despite this, the number of professional fishermen mentioned in the sources is surprisingly low and evidently applies only to those engaged in fishing in open waters with boats and drag-nets which require considerable investment and expertise. Even these fishermen were in general employed by the large waterside estates and were entitled only to the smaller part of the catch. Fishing was for the most part a side-occupation supplementing peasant farming and filling the dead periods of agriculture; it was at the same time a compulsory form of feudal socage. As such it formed an organic part of complex water utilisation but, owing to the large-scale draining projects of the eighteenth to nineteenth centuries, it went out of use to such an extent that its characteristic features were brought to light only by most recent historical research.

The essence of this utilisation was the connection of the dead channels to the main course by means of the so-called *fok* (meaning 'eye'), which was a narrow channel cut through the alluvial bank. In this way it was possible to distribute and restrain the flood waters and to protect the banks from destruction, and, what was most important, to let water into the dead channels threatened by stagnation. The principal form of fishing was the temporary blocking of the 'eyes' whereby the big fish remained trapped while the new brood produced in the flood area was carried back to the main bed by the receding water. In winter fish were caught when they gathered at the holes cut in the ice cover. Thus the proverbial plenty of fish in the flood areas was not simply a gift of nature; on the contrary it resulted from the regular opening-up and blocking of the 'eyes', and their constant maintenance. This was hard work, and entire village communities were mobilised for it. However, the result was that the people were able to supply large areas with live water continuously, and to maintain in this way the ash- and oak-woods on the islands, as well as the orchards improved by grafting and mentioned in documents from the thirteenth century (these orchards consisted of apple, pear, plum and hazelnut indigenous to the Carpathian basin, and of walnut and sour-cherry introduced by the Romans); they could grow grain on the constantly dry spots, could keep herds of half-wild horses, cattle and swine practically without human tending on occasionally flooded fields and pastures and in forests. Quite a number of water-plants provided either human and animal foods, or raw material for home crafts.

Although fishing, animal-breeding and the home crafts produced surplus that could be put on the market, it was the utilisation of flood areas that actually remained – exactly because of its many-sidedness – the principal form of extensive and self-contained peasant agriculture in Hungary. This was due particularly to the fact that the possibilities of growing grain were limited on account of the changing movement of waters and because tillage was considered less important than animal husbandry. That this form of agriculture nevertheless survived up to the eighteenth century can be ascribed mainly to the fact that from the middle of the sixteenth to the end of the seventeenth century most of the Danube and Tisza region was under Turkish occupation, and that the

Turkish authorities levied taxes but did not interfere with agricultural activities as the Hungarian landlords did. From the middle of the sixteenth century the latter established their demesne farms under their own management but worked them with tenant labour, and subsequently established a monopoly system that crippled the peasants' own agricultural activity, for example by exclusive or temporary keeping of inns and slaughter houses by the landlord, compulsory purchase of wine and grain, prohibition of the free use of fishing-waters and acorn-bearing woods, etc.[4] Negative consequences of all this had appeared already by the seventeenth century in the flood-area regions that remained under Hungarian rule (the plain in north-western Hungary and the upper Tisza region): the peasants in many places neglected maintenance of the 'eyes' and the dead channels turned into marsh. This situation was aggravated by a considerable change in the weather: after the relatively dry weather of the fifteenth century, disastrous floods were recorded in two-thirds of the sixteenth century, and there are reports about ploughland having become permanently unusable because of floods at the beginning of the seventeenth century, e.g., in the region of Pozsony which till then was renowned for the richest wheat crops in the country, and was the only region from which grain was exported. The utilisation of flood areas was actually an archaic phenomenon which was appropriate only in the exceptional circumstances of Turkish occupation, including the sparse population (due to wars) and last but not least, the need for protection from armies.

Although both the French friar at the beginning of the fourteenth century and the English traveller at the end of the seventeenth century praised Hungarian bread, this country's agriculture was during the entire period much less based on grain than that of the neighbouring northern and western countries. True, tillage was promoted by regular crop rotation and by the introduction of the heavy plough, and was extended by continuous deforestation both in the hilly and mountain regions. There was growth both qualitatively and quantitatively. The peopling of the highlands extended the land used for rye and oats, but wheat became dominant in the hilly regions and on the plains, increasingly replacing millet, the principal crop of the newly cleared woodland, and appearing rarely together with rye, mostly on sandy soil. Depending on weather conditions, 50 to 90 per cent of the peasants' grain crop had become wheat by the fifteenth century, and the yield ratio varied between three and four, or sometimes five in the sixteenth century, compared to two to three in the fourteenth. Yet counter-forces were acting at the same time. Data available from the fifteenth century show that ploughland took up no more than 25 to 50 per cent of the area even in hilly villages of clearly agrarian character, a part of which percentage was recorded as new clearings. Grassland and forests taken together amounted to half, or rather more, of the area and consequently animal husbandry was not yet subordinated to tillage.[5]

The abandonment of cultivation took place in the fifteenth century in

Hungary as in other parts of Europe; large numbers of small villages became completely depopulated, and one-third or half of the farms were deserted. The population migrated to the towns, mainly to the centres of agricultural commodity production; these were the so-called market-towns (*oppida*) under seigniorial authority, but enjoying at the same time an autonomy, mainly the right of holding markets. By the end of the sixteenth century the nearly 20,000 rural settlements of Hungary had an average population of not more than 17 families, while the approximately 300 market-towns averaged 200 each, and the 30 free towns 500 and more. The depopulation of the villages was detrimental to grain production because the inhabitants of towns and market-towns were engaged (in addition to a moderate amount of handicraft) primarily in viticulture and in raising cattle, for which hired workers were required.[6]

From the first third of the sixteenth century, the grain crops estimated on the basis of the tithe register showed a nation-wide increase. The crop of some tithe-payers, counted in sheaves, had increased twofold, sometimes threefold, by 1570. There was a halt at this point, and by 1620 production had fallen back to the initial level, to stagnate here until the end of the century. From the threshing results it appears on the other hand that while in about 1570 one sheaf yielded 3 litres of grain and in about 1620 only two, 3 litres per sheaf were attained, even surpassed, by the end of the century. The only explanation for this is that the peasants of Hungary, encouraged by the European grain boom, extended sowing to lands of poorer quality; this resulted in a fall in productivity which could then be compensated for only by a reduction in the sowing area.[7]

Thus grain production fluctuated both in extent and productivity during the four centuries in question, and, though it was not missing from any of the land types of the Carpathian basin, it became a dominant branch of production only in certain regions, mainly those bordering on areas where cattle-breeding or vine-growing monocultures had developed and which were therefore in need of grain imports. Otherwise bread met at most half the calorific requirements for the nutrition of the Hungarian people in the seventeenth century while in the Western and neighbouring Northern countries it met two-thirds at least.[8]

The vine played a much more conspicuous and dynamic role than grain in the making of the economic landscape. By the beginning of the fourteenth century viticulture had reached Hungary's northern and eastern borders, beyond which vines were not grown even in neighbouring countries; but through constant deforestation viticulture steadily spread within Hungary's borders. In the fourteenth to fifteenth centuries the wines of Syrmia, between the Danube and the Save, and of the hilly country west of the Danube were most liked; the Great Plain was supplied from here, and wine was exported to Silesia. The wines of the north-eastern district extending on the Gyöngyös–Eger–Miskolc–Tokaj–Beregszász line equalled these by the end of the fifteenth century and even outrivalled them during the sixteenth century because of an important technical innovation. The soil was well prepared by embanking and manuring, and new methods of dressing were introduced, but the most important factor was the postponement of the vintage until the end of October so that the grapes dried and underwent the 'noble rot' on the vine. An essence was made from these grapes with the addition of which the average wine became the famous *aszu* of Tokaj. The 20 small vine-growing towns of the Tokaj district introduced a common regulation with strict prescriptions regarding production as early as 1561. Through the rapid increase of exports to Poland, the hilly country of Tokaj took the lead in the Hungarian wine trade by the end of the century, surpassing with its exportation of some 30,000 hectolitres the still important wine district of Rohonc–Sopron–Modor which exported 20,000 litres annually. Wine was also, needless to say, an important commodity on the domestic market. Although the landlords had few vines cultivated under their own management, they had so much wine coming from the wine delivery of the serfs and compulsory purchases that the proceeds of the seigniorial inns were by far the highest among the incomes of the large estates. Vines were grown in all suitable regions of the country, in some places as a monoculture which completely ousted grain. The territory under the rule of the Turks, who drank no wine but nevertheless levied heavy taxes on it, was no exception; south of Lake Balaton the famous medieval vineyards on the hills not only survived but were enlarged by new plantations, and the market-towns of the Great Plain began at the time of the Turkish occupation to introduce on sandy soil the vines that till then had grown only in the hilly areas.[9]

The market-towns of the hilly country became centres of the wine trade as their citizens leased the vineyards of the neighbouring, partly depopulated, villages, and not only traded in wine, but also produced it. Other towns monopolised the trade in cattle, and virtually monopolised stock-raising, expanding the land available for pasture by leasing the fields of deserted villages. Excellent breeding stock was provided for this purpose by the heavy-bodied cattle of the nomadic Cumanians, who in the second half of the thirteenth century migrated from the eastern steppes to the Great Hungarian Plain. These cattle belonged to the *primigenius* type which was more closely related to the aurochs than the *brachycerous* type indigenous at that time in Central Europe and also in Hungary. The Cumanians were soon Magyarised, their leading stratum was ennobled, the common people became free peasants, and very many of them migrated to the market-towns of the Great Plain where they entered service with the Hungarian citizens who undertook large-scale cattle-breeding. The body weight of the Cumanian cattle, which were mouse-grey in colour and had forking horns, was steadily increased by careful breeding. By the end of the sixteenth century Hungarian cattle had surpassed the average European weight of 200 kg and weighed about 350 kg; we even know of weights as heavy as 450–500 kg in the middle of the seventeenth century. The sandy steppes of Little and Great Cumania within the flood areas of the Great Plain had been, and continued to be in the period under survey, the practically exclusive breeding areas of cattle exported abroad. Exportation

to the south-German and north-Italian markets started as early as the middle
of the fourteenth century and reached its peak in the middle of the sixteenth:
some 50,000 oxen in 1562 and some 130,000 in 1587 were driven by the
market-towns of the Great Plain under Turkish rule to the West through the
customs houses of the Kingdom of Hungary.[10]

It appears both from what has been said and from a comparison of the
itineraries we have quoted that the transformation of peasant subsistence
farming into commodity production directed at domestic and foreign markets
affected only certain branches of the economy, but promoted these vigorously
and so produced a considerable reshaping of economic landscapes. Within the
Carpathian basin, for example, the traveller would have seen more vineyards
but also more animals at the end of the seventeenth century than had existed in
about 1300, while the cultivation of cereals – even if it had increased in absolute
terms – might have seemed static compared with wine production and
stock-breeding. The seigniorial demesne farms, producing mainly grain and
employing labour services, which emerged in the middle of the sixteenth
century and extended in the seventeenth century to some 15–20 per cent of
ploughland in the Kingdom of Hungary and in Transylvania, were responsible
for no innovations, either quantitatively or qualitatively, because they employed
peasant labour and peasant methods. The Mediterranean and continental
features of the Carpathian basin, which was essentially part of the Atlantic
forest zone, were thus emphasised by a closer interconnection with the
all-European market. While tillage – bringing the Carpathian basin into
relationship with its western and northern neighbours – became part of the
self-contained feudal structure, the viticulture and stock-breeding connected
with the southern and eastern neighbourhood not only formed the economic
landscape but also developed into the basis of the capitalist economy and
production for export. To sum up, Hungary, taking part in the international
division of labour through the exportation of wine and cattle, joined the
emerging world market in this particular way, and so could continue, up to
the new European grain boom in the middle of the eighteenth century, as an
economic region devoting most of her territory to the keeping of animals, since
viticulture is a branch of production that requires relatively small areas but
is of high labour-intensity, just the opposite of stock-breeding.

Consequently, cattle and other animals assumed considerable importance
and occupied large territories. According to a registration of landlords
comprising about 32,000 households of serfs in the market-towns and villages
of the Kingdom of Hungary and Transylvania (no adequate data are available
on the third zone under Turkish occupation), in about 1640 every peasant
family, including the completely landless, had on average 2.5 draught-oxen
and as many cows, in alpine regions 2 draught-oxen and as many cows, and
in the intensely viticultural regions 1.5 draught-oxen and 1 cow. Only about
40 per cent of the peasant farms were able to set up a complete team for
ploughing, which required 4–6 oxen, while the rest lived as cottars on day-wages,

or cultivated small vineyards, or bred animals for meat. Horses were used for plough-drawing only in areas of German settlements, yet peasants specialised in cartage kept horses in larger numbers. Not more than 0.5 horse was the average per peasant family. Swine, on the other hand, were raised in great numbers everywhere, 3 per family on average, but in certain regions rich in acorn-bearing woods the population specialised in pig-breeding. Sheep-raising was still more region dependent. Regional varieties and methods differed: the Hungarians of the Great Plain raised the curly *racka* sheep with twisted horns – mentioned in the itinerary of Edward Browne – mainly for its meat and the wool that provided the material for the coarse cloth of the commonly worn long cloaks, while in the mountain region the Romanians, Slovaks and Ruthenians raised the *purzsa* variety, largely for its milk and the salty curd which was a main part of the common diet. On average there were 4.4 sheep per peasant family, but in actual fact 20–40 sheep, or very occasionally more, were kept by only a fifth of these families. By the end of the fifteenth century the population of the alpine regions had grown so much that transhumant shepherding was no longer able to support the increased population, and the Romanian, Slovak and Ruthenian surplus population began to move to the hilly country, to the abandoned Hungarian villages where they changed over to tillage.[11]

The alpine regions were important, not only for pig and sheep breeding but also for mining. In the period under survey, Hungary was rich in salt, silver, gold and most of all copper. A particular economic landscape took shape in the fourteenth century near the mining towns with their hydraulic ore crushers, smelteries and foundries, but in the fifteenth century there arose the need for deep working which could be met only by foreign expertise and capital. It was in this way that Hungarian mining fell into the hands of south-German merchant capitalists who exported copper, the main mining product, unprocessed.[12] As with the wool of Hungarian sheep which was unfit for making finer cloth, the Hungarian mining products could not become the basis of local industrialisation. Thus the highlands of the Carpathian basin did not combine with the hilly country and the plains to form a single economic structure, and accordingly urbanisation did not take place to combine the regions into a unit. The free towns were situated along the Carpathians near the borders and, with their German ethnic population, became isolated from the villages and market-towns; their intermediate trade served only to consolidate the feudal system, for industries were initiated that they were not able to develop because of the competition of textile – and metal – industry imports from the Western trade partners who required Hungary's agricultural produce.[13] The Carpathian basin thus remained an ensemble of preponderantly agrarian economic landscapes, and this agrarian character persisted for a long time because of the international division of labour which became established with the development of the world market.

3 ✷ Economic landscapes: Poland from the fourteenth to the seventeenth century

ANDRZEJ WYROBISZ

The Polish state in the first half of the fourteenth century constituted a territory of up to 150,000 sq km inhabited by a population of around 1 to 1.25 million. In 1634, when after the signing of the Polanow peace treaty the Polish Commonwealth attained the most extended borders in all its history, the Polish–Lithuanian state constituted an area of 990,000 sq km with around 10 million inhabitants. This tremendous increase of territory and population was the consequence of a unification of the Polish lands under the rule of the last two monarchs of the Piast and the Jagiellonian dynasties and, above all, of the Polish–Lithuanian union (established in 1386 and finally consolidated in 1569) as a result of which Poland was joined by the Grand Duchy of Lithuania which was several times larger. In the seventeenth century Poland was territorially one of the largest states in Europe (exceeded only by Russia) but her demographic potential remained below the European average. Although the mean population density in the Polish part of the country in the first half of the seventeenth century (20 inhabitants per sq km) exceeded the European average, it was far below the indices of the most populous countries of Western Europe, while the average population density in the Grand Duchy (6 inhabitants per sq km) was among the lowest in Europe. Moreover, the population of the Commonwealth was distributed very unevenly. Alongside large and almost unpopulated territories (the Ukraine had 3 inhabitants per sq km) there occurred large population conglomerations (areas of the biggest Polish towns: Cracow, Gdańsk, Toruń, Elbląg and also a part of Mazovia) where population density approached the highest European indices (30–40 inhabitants per sq km). One should, however, recall the enormous losses of population suffered by the Ukraine as a result of the Cossack uprising in 1648 and by Poland as a whole during the 1655–60 wars with Sweden, at which time the losses amounted to at least 25 per cent of the pre-war population, in certain regions perhaps even more than 60 per cent.[1]

An increase of state territory and population brought about an increase of raw materials and labour force and consequently also of production potentials

36

as well as a widening of the domestic market. Within the borders of the Polish–Lithuanian state in the sixteenth–seventeenth centuries there existed territories extremely varied both physiographically and geologically: mountains and highlands, lowlands and valleys, lake districts and the steppe. These were divided by several large river systems belonging to two basins: the Baltic and the Black Sea. Here one also encountered soil of varying fertility and cultivability and even differences of climate, length of vegetation period and rainfall. This very varied area contained natural resources which could be exploited and dominated by man at the given stage of technology.

One of the most important natural resources of Poland in the period from the fourteenth to the seventeenth century was its forests; these supplied meat, fur and hides, wax and honey, other foodstuffs (such as fruit and mushrooms) and fodder, but, above all, timber which was at that time the basic building material, practically the only fuel and one of the most universally used raw materials in many branches of industrial production. Nearly every branch of artisanship utilised timber in the form of raw material, as tools or fuel. The precise area occupied by forests in Poland during the late Middle Ages and modern times is not known; the same pertains to the composition of the forests. In Greater Poland, during the 1580–1600 period, the forest area is calculated to have been 13,260 sq km, while for the entire country the accepted figure is 150,000 sq km. In the Middle Ages the forest area had most certainly been larger since deforestation had gradually taken place through progress in rural colonisation and the exploitation of the forests. In Greater Poland the area of forests and marshlands from the end of the fourteenth to the end of the sixteenth century decreased from *c.* 50 per cent to *c.* 40 per cent of the entire territory and in the Lvov region from the beginning of the fifteenth to the end of the sixteenth century from *c.* 46 per cent to *c.* 44 per cent. However, in the seventeenth century there still existed in the Polish Commonwealth enormous and practically untouched wooded areas, e.g., in the Carpathian and Świętokrzyskie mountains, on the border between Mazovia and the Duchy of Prussia (the Kurpie forests), in Podlasie and, above all, in Lithuania.

At the end of the sixteenth century and in the first half of the seventeenth the threat of forest devastation as a result of excessive exploitation was already noticed. It was expressed both in literature – in political and economic writings as well as in various ordinances and organisational undertakings having as their aim to limit or rationalise tree-felling – and also in attempts to introduce new technologies which would guarantee a more economical use of fuel (for example, in salt works) or simply to liquidate those industrial establishments which used especially large amounts of fuel, such as foundries and glass works.[2]

Simultaneously, however, a very high and profitable export of timber for shipbuilding and other constructions as well as of wood by-products (tar, potash) was not only maintained but even expanded. Although in the first half of the seventeenth century the export of forest products through Gdańsk decreased, at the same time the rafting of Lithuanian wood towards Riga, Labiau and Königsberg increased.[3] Thus there arose a paradoxical situation in which Poland was one of the most important exporters of wood in Europe from the fifteenth to the seventeenth century while simultaneously various fields of her own industry felt the lack of this raw material. Deforestation occurred especially alongside navigable rivers: the Vistula, the Niemen and the Dvina. As a result of excessive and irrational tree felling, certain valuable species of trees (e.g. the yew) and of animals disappeared (the aurochs, *Bos primigenius*, completely died out in the seventeenth century). It also caused soil erosion and denudation, especially in the loess areas of the Lublin and Little Poland highlands as well as in a part of the Carpathian highlands. In deforested areas the level of ground water became lower, the threat of floods increased and thus the conditions for the development of agriculture worsened.

Agriculture was the main area of the Polish economy during the entire period under discussion. The climate and soil conditions meant that it was possible to cultivate all parts of the Polish Commonwealth. Inferior agricultural tools, however, led in the fourteenth century to certain very fertile areas with heavy soil remaining uncultivated. This state of affairs changed in the fifteenth to sixteenth century, partly owing to the improvement of tools but even more to the market which opened up to Polish cereals in Western Europe, for the potential profits induced the Polish gentry to use the land to the full for grain production. This also resulted in a division into regions of agricultural production in the sixteenth to seventeenth century. Whereas it would be difficult to point out any regional differentiation in agriculture and crop structure in the late Middle Ages, in the sixteenth and seventeenth centuries regions of more intensive agriculture began to appear. The influential factor was not the fertility of the soil or climatic conditions of these areas, however, but the possession of navigable rivers which facilitated grain delivery to Gdańsk. Such areas were the Vistula basin including the Bug and the Narew, and to a lesser degree the Warta basin; in Lithuania, export of grain developed along the Niemen and lower Dvina. Great rivers crossing the then territory of the Polish–Lithuanian state such as the Dnieper and Dniester, because of a lack of connections with the grain markets of Europe, did not play a stimulating role in the development of agriculture. As a result agriculture developed at times very strongly in areas with soil of low or medium quality. Mazovia is an example of this, and in the second half of the sixteenth and first half of the seventeenth century the Podlasie and Sieradz regions were included into export production while the extremely fertile Ukraine represented only a low level of agriculture. In the crop structure of the late Middle Ages rye constituted *c.* 40 per cent, oats *c.* 38 per cent, wheat *c.* 9 per cent and barley *c.* 6 per cent, which reflected local consumption needs. From the fifteenth century onwards the crop structure began to undergo certain changes, adapting itself in those regions working for export production towards the demands of the European markets and elsewhere towards the needs of the food industries. Hence, in the sixteenth and seventeenth centuries the cultivation of rye comprised from 35 per cent of arable land up to 60 per cent in regions exporting grain. Wheat was sown on from 2 to 20 per cent of the fields. Barley comprised 5 to 10 per cent of the crops and the amounts of this grain were visibly larger in areas where breweries developed (parts of Mazovia and the Carpathian highlands). Twenty-five per cent to 35 per cent of the fields remained sown with oats, more in regions of intensive animal husbandry and wherever soil conditions or the climate made it difficult to cultivate other grains (the Carpathian highlands, the Świętokrzyskie mountains, Podlasie). The cultivation of millet was of little significance, and occurred mainly in the central and southern parts of the country; the same pertained to buckwheat. After the wars in the middle of the seventeenth century there occurred a certain decrease in the cultivation of rye connected with export difficulties, while the production of barley and oats for domestic consumption increased. Grain production during the entire period totally satisfied the needs of the domestic market (the apparent deficiency of rye in Little Poland in the sixteenth century could easily have been supplemented by surplus production from the remaining regions), while from the middle of the fifteenth century it furnished very significant amounts of grain (above all, rye) to the Western European markets. When exports reached their peak, during the first half of the seventeenth century, Poland sent through Gdańsk 70,000 to 90,000 lasts of grain annually.[4]

The cultivation of fruit and vegetables was not considerable but it satisfied the equally small demand of the home market. Because of climatic conditions, southern Poland had larger orchard areas. Grapes introduced into Poland in the early Middle Ages by monks were cultivated in exceptional cases and had no economic significance despite the fact that they were frequently mentioned in descriptions of manorial farms. Wine was imported from abroad, mainly from Hungary, and this import grew in the sixteenth and seventeenth centuries.

On the other hand, essential economic importance was given to the cultivation of fibrous plants – flax and hemp – as well as dyestuff plants which, although involving areas smaller than those devoted to grain, guaranteed a sufficient supply of these raw materials for domestic textile production and even created possibilities for export. Flax was cultivated in the entire Commonwealth but because of its climatic and soil demands it did not succeed equally in all areas, as a result of which there appeared several basic regions of intensive cultivation: Pomerania, Lithuania and Samogitia, Livonia, the Carpathian highlands and from the sixteenth century also Greater Poland. Hemp was grown mainly in Prussia, Mazovia, north-eastern Little Poland and Lithuania. During the second half of the sixteenth century and during the seventeenth century there existed in Lithuania whole areas in which hemp was the main crop produced both by the gentry and the peasants; from here most of the hemp was exported, through Königsberg, among other towns. The area under cultivation of hemp and flax in the Commonwealth in the middle of the seventeenth century is estimated to have been approximately 300,000 ha.

In the textile industry various barks and plants such as the bark of birches, alder, oak, apple tree, barberry, greenweed, dyer's rocket and buckthorn were utilised as dyes. Special dyestuff plants such as madder and pastel were cultivated. Of greatest importance in dyeing was the scale insect (*Coccus polonicus*) – the larvae of this insect belonging to the species which feeds upon the roots of the scleranth (*Scerantus parennis*) and on other weeds which provided a red dye highly valued in the textile industry all over Europe. In Poland–Lithuania there existed special plantations of this insect. At the beginning of the sixteenth century approximately 5,000 hundredweight were collected, a large part of which was exported (in the years 1533–43 *c.* 60,000 kg was sent through Poznań and *c.* 8,000 kg through Cracow). After the discovery of America, the Polish scale insect was replaced by the American cochineal which was twenty times more productive, and the cultivation of the scale insect in Poland as well as the trade connected with it almost completely disappeared in the second half of the sixteenth century. The decline of this cultivation was probably also the result of the development of cattle-breeding and the cultivation of grain, since the two were irreconcilable. The scale insect was pushed out of the market even in regions of a medium-intensive agricultural and animal-breeding economy; it was retained slightly longer in the Ukraine and the Carpathian highlands where it was only of a local and slight significance.[5]

The extensive demesne economy based on grain production led to a reduction of stock-raising, above all because the cultivation of grain took over pastures, waste and virgin lands and thus reduced the fodder supply. This is the reason why in central Poland, where the manorial system and grain production were particularly highly developed, cattle-breeding remained at a low level. The scope of animal husbandry was meagre in the fertile Vistula fens, which were distinguished by high agricultural production. On the other hand, in regions beyond the Vistula basin and cut off from the Gdańsk market where grain production was less profitable, cattle-breeding developed on a grand scale. In the sixteenth century one can even observe a shift of the cattle-breeding areas to the eastern and southern borders proportional to the expansion of the grain-producing manors. The most important regions of cattle-breeding in Poland in the sixteenth to seventeenth century with their excellent conditions for fodder production were the Ukraine, Podole, the southern part of Red Ruthenia from the Stryj–Trembowla line and, to a slightly lesser degree, Volhynia. In these areas, animal husbandry meant the breeding of oxen of the grey-steppe variety (Podole cattle), which both in weight and size were considerably superior to cattle bred in other regions of the country, as well as the raising of the superior Wallachian cattle. Animal production in those regions exceeded local and even domestic needs of meat and hides, and a large part was intended for export, primarily to Germany. In the first half of the seventeenth century, according to calculations made by M. Horn, 27,000–33,000 oxen were driven annually from these regions to Silesia and further to the west. There was fairly significant animal husbandry in Mazovia and Podlasie where soil did not favour a high grain production; here, however, the fodder production was also smaller than in Podole and the Ukraine and the breed of cattle (Polish red cattle) was inferior. Generally one can say that the intensity of cattle-breeding was inversely proportional to the level of grain cultivation and the amount of land devoted to that cultivation.

Pig-breeding played an insignificant role in Poland from the fourteenth to the seventeenth century while a large and universal importance was attached to sheep-breeding which supplied skins, meat, milk products and above all wool, the basic raw material for textiles. Sheep were bred in the whole of Poland. In the sixteenth and seventeenth century, Greater Poland, Pomerania and the Carpathian highlands were foremost in wool production. A sharp increase in the number of sheep occurred at the turn of the fourteenth century and then in the sixteenth century when in Greater Poland there emerged large centres of cloth production; the next increase took place in the 1630s when the Greater Poland gentry became interested in sheep-breeding.

The total number of sheep in Poland (without Lithuania and the eastern part of the 'Crown', i.e., the Ukraine and Red Ruthenia) is calculated at approximately 1.7 million at the end of the sixteenth century. These were sheep of the domestic lowland variety (only in the Carpathians were there Polish mountain sheep); at the end of the sixteenth century attempts were made to improve this breed by introducing Hungarian rams into Little Poland. The annual production per sheep was 500–600 grams of wool (in Greater Poland perhaps even 800 grams) which meant an annual total production amounting to 3,500,000 to 4,200,000 kg. However, since a large part of this production (15 per cent to 20 per cent in the first half of the sixteenth century and 45 per cent in the latter half) was exported to Brandenburg, Silesia, Bohemia and even to England and Holland, the Polish cloth industry felt a lack of this raw material.[6]

In the 1640s mulberry bushes were planted and silkworms began to be cultivated around Brody for the silk factory belonging to Stanisław Koniecpolski. Perhaps similar attempts were undertaken in other regions in the south of Poland but they were of no economic importance and were unable to guarantee domestic workshops a supply of raw material.

Poland was self-sufficient in organic raw materials and was even able to export considerable amounts of them, being the main supplier of timber and grain and to a certain extent also of livestock, hides, wool, flax and hemp to Western Europe, at least from the middle of the fifteenth up to the middle of the seventeenth century. On the other hand, mineral raw materials appeared or were exploited in insufficient quantities and often the only solution was to import them. The more important mineral deposits exploited in the fourteenth to the seventeenth century were found in the southern regions of the Commonwealth, i.e., in Little Poland and in Red Ruthenia; in the remaining territories there was small-scale mining of minerals which was of little economic significance. The greatest economic role was played by salt and lead.

In the fourteenth to the seventeenth century salt was mined only in the southern parts of the Commonwealth and in two centres: these were the salt mines in Wieliczka and Bochnia near Cracow and the salt springs in Red Ruthenia (Stara Sól, Drohobycz and others). Here salt had already been mined earlier in the Middle Ages. In the fourteenth century the mining of salt developed, reaching particularly large proportions in 1500–1650, particularly in the mines of the Cracow region. The exploitation of shallow deposits gradually led to deeper mining; at the beginning of the sixteenth century miners in Wieliczka descended to from 60 to 70 metres while at the end of the same century work was conducted at a depth of 100 to 120 metres. Simultaneously, attempts were made to increase exploitation by sinking new shafts at the beginning of the seventeenth century (three shafts were working in Wieliczka in the fifteenth century, six at the end of the sixteenth and ten in the middle of the seventeenth century). As a result of these undertakings the production in the Wieliczka salt mines increased in the period from 1500 to 1650 practically fivefold. Both mines in the Cracow region produced annually *c.* 20,000 to 22,000 tons at the beginning of the sixteenth century, *c.* 30,000 tons at the turn of the sixteenth and *c.* 40,000 tons annually in the middle of the seventeenth century. On the other hand, the annual salt production of the Red Ruthenia mines in the middle of the sixteenth century attained *c.* 7,000 tons but later never exceeded 10,000 tons. A large part of the salt (originally 40 per cent and subsequently 20 per cent) was exported to Slovakia and Hungary, Silesia and Moravia, and for this reason domestic production could not meet the total demand of the home market. Northern and central Poland had to import French, Portuguese and Frisian salt through Gdańsk.[7]

Lead was found together with silver and zinc in deposits in Silesia and around Cracow which were the largest in Poland and one of the most sizeable sources of lead in Europe. It was also found in the Kielce–Chęciny region. Exploitation which had already begun in the thirteenth century passed through a stage of great development in the fourteenth century and at the end of the fifteenth century entered into a period of long-lasting crisis caused by the total depletion of the shallow, easily accessible deposits. This crisis was overcome in the middle of the sixteenth century by the use of new methods of gravitational mine draining (the construction of galleries) making it possible to mine deeper deposits (50–60 m and locally as much as 80 m deep). Hence lead production doubled in the second half of the sixteenth century and in the first half of the seventeenth it even increased eightfold, compared with the first half of the sixteenth century. This increase was connected with a complete change in the organisation and financing of ore mining; instead of the former miners' guilds, establishments financed by the kings, magnates and wealthy Olkusz and Cracow burghers took over exploitation in the second half of the sixteenth and in the seventeenth century. Olkusz was the main lead-mining centre in the Silesia–Cracow deposit area while in the first half of the sixteenth century Tarnowskie Góry, also within this region but already beyond the borders of the Polish state, became increasingly important. From the middle of the sixteenth century additional exploitation of calamine (oxidized zinc ore), previously not mined, was undertaken in the Silesia–Cracow deposit area. Moreover copper was being exploited in the Kielce–Chęciny region (where lead was also mined) as well as to a slight degree in the Tatra mountains. Lead production in the Olkusz mines, in the peak period of their development at the end of the sixteenth and the first half of the seventeenth century, reached up to 3,500 tons annually. A few hundred tons were obtained annually from the Kielce–Chęciny mines; 80 per cent of this was exported to Slovakia and Bohemia in the sixteenth century and through Gdańsk to Western Europe in the seventeenth century while the remainder was designated for domestic needs. A part of the calamine was also exported; its exploitation in the Olkusz region can be estimated at from 600 to 1,200 tons annually. On the other hand, the production of copper in the Kielce–Chęciny region was only 120 to 180 tons, which could not satisfy the home market and thus copper was imported from Slovakia. In the late Middle Ages as well as in modern times gold was not mined in Poland and the exploitation of silver, which appeared together with lead, was small; in the middle of the sixteenth century Olkusz supplied annually 600 kg of silver, 1,200 kg at the end of the century and first half of the seventeenth while the Tatra and Kielce–Chęciny deposits gave a few score kgs of silver. For minting and goldsmithing silver was imported from abroad, mainly from Bohemia and Slovakia, in exchange for Polish lead. There was a total lack of zinc and mercury which also had to be imported.[8]

The supplies of iron ore in medieval Poland, and to a large extent in modern times, were sod ores found just below ground surface which were distributed in small quantities throughout the country; these were exploited by simple digging. In the sixteenth to seventeenth centuries the exploitation of siderites and limonite deposits became increasingly important; this took place at greater depths of 30–40 m which called for underground exploitation and the construction of suitable mines. This resulted in a regional concentration of iron-ore mining in modern times in comparison to its dissemination during the medieval period. Larger iron-ore mining centres were concentrated during the sixteenth and first half of the seventeenth century in the Częstochowa region (of prime importance in the sixteenth century), the Kielce–Chęciny region (which came into prominence at the beginning of the seventeenth century), and the Cracow–Upper Silesian and Carpathian regions; less important ones existed in Pomerania. The peak development of iron production occurred in the second half of the sixteenth century when the exploitation of iron in the Commonwealth reached 9,800 tons annually (5,000 tons from Little Poland, 800 from Mazovia, 1,300 from Greater Poland). In the first half of the seventeenth century there was a decrease in exploitation and a decline in the development of iron-ore mining. The output from the iron-ore mines was entirely absorbed by the domestic industry. Amounts produced in the country were insufficient and thus iron was imported from Slovakia, Moravia, Styria, Silesia and Sweden.

The largest and most important deposits of mineral resources, i.e., coal and sulphur in the contemporary Polish economy, either remained unknown from the fourteenth to seventeenth centuries or their exploitation was not undertaken for technological reasons. In the middle of the seventeenth century a certain amount of coal was dug from shallow deposits in Upper Silesia near Murcki and in the Cracow region near Tenczynek; in 1657 attempts were even made at using it for the production of iron. But it was of no economic importance since the technology of the period made it impossible either to develop coal mining or to utilise coal as a source of energy or as a chemical raw material in industry. Sulphur was exploited in Swoszowice and other villages near Cracow. Sulphur deposits in Czarkowy on the River Nida known at that time were not mined because of unfavourable geological conditions. The annual sulphur production at the end of the sixteenth and first half of the seventeenth century is calculated at 80 tons, which entirely satisfied domestic needs and even made export possible.[9] In the sixteenth century the search was begun for saltpetre, alum and vitriol, known as copperas – raw materials indispensable for the production of gunpowder as well as in the paper industry, textile dyestuffs and tanneries. Saltpetre was exploited in many parts of the Carpathian highlands. Alum was found in small amounts in the springs of Drohobycz. Before 1547, deposits of alum and vitriol were discovered in Kozielec in Pomerania. Exploitation was organised by Toruń merchants and then taken over by the Loitz family of bankers from Szczecin and Gdańsk; this exploitation was forsaken probably at their financial downfall in 1572. It was carried on by surface mining and could yield c. 12,000 kg of alum a year. The production of saltpetre and alum was sufficient for domestic needs and these raw materials were even exported (alum was imported in the first half of the seventeenth century) although vitriol was always brought in from abroad. From the middle of the sixteenth century there grew in Poland an interest in oil and paraffin wax found in the Carpathian highlands, but these raw materials were utilised only as medicine and emollients; no other use was found for them. In the sixteenth century the deposits of amber on the Gdańsk coast, famous since antiquity, started to become depleted. The Gdańsk amber workshops which had flourished in the second half of the sixteenth and in the early seventeenth century were forced to bring raw materials from the Duchy of Prussia, Denmark and Kurland.

As regards building materials, Poland had at her disposal above all large resources of timber, as has been already mentioned above. Hence, the majority of buildings constructed from the fourteenth to the seventeenth centuries were made from wood, while in the seventeenth century the role of timber as building material, since it was easy to obtain and required less-skilled craftsmen for its use, even increased. At least 90 per cent of all buildings were wooden, including all residential and farm buildings in the countryside (with the exception of a very few brick or stone manor houses, above all in Little Poland) and in the small towns and the majority of houses in medium-sized or large towns. In Warsaw, in the second half of the eighteenth century wooden houses still constituted around 75 per cent of all constructions. Many churches, public buildings and even residential homes were built of timber (the favourite residence of King Sigismund Augustus in Knyszyn was also wooden). Only some houses in medium and large cities were of brick; of brick too were defence constructions (although there were wooden palisades and earthworks), the majority of royal and magnate residences, monasteries and churches.[10] Raw materials indispensable for brick production such as clay, sand, water and firewood were available over the entire country. Despite this, certain amounts of brick and roof tiles of high quality were imported from Holland. In large urban centres with intensive building activity (among others Warsaw, Cracow and Lublin at the turn of the sixteenth and seventeenth centuries) there was a permanent lack of bricks. Stone was used only for architectural details and decoration, and it appeared very rarely as the basic construction material since there were few deposits of stone suitable for construction in Poland and they were concentrated almost exclusively in Little Poland and Red Ruthenia. The development of Renaissance and Baroque architecture as well as sculpture connected with it resulted in a significant increase in demand for marble, limestone and sandstone. In the sixteenth century an old and important centre for the exploitation of limestone in Pinczów was developed which supplied almost all of Poland with excellent raw material for sculpture and architectural details. The Pinczów limestone was transported by river, hence its distribution was closely linked with the river network, primarily with the Vistula basin. At the beginning of the seventeenth century there emerged a number of new centres for the exploitation of sandstone in Little Poland. In Dębnik near Cracow at the end of the sixteenth century, quarries of black marble were active, a raw material very much sought after by sculptors and architects of the Baroque period. At the same time the quarrying of multi-coloured marble was begun in the region of Chęciny.

Despite the lack of zinc and an insufficient amount of iron and copper as well as of building stone, Poland in the late Middle Ages and even more so in the sixteenth to seventeenth century, when the territory of the state was increased by the addition of Lithuanian–Ruthenian lands, possessed sufficiently rich supplies of natural resources indispensable for the development of all fields of the economy. Since Poland enjoyed a surplus of many of these resources, she was able to export them without detriment to the economy. If an insufficiency of certain resources was felt (for instance salt, and from the end of the sixteenth century timber or wool), this was remedied by importing them or limiting their use; the case arose not so much because of an actual lack but because of insufficiently developed exploitation, irrational management or excessive export. It was not difficult to substitute brick for stone, and insufficient metal ores could be supplemented by imports, which was the more easy considering that Poland participated in international trade and in particular acted as an intermediary in the trade in Slovak copper. In the sixteenth to seventeenth centuries and in certain cases somewhat earlier, Poland was above all a supplier of raw materials to the countries of Western Europe and this was the basis of her wealth in the sixteenth century. However, in the long run neglect of industrial production caused the economic ruin of the country.[11] In adapting to Polish conditions the model presented by Ruggiero Romano in his book *Tra due crisi: l'Italia del Rinascimento*,[12] one can say that the fourteenth-century crisis did not affect Poland. On the contrary, it was precisely then that the gap between it and the most developed countries in Europe began to decrease. In the sixteenth century Poland experienced a period of prosperity based on the weak foundations of extensive exploitation of natural resources, while the economic crisis of the seventeenth century was here particularly acute. Throughout this whole period feudal economic structures remained unchanged.

4 ❧ The demographic landscape of East-Central Europe

ERIC FÜGEDI

quidquid delirant reges, plectuntur Achivi
(For every folly of their rulers the Greeks feel the lash)

(Horace)

The demographic evolution of East-Central Europe between 1300 and 1700 is really rather like a landscape: a landscape, plunged into darkness, where here and there light is thrown. Some of the parts are given a strong light, some stay in a faint light, where only shadowy outlines can be discerned. The illuminated parts – however strong or faint the light is – do not present a pleasant picture: usually they refer to demographic disasters and show their distressing consequences. One has the impression that the picture would not be more pleasant if one could take in the whole scenery at a glance; it would not reflect peaceful growth of the population, but the aftermath of war and epidemics, in short, the decline of population.

How much light is thrown on the parts of this landscape depends more on the nature of the sources than on the efforts of historical demographers. Complete census data would be the best basis for a comprehensive picture of the population, but in this part of the continent rulers began to take censuses only in the second half of the eighteenth century. In Bohemia and the other 'hereditary' provinces of the Habsburg empire, already familiar with loyalty and obedience, they succeeded as early as 1754, in recalcitrant Hungary only in 1784; in Poland the Great Diet managed to take a census in 1789 of what remained of the country after the first partition.[1] Demographers have up to now tried to draw conclusions from the more reliable data of these early censuses concerning previous periods, and one may hope that this method will be improved and that one day the demographic conditions of the seventeenth century will be better known from the censuses of the late eighteenth century. For the time being we are still far from that.

The ingenious French method of family reconstitution from parish registers does not help to form a comprehensive demographic picture of East-Central Europe. In Hungary from the beginning of our period we must take into

47

account the existence of a minority of Orthodox Christians while in Poland the union with Lithuania incorporated many more. In the Orthodox Church, parish registers were unknown and when at the end of the eighteenth century the state compelled the priests to establish registers, tradition and theological considerations prevailed over practical necessities, so that the data contained in the newly drawn-up registers does not allow families to be reconstituted. Parish registers were generally introduced by the Catholics in the late sixteenth century in all three countries and the practice was adopted by the Protestants too. As a result of the Reformation and Counter-Reformation, in this part of Europe the religious unity favoured by the enlightened monarchies never materialised and the denominations became consolidated in their different proportions. One extreme is illustrated by Bohemia, where the Counter-Reformation was completely successful, at least in theory; in Hungary, on the other hand, where even full state support could not reconquer the population for Catholicism, an essential part of the people remained Protestant, but were divided into Lutherans, Calvinists and Unitarians. The fluctuations of the religious conflict, and zealous attempts to hinder free exercise of any other religion resulted many a time in the loss or destruction of early parish registers, and even at a much later period religious minorities were likely to be left out.

It is generally the case in the whole of East-Central Europe that in the Catholic Church continuous registration began in the middle of the seventeenth century and – like anything new – worked irregularly; the regulations of the *Rituale Romanum* introduced by Pope Paul V in 1614 did not fully succeed. Difficulties were great even in the territories where religious unity had been restored. The vastness of the parishes (sometimes even 200 sq km in area), an uneducated and undisciplined clergy, lack of control and the high fees claimed for administering the sacraments prevented the regular keeping of parish registers in Poland during the seventeenth century. The inhabitants of towns, however, had long been accustomed to establishing and keeping various registers, descriptions and lists, and it is therefore little wonder that parish registers were drawn up in Jáchymov in 1531, in Cracow in 1548 and so on, and have been kept regularly ever since.

Considering that taxation returns are 'the most common indicators of population levels before the period of censuses',[2] the scholar is inclined to look for those which cover large areas, possibly whole countries. For the beginning of the fourteenth century, papal tax returns seemed for some time to be the suitable source. In Poland (in 1318) and in the Silesian duchies (much later, in 1353–9) the papal taxation system of Peter's Pence was adopted.[3] In Hungary some kind of connection could surely be made between the sum of the tithe and the population figures (more exactly the number of tithe-payers); if, that is, the precise boundaries of the parishes were known, and also historians were able to sort out which of the parishes possessed revenues from pious foundations or from any other source. As neither of these problems seems likely to be solved, given the state of preservation of Hungarian sources, for the time being the papal tax returns do not seem useful for demographic purposes in Hungary either.

A few decades ago Hungarian historians had a sudden ray of hope when they came into possession of extraordinary sources concerning those parts of the country which from 1542 to 1686 were under Turkish domination. At first glance the Turkish taxation returns, the so-called *tahrir defters*, show a great many advantages, and particularly if compared with earlier Christian ones. The different sorts of landowners – king, Church, nobles – disappeared and all the people were subjects of the sultanship. Taxes were standardised, the collectors all trained in the same way. The first lists were drawn up early, in the fourth year of domination (1546). They were several times brought up to date, sometimes even taking the early version into consideration, and the differences written down. Many *defters* survived and, following the pioneer work of L. Fekete, many were published and processed. In spite of all these advantages, the initial enthusiasm cooled, partly because historians and turcologists failed to evaluate the tax system for demographic purposes. We do not know what kind of people were omitted, or at what age boys were considered to have reached manhood and entered on the lists.[4] The other difficulty lies in the social evolution of Hungary. Peasant family names became firmly established only in the eighteenth century; until then they changed continuously and freely, so that persons appearing in the lists cannot be identified.

We may say that for the whole period feudalism created rather small territorial units and that in consequence a diocese, a town, or a domain usually produced good, or at least better, sources from the point of view of demography, even if the purpose of the list was purely fiscal or administrative. From 1629 onwards, for example, the archbishop of Prague had special lists of inhabitants made at the time of Easter Communion. The surviving lists are not of equal value, but those most detailed ascertained the family structure, included servants, noted the degree of relation to the head of the household, broke down the population according to social groups, gave information on profession and exceptionally on denomination. The same can be said of the Polish *status animarum*, the first of which was drawn up in 1695.

All in all, we do have well-compiled extant sources which shed light on the demographic conditions of small territories, sometimes of a single estate or town, usually at one point of time or for a very short period. However ambitious it seems, I will try to draw these details into a coherent picture for the three countries in question.

The demographic situation at the starting point seems to be fairly clear, though not free of contradictions. The population in the provinces of the Crown of Bohemia ranged from between two and three million, but certainly did not reach three million, Hungary had a population of two million, and Poland (not yet in union with Lithuania) between 1.2 and 1.5 million.[5] The settlement shows a great deal of similarity in all three countries. The overwhelming majority of the population was everywhere agrarian in spite of the fact that all three countries profited from mining: in Bohemia of silver, in Hungary of silver and gold, in Poland of lead and salt.

The peasant population lived in small villages, the average consisting in Bohemia, according to V. Davidek, of 74 persons, and in Hungary, according to I. Szabó's estimation, 130 persons, i.e., 8–10 households. Taking into consideration that according to Czech historians Davidek overestimated the number of villages, the average population of a village could not differ very much in the two countries. The three countries were similar to one another in other respects too. There was plenty of potential agricultural land, chiefly forests that could be made arable. Partly in connection with that surplus land, settlers had been called in by the kings and ecclesiastical and lay lords to set up new villages. In Bohemia the process had taken place in the thirteenth century, but in Poland and Hungary it continued in the fourteenth. It was chiefly German settlers who came to Poland and Bohemia, while in Hungary immigrants arrived from every part of the continent. In consequence the countries became nationally mixed and this feature – changing in quantity and quality during the centuries to come – never ceased to play its role. German immigrants founded many towns in East-Central Europe and the population of the towns was until the mid-sixteenth century usually partly German, and continually attracting new immigrants. The difference in nationality and different economic activities of the population in the towns brought about sharp conflicts with the rural population, with the townspeople forming something of a foreign body within the region. The most important and most populous towns were the capitals, Buda, Prague, Brno and Cracow. The largest proportion of the urban population was to be found in Bohemia, where several hundred towns existed, though many of them were small.

The peaceful picture of these countries and their population that is sometimes painted is perhaps the illusion of the historian, who does not have to wait long for the first great demographic event. At the end of 1347 Europe was invaded from the sea by the Black Death taking its toll of human lives. Of our three countries only Hungary had at the time some, rather weak, connections with the sea, and the epidemic had to use the slower land routes. At the end of 1349 the plague arrived in Hungary and Bohemia, where it caused losses in 1350. It seems to have kept away from Poland altogether and, according to the unanimous opinion of scholars, its impact in the East was not comparable to that experienced in the West, with the exception of Moravia and Silesia, or rather the chief towns, Brno, Znojmo and Wrocław.

To explain this contrast, we must first note the relative sparseness of population in the East. In the case of Hungary and Poland, one may argue that the corn production, animal husbandry and fishing formed a stable equilibrium, famine was extremely exceptional and the Black Death did not catch the population in such poor health as in the Western countries. Recently two biological arguments have been put forward to explain the light losses. J. C. Russell has pointed out that a continental climate is less favourable to plague than an oceanic climate, and J. Nemeskéri launched the idea – at least for Hungary – that its population belonged to the blood-group B, which shows a greater power of resistance to epidemics. Whatever the explanation, much smaller losses than in Western Europe seem to characterise the demographic history of East-Central Europe in the fourteenth century.[6] In one respect, nevertheless, it shared the fate of the Western parts of the continent: from that time on plague was always present, even if there were no severe outbreaks in the next two centuries. Evidence of this is the death from bubonic plague in Prague in 1457 of Ladislaus king of Hungary and Bohemia.

The rest of the fourteenth century brought peaceful development under three exceptionally capable kings: Charles IV, king of Bohemia and emperor, Louis the Great of Hungary, and Casimir the Great of Poland. The trends differed in the three countries, however: in Bohemia crafts and trade (i.e., the towns) benefited more from this growth, in the other two countries the rural population.

Political events first disturbed this peaceful development in Bohemia. The usual – and unfortunately incalculable – losses of the Hussite revolution were augmented by the expulsion of the German population. Though some of these Germans soon returned, the political situation was not resolved and there was war in Bohemia and in northern Hungary throughout the fifteenth century. Two points deserve emphasis: (1) in this part of Europe religious conviction appeared on the scene for the first time as a factor influencing demography (through both emigration and expulsion); (2) during the long wars Hussite tactics were developed to perfection and from the mid-fifteenth century Bohemian mercenaries were much in demand as well-trained and battle-tested warriors. These two factors, having once made their entrance, proved to be inseparable companions. The question of religion remained influential until the end of our period and the Bohemian population even in the Thirty Years' War continued to provide various armies with mercenaries, in that way losing a not inconsiderable number of its men in their prime.

In Hungary social and economic development brought transformations in the structure of settlement. The rural population began to abandon the villages and migrate into the privileged centres of the great estates or into settlements where monoculture – usually vinegrowing – prevailed and the inhabitants enjoyed more freedom and self-government. The average population per village dropped from 130 to 115 persons; many farms were vacated and were conveyed by the landlords to lessees or remained uncultivated. The number of privileged settlements (*oppida*) was estimated officially at 800. This sounds an exaggeration, but their population certainly ranged from 500 to 600, which

CARLYLE CAMPBELL LIBRARY
MEREDITH COLLEGE

means that they contained 16–20 per cent of the total peasant population. Whereas in Bohemia, as mentioned before, trade and crafts were giving strength to the towns, in Hungary this was far from the case because the Hungarian *oppida* were gathering-places of the agrarian population, and few craftsmen and even fewer merchants were to be found in them.[7] In Hungary the peasantry made up 97 per cent of the total population at the close of the fifteenth century and the nobility about 1 per cent, leaving 2 per cent for the towns.

There is an unexpected illumination of the dark landscape in the middle of the sixteenth century. In 1551 a small town (one of the *oppida*), Szigetvár, expecting a Turkish siege, made a 'census' of its inhabitants, listing all persons within its walls, enumerating all members household by household, recording their relation to the head and specifying their food and stock. The list, containing 371 households, proves that the majority (62.4 per cent) lived within the framework of the nuclear family; there were absolutely no families consisting of three generations. Most of the families with children (67.3 per cent) had only one or two offspring; the highest number of children was six and consequently the average family contained 3.6 persons. This demographic situation, of course, was heavily influenced by the expected Turkish attack. The population was inflated by the stream of fugitive villagers; 42.3 per cent of the families were incomplete, 36.6 per cent headed by the mother, the father having been *a Thurcis...interfectus* or *captus a Thurcis*. In brief, the census of Szigetvár reflects the circumstances of a territory remaining under Christian domination but exposed to repeated Turkish raids. F. Szakály, who analysed these data, rightly supposes that the average family must have been more numerous in those parts of the country where the Turkish threat did not exist. This supposition has been proved by I. Hunyadi. For Keresztur, a small village in the western part of the country, a more detailed census of 1542 has survived. The population amounted to 294 in 46 households, i.e., an average of 6.4 persons per household. The enumeration of draught animals makes it possible to classify households according to their financial situation. In prosperous households (owning four or more draught animals), which make up 27.7 per cent of the total, there are always 2–3 men to be found; in the others only one. With 2–3 men we may assume 1 or 2 servants, and it seems to be typical that at Szigetvár 20.8 per cent of the households listed servants. Perhaps we may draw the general conclusions that in Hungary the nuclear family prevailed and that about one-fifth of the rural households contained servants.

The prevalence of the nuclear family has astonished scholars, particularly ethnographers, who considered the extended family the ancient family form of the Hungarians. Such extended families really characterised Hungary during the eighteenth and nineteenth century, but they were born not out of tradition but of economic necessity, caused first of all by the Turkish domination. Though – as has already been said – proper demographic conclusions cannot be reached on the basis of the *defters*, their study has thrown considerable light on the conditions under which the population of two-thirds of Hungary lived from 1542 on. There can be no doubt about the final result of the Turkish domination: the population was almost totally exterminated. After the Turks had been driven out at the end of the seventeenth century, the population of the whole country amounted, according to various – and hotly debated – estimates, to 2.5 to 3 million against four million at the close of the fifteenth century.

This tragic destruction did not sweep the entire area of Turkish domination with the same cruelty. The Hungarian Plains – their southern parts today belonging to Yugoslavia and Romania – suffered the heaviest losses. However, even in these parts one cannot exclude the possibility that the Turks moved the Christian population into their more secure Balkan provinces. Villages lying on the great routes were soon depopulated in the course of repeated Turkish assaults. The villages of the new Hungarian–Turkish frontier did not fare any better: sieges of castles and towns, raids from both sides and particularly the fact that taxes were collected by both sides forced the population to flee. Excessively complicated and heavy taxation forced other villagers to migrate to the towns which were in a better position to defend themselves and their interests. The big 'peasant-towns' in the Hungarian Plain came into being during this period. As a consequence of this movement, the territory of the abandoned villages came into the possession of the swollen towns, first as leases, later as incorporated land.

The development of vast border areas brought changes in the rural economy: corn gave way to livestock, chiefly cattle and sheep. Within six months of 1563–4 (including the chief season of cattle droving from August to October) 30 thousand oxen and 25 thousand sheep were exported at one – admittedly the most important – Turkish custom-house. Live cattle and animal products made up 99.9 per cent of the customs revenue.

Slavs from the Balkans took the place of the Hungarians who had fled or been exterminated, and Turkish craftsmen migrated to the towns, forming a Moslem community together with stranded soldiers and civil servants. The series of surviving *defters* prove that the population declined most sharply during the seventeenth century. Unbelievable losses were caused by a combination of factors. In 1591 war broke out between the Turks and the Christian part of Hungary (so-called Royal Hungary) and lasted fifteen years. Scores of thousands of Habsburg troops and Turkish armies more than a hundred thousand strong assembled and advanced, besieged fortresses, fought fierce battles, with all the accompanying disruption of which pillage had the worst effect. There was not much difference in the behaviour of the various troops of either side, but it proved to be a disaster that from 1597 onwards the Turks put Mongols in the field, who as nomads sometimes passed the winter there. Their advance was characterised by massacre and destruction beyond all reason; they depopulated whole counties, more than once those of their own master.

The Fifteen Years' War came to an end in 1606, but the remaining years of the century brought little relief. War continued with some intermissions and in 1683 the Turks again sent Mongols to Hungary. What had managed to be saved during the long Turkish domination was destroyed by the mercenaries of the liberating army. Plague affected the whole of the country in 1621–2, 1644–5 and 1660–2, but it never disappeared totally. The plague of 1690–2 was imported by wounded soldiers; it claimed 30 thousand dead.[8]

The Turks were driven away in 1686, and the estimate that only 10 per cent of the population from the beginning of the sixteenth century survived till the end of the Turkish domination does not seem exaggerated. The losses of the Magyar population were even heavier, as an important part of the 10 per cent was made up of immigrants from the Balkans. Its economy did not fare better. Forests were destroyed, rivers ran wild, new large marshes came into being on land which in the other areas provided extensive animal husbandry.

About the demographic evolution of Royal Hungary and Transylvania, which became a more-or-less independent duchy in the middle of the sixteenth century, we know nothing. Recent estimates of I. Bakács and I. N. Kiss seem questionable. The combination of war and epidemics did not spare this part of the country either; nevertheless it is likely that it suffered no diminution in its population figures from the beginning of the sixteenth century.

It was mentioned above that in about 1300 the three countries differed very little. However, summing up Hungary's situation in the sixteenth to the seventeenth century, it has to be said that that country with its patchy agriculture, worked-out mines and thin population lagged far behind Bohemia and Poland.

Bohemia seems to have recovered from the losses caused by the Hussite revolution and the following wars. By the end of the sixteenth century the population had reached four million. The rate of growth reached its peak in the first half of the sixteenth century, at the time of economic boom, and was brought about not only by natural reproduction but by immigration. New mines were opened to exploit the mountains' precious metals. The development of the chief mining town, Jáchymov, illustrates the close connection between economic and population growth. The town was founded beside a silver mine in 1516 and already had 16,000 inhabitants in 1533, at the peak of silver production.

The economic boom initiated a development similar to that in Hungary a century earlier. Villages, forming the centres of estates, became small towns by multiplying their population and strengthening their economic activities. The landlords were eager to help their development and tried to make them centres of trade and crafts. The growth in population was caused by peasants escaping from the increasing pressure of taxes and serf labour.

Fortunately we possess 'inventories' from this period of a small town, Prachatice (made in 1585), and of two estates, Vysoký Chlumec and Jistebnice (written down in 1617). The inventories include not only 346 households of 4 smaller towns, but also 519 households of 87 villages and therefore enable us to take a look at the demographic situation of both peasants and townspeople. There is a marked contrast with Hungary. The Czech villages – at least in the region referred to – were smaller: the number of households ranged mostly from 3 to 13, exceeding 20 in only one of them. The four towns were also smaller than Szigetvár, even if we take into consideration that the latter had been swollen with escaping peasants. In contrast to Hungary where small towns kept their rural character longer, the Czech towns became real centres of trade and crafts. At the end of the sixteenth century in Bohemia there were 56 royal towns, and this number has to be augmented by 77 towns of private landlords in which the number of the houses exceeded 100. In Moravia only 9 royal towns can be found, but the number of small towns was astonishingly high. In Bohemia at least one-fourth, in Moravia one-fifth, of the population lived in towns.

Households in towns, with an average of 5.1 to 6.3 persons (not including servants), were smaller than in the villages where the average size was 8.2 (again not including servants). The wealthy and the poor differed, of course, in both towns and villages. The wealthy of the towns had a family average of 2.7, and of the villages 3.6 persons; there was a similar pattern for the poor: 2.1 in towns and 2.3 in the villages. The average number of children per family in the towns was 2.22 and in the villages 3 to 4. On the whole these figures are similar to those of Hungary but are a little more favourable. Rapid growth cannot be concluded from the indices, even if we suppose that they can be generalised for the whole of the country. Perhaps more immigrants were attracted by the economic boom than is usually supposed.

The demographic disaster in Bohemia, as in Hungary, was the result of politics. The centralising and absolutist ambitions of the Habsburgs had already led to strained relations with the Bohemian estates in the 1540s. The tension resulted in the outbreak of an armed uprising in 1618 and ended in 1620 at the White Mountain with a crushing defeat of the estates. The uprising was not isolated, but was a part of the Thirty Years' War. The presence of foreign troops was established for the lifetime of a generation; they left only after the treaty of Westphalia. Epidemics proved to be companions of war in Bohemia too; plague swept over the country in four big waves, 1622–6, 1633–5, 1639–40 and 1648–9. Emigration joined with war and epidemics to diminish the population. The vengeance following the battle of the White Mountain affected not only the leaders and the members of the ruling class; every peasant and burgher who was not willing to give up his Hussite or Protestant religion became involved in it. Deportation and voluntary emigration, chiefly of Czechs, reduced the population.

Czech historians do not agree about the relative importance of the three factors. Formerly the consequences of the war and of the presence of mercenaries were placed first, emigration second and epidemics third. Recently the order has been reversed. O. Placht has pointed out that many of the emigrants returned after only a short time in exile; the greatest losses were caused by epidemics. In spite of his revaluation of the causes, he also thinks that the losses of the population were extremely heavy. Bohemia lost 45 per cent of its population (770 thousand) and Moravia 25 per cent (200 thousand), so that the population of the two was reduced from 2.5 million at the beginning of the seventeenth century to little over 1.5 million by the end, that is, one has to reckon with the loss of some 40 per cent. Placht emphasises that it was the size of households that decreased most drastically and that the average number of children per family – both in town and country – dropped to half that at the beginning of the century.

Another step forward in estimating the losses was made by J. Petráň and V. Davidek. In their view only a third of the population was lost. Their estimates are based on the economic situation. E. Maur worked on the previously mentioned communion lists of the archdiocese of Prague from 1651.[9] His aim was not so much to assess the losses as to establish the demographic structure of the population that had survived the wars. The communion lists of this year are like real censuses; all adults required to go to confession are included with their ages, and in some cases children not old enough to confess and even babies. In spite of all the defects of pre-statistical censuses, in recording ages, for example, 'on the national scale the list seems on the whole to give reliable information about the peasants and townspeople'.[10] It should be added, however, that not the whole list, but only parts of it have been analysed: 'the number of samples taken is not sufficient at all; some regions are over-represented, some under-represented, others are left out entirely'.[11]

The consequences of the war show themselves in almost every respect, the sex ratio being one. Though in the countryside to every 100 men there were at most 110 women, in the towns they exceeded 120, and in some cases reached 150. In the countryside a quarter of women of child-bearing age could not find a husband and in the towns there were as many as a third of such unfortunate women. The great shortage of men was due chiefly to the recruitment of mercenaries and only partly due to the biological weakness of the males. In the countryside 25–30 per cent of women in the 15- to 19-year-old category were already married, in the towns at best only 15 per cent; consequently in the towns 3–7 per cent of the babies were born out of wedlock. In spite of women marrying at an early age, there were few children: 2–3 per family on average and in the areas severely affected by the war even less, 1.5 to 2. 'The lowest age groups are among the most affected.'[12]

If we speak of the average, it should be added that the distribution of the phenomena was very unequal. There were regions almost totally destroyed by the war, but some were very quickly repopulated. In the border regions migration was responsible for large reductions, and it seems likely that nationality also influenced demographic behaviour. The provinces of the Crown of Bohemia, we may therefore conclude, lost between 1620 and 1650 at least a third, maybe even more, of their population as a consequence of war, epidemics and migration – heavy losses of course, but much less so than in Hungary. Recovery began partly by immigration, partly by increasing natural reproduction, and the country also had the advantage of not being excluded from European economic development.

In Poland peaceful development continued in the sixteenth century and as a result the population reached 3.2 million. The more abundant sources of the sixteenth century than of previous times allow family and household sizes at that period to be determined. An enquiry into 12 villages (7 from Great Poland, 5 from Little Poland) shows that the average number of children per family was 3.5–3.6, which partly explains the increased population. The households were completed by servants, so the size of the household depended chiefly upon the material base, i.e., on the dimension of land at its disposal. According to A. Wyczański's calculation, in the case of a one-mansus farm (1 mansus = 16.8 ha) there was an average of 2.8 servants per household, in the case of one-half mansus 2.4, in that of a one-quarter only 0.9. Corresponding with that, the size of a peasant household ranged from 6.6 to 8.7 persons.

The peaceful development of the sixteenth century in Poland–Lithuania was interrupted by political events, by prolonged or intermittent wars with the Tartars, Cossacks, Transylvania, Muscovy or the Swedes, leading in 1655–60 to what has been called a 'Deluge'. By European standards, the Swedes and their allies proved to be ruthless belligerents too; in Mazovia, out of 43 royal towns no fewer than 15 were burnt down. War was accompanied by epidemics; according to some estimates, usually considered exaggerated, 400 thousand people fell victim to them. They ravaged the towns chiefly, where the crowded population living in unsanitary conditions suffered heavy losses. Epidemics were encouraged by catastrophic harvests: the production of peasant farms fell back to a third the level of a hundred years before, those of the great landlords to 45 per cent. The three factors – wars, epidemics and famine – carried off a third of the population or perhaps even more.[13] The increase of the previous hundred years was lost. The losses were not uniform over the whole country: they were the smallest, 23 per cent, in Little Poland, the highest in Mazovia, where 40 per cent of the rural and 70 per cent of the urban population perished.

The few illuminated patches help us to draw some conclusions about the demographic evolution of East-Central Europe as a whole. The evolution of Western Europe – and particularly that of England – was characterised by the fact that, after the ravages of the Black Death in 1348,

At the end of the fifteenth century population again began to rise and by the time that parish registers were first kept in 1538 population was rising fast in most parishes. It continued to do so until the middle decade of the seventeenth century, when this second wave of growth was played out and for a century population nationally showed no decisive trend.[14]

In East-Central Europe the Black Death did not take a heavy toll of the population and in the fifteenth century slow growth took place there, perhaps with the exception of Bohemia. The first disaster affected Hungary at the end of the sixteenth century, thirty years later Bohemia was involved in a demographic catastrophe, and Poland followed soon after. In all three countries the population suffered extremely heavy losses, similar to the Black Death of the fourteenth century in the Western part of the continent, and in all three cases politics initiated them. The disaster consisted not only in the combination of the three factors – war, epidemics and famine (with resulting emigration) – but in the continued presence of this combination for more decades. In Hungary it took the last 90 years of Turkish domination, in Bohemia 30, in Poland 20 years before things finally settled down. If we assume that there was a peaceful development and slow growth from 1350 till the end of the sixteenth century in spite of the delicate demographic structure, the seventeenth century has to be considered as disastrous. The effects of the disasters were the heavier because they came late, the productive forces diminished just at a time when they were most needed. In this respect, as well as in that of nationality, the price of the disasters had to be paid by the centuries to come. Lost also was the relative uniformity of the economic, social and demographic situation that had characterised the three countries at the beginning of our period, and with it mutual understanding between different nationalities was reduced.

5 ✝ Trends of agrarian economy in Poland, Bohemia and Hungary from the middle of the fifteenth to the middle of the seventeenth century

LEONID ŻYTKOWICZ

The countries mentioned in the title of this article constituted a very extensive area. Stretching from the southern coastline of the Baltic up to the Dalmatian coast of the Adriatic, it divided the whole of Europe asymmetrically. The union between Poland and Lithuania in 1569 increased this area considerably up to the Dnieper basin in the east and the Dvina in the north. From the point of view of the dynastic successes of the Jagiellonians, one can describe this whole region as Jagiellonian Europe. But it is not this aspect which leads us to attempt a cohesive examination of the development of conditions for the grain economy in these countries.

These were countries which lay to the east of the most developed and densely populated areas of Europe at that period. Expansive lowlands and climatic conditions predestined them to the role of great producers of grain. Simultaneously, in the sixteenth century and perhaps even earlier, Europe found itself under the influence of a large demand for agrarian products, especially grain, which was felt particularly acutely, although not solely, in the most developed countries of Western Europe. The increase of demand and favourable prices for agrarian products formed, we believe, the main premise for an economic activisation of the feudal class in the region which is of interest to us.[1] At this point one should stress the fact that the feudal class in these countries had a monopoly of landownership and that the rural population which subsisted on work in agriculture was dependent upon it.

However, the situation and conditions for the development of each of the above-mentioned countries were not identical. Poland constituted an integral and, from the economic point of view, a most important component of the 'Baltic zone'. The role and function of this area in the European economy, at the dawn of the modern era, can be described as that of a territory supplying Western Europe with agricultural and animal products, as a result of which it became the object of interest to Western capital. 'Baltic' grain, in reality grain from the northern parts of Poland (up to 1454 from those areas which remained under the rule of the Teutonic Order), played a significant role in

59

supplying food for the towns of Flanders and Brabant already in the fifteenth century.[2] This does not concern either Bohemia or Hungary although the export of Hungarian oxen played a considerable role in the economy of that country.

I

As we have mentioned, Poland possessed both the natural and transportation conditions for becoming a great exporter of grain. Moreover the social and political dominance of the feudal class and the structure of landownership facilitated the organisation of the production of grain for the market and guaranteed a favourable division of the social income. A relatively low level of urbanisation as well as the fact that a part of the town population was engaged in agriculture should have made possible the sending to distant markets of a considerable part of the production surplus. These factors were the main reasons for the reconstruction of an agrarian system in Poland aimed towards the development of serf-labour economy. This also signified far-reaching changes not only in the agrarian structure of the country but also in the economic, social and legal status of the rural population.

The existing economic system in Poland limited the role and income of the landowner to the collection of monetary payments, payments in kind as well as those resulting from feudal privileges. The estate of the lord of the manor, i.e., the *praedium* (later known as the *praedium antiquum* as distinct from the demesne producing for the market) was to satisfy the needs of the landowner himself and his household. The producer of grain and supplier to the market was the peasant farmstead. It was capable of supplying a surplus to the town and local market. Considering the technical conditions of transportation at the time, the supply of grain to a distant market was undoubtedly not less difficult and perhaps even more costly than its production. Despite appearances, river transportation was not cheap and could amount to 10 to 20, even 30 per cent of the value of the grain, depending on the distance. Naturally, the transportation of large amounts of grain was more profitable than of small ones. The mediation of the merchant also deprived the producer of a part of the profits gained from the sale. The problem of distance resulted from the fact that it was the foreign, external market which was so vital, since neighbouring countries, as a result of a similar economic structure, were not able to become importers of Polish grain on a large scale. Only neighbouring Silesia, which at that time belonged to Bohemia and after 1526–9 became a part of the Habsburg monarchy, imported certain amounts of grain from Great Poland, but this was local trade and not export on a large scale. Only its own production and organisation of sales of surplus grain could ensure the feudal class higher incomes than was possible under the rent system.

This was why the feudal class strove towards its own organisation of both the production and transportation of grain to the sea ports and especially to Gdańsk and, with this aim in mind, towards the establishment of a fleet of river boats. Moreover, a nobleman, and especially a magnate, a great landowner, could use free peasant transport in order to bring the grain to the river docks, which in turn made it possible to increase the supply radius to areas beyond the Vistula basin and, above all, to Volhynia and Red Ruthenia and even further. It is understandable that the owner of a great estate found himself in a better situation than the squire who possessed only one or two manors. From the beginning of the seventeenth century this became one of the reasons for the process of concentration of landed property in the hands of larger owners, at the expense of the middle and lesser gentry. Such a process had far-reaching social and political consequences since it created premises for an increase in the importance of the magnates and, in the future, for the rule of a magnate oligarchy.

Let us, however, return to the village and manor. In order to organise serf-labour agrarian production it was indispensable to have arable land, human labour, draft animals, tools and farm buildings. Land did not present a problem. So-called vacant (waste) lands, i.e., lands uninhabited or for various reasons deserted by settlers, were a universal phenomenon, not a purely Polish one. Moreover, it was possible to confiscate the better land from the peasants, transferring them to either inferior or totally waste lands. It was also possible to decrease the areas of the peasant farmsteads. During a period of an intensive development of the manor and of serf labour, landowners considered farmsteads of one-half mansus to be of optimum size and self-sufficient; in other words, capable of maintaining a peasant family as well as its draught animals and in addition able to supply a surplus of labour, both human and animal. Finally, it was possible to gain lands for the manor by clearing woodlands and generally by cultivating the *agri novales*, i.e., lands heretofore unexploited in agriculture. On the other hand, there did not occur in Poland the development of total relegation, that is the ousting of peasants from villages, since this would have been contrary to the interests of the landowner.[3]

And labour itself? As a rule it took the form of compulsory unpaid labour by the rural population, universally known as *pańszczyzna* (serf labour). The view which claims that the manor in Poland during the first stage of its development was of a hired-labour character has been abandoned. The more effective but costly hired labour could have been more widely applied wherever the manor had better conditions for development and especially more favourable conditions for the sale of agricultural products, and thus at its disposal larger financial resources, for example, in the fertile Żuławy region of the Vistula estuary or in the regions near the more important towns. But even there the costs of hiring labour were very high in relation to the value of the crops, despite the fact that free labour was also partly used. For example, in the above-mentioned Żuławy region, which belonged to Malbork Castle (royal property) in the years 1561–4, these costs constituted 34 per cent of production value (including the consumption of the manor itself, but without seed for sowing). On the other hand, the costs of grain transportation were relatively low since they amounted to only a few per cent in relation to sums gained from sales of grain. In the suburban manors of Poznań in the years 1585–1639 hiring labour absorbed 20 to 40 per cent of the cost of production, depending on a given year. This unfavourable proportion between hiring costs and crop value, was the result of the low yield ratio which usually did not exceed 2 to 4. This was the situation during the long period from the sixteenth to the middle of the eighteenth century.

Low yields, their considerable variability, the frequent years of poor harvest as a result of weather conditions, hence an uncertainty as regards the crops, were the main if not the sole causes for the serf-labour organisation of the manors. Production risks became smaller and even a slight commodity surplus which could be sold was decisive for the 'profitability' of a farm. In research on the origin of the serf-labour manor in Poland insufficient attention has as yet been paid to the level of the productive forces, or, in this case, the low productivity of labour in agriculture. Unpaid serf labour could have influenced the level of sales prices of Polish grain abroad. One automatically asks the question, to which it is extremely hard to find an answer, whether in the conditions of a general use of hired labour the bulk export of Polish grain would have been possible or whether the price would not have been too high for the foreign buyer. The serf labourer used his own tools and his own draught animals. This made it possible to reduce to a minimum the investment expenditure on the part of the landlord. One should remember the social–constitutional conditions of the period which made it impossible to develop a labour market in agriculture. The spread of hired labour would have had to lead to the loosening or even the disintegration of serfdom and this was not in the least in the interests of the feudal class.[4]

Total grain production did not correspond to the great expanse of the country. The reasons for this were low productivity, the extensive character of Polish agriculture, a fallow system of land cultivation (in principle the three-field but in certain areas the two-field system) as well as the fact that, according to the estimates made by A. Wyczański, in the main regions of the country (Mazovia, Little and Great Poland) only 18.7, 14.3 and 26.2 per cent of land was under cultivation and only in Royal Prussia as much as 40.7 per cent of the total land (including fallow). According to the estimates made by A. Wyczański, in 1580 despite the very high yield ratio, the production of the main grains, with the exception of oats, in the four regions mentioned above (totalling approximately 165,000 sq km with a population of 3.4 million) amounted to 1,500,000 tons (of which 986,000 tons were of rye). The inclusion of oats, which was economically less important since it was not a bread grain, might have made it possible to raise this amount to 2,000,000 tons. In the remaining regions of the country grain production must have been even lower in relation to its area, primarily as a result of a low density of population, a low degree of urbanisation and poor communications.

The structure of grain cultivation was to a large extent regulated by the three-crop rotation system, which meant that as a rule the areas of winter and summer crops had to be equal. In the two-field system there existed a greater freedom in shaping the proportion of both these grains since first one and then the other was planted on fallow lands. However, a general tendency could be noted towards increasing the area under winter crops at the expense of summer crops and perhaps of fallow lands too. These winter crops were the bread grains for which demand on the market was the greatest, and possibly also on the farmstead itself. Because of the soil and the level of agricultural technology, it was mainly rye rather than wheat which was grown. Among the summer grains, oats were cultivated most widely, giving, as a rule, the lowest yield. Barley was in great demand as a result of a high consumption of beer. The production of barley was probably insufficient since numerous sources of information available indicate that rye and oats were also used for beer-making.

Rye and oats together generally speaking constituted over 80 per cent of grain sown. One of the rare exceptions was the already-mentioned Malbork property, where large amounts of barley were cultivated. Of course, one can find examples of manors where more wheat was grown (and at the same time less oats), e.g., on the fertile lands of the Sandomierz voivodship (Little Poland) or the Ruthenian voivodship. The composition of the harvest was as a rule slightly different, mainly because of the lower yield of oats. Perhaps it was sown on worse land and as a rule unfertilised because it was on the stubble fields. But part of it could have been used for fodder in an unthreshed form, and as a result all of its yield not registered. Low grain harvests in Poland did not constitute a specifically local phenomenon and in this respect significant differences between Poland and the neighbouring countries did not occur.

Research into the production of peasant farms is more difficult than into that of the great estates. As a result of a lack of statistics one has to make use of indirect data, such as the size of a farmstead, the area under cultivation (which can be determined only hypothetically) and crop yields. Under these circumstances calculations can differ and there exists the danger of schematic reasoning. Mrs A. Wawrzyńczyk gave a very high estimate for the production of a one-half mansus peasant farmstead in Mazovia in the mid-sixteenth century, i.e., of 214 Gdańsk scheffel of the four basic grains, which amounts to practically 7,000 kilograms. That author assumed a very high yield ratio averaging 9 to 1 for the four grains.[5] This would prove great prosperity for the Mazovian peasant in the early period of the serf-labour system. A different result was attained in an attempt to calculate the productivity of the one-half mansus peasant farmstead in Mazovia in the middle of the seventeenth century on the basis of tithe registers: it amounted to 1,800–2,700 kilograms of grain gross, depending on the harvest. Only in a year of a relatively good harvest could such a production satisfy the needs of a farmstead, and the market surplus was minimal. In worse years there occurred a deficit.[6]

Reality was certainly much more complicated. During the period of feudal economy harvests were subject to steady and practically annual fluctuations. Production surplus, and especially the part intended for sale, was subject to multiple fluctuation since certain items of grain expenditure were permanent. In order to counteract these insufficiencies, peasants tried to make more intensive use of their own plots which lay close to the farm buildings. It would be difficult to say how much and what was gained by this but the fact itself is significant. Some profit must have been made on the cultivation of such crops as rape seed, flax, hemp, buckwheat and millet. A certain amount of the produce must have made its way to the markets. Moreover, as the samples studied by A. Wyczański shows, Polish peasants were often active outside their own farms, renting various demesne lands, as a rule arable lands. Naturally this led to a widening of differences in income and greater changes in the social stratification of the rural population. In addition, peasants expanded their own farms by the cultivation of woodlands and waste lands without seeking the approval of the landlord.

Even today we do not know what the share of the Polish peasant was in supplying produce for the home market in the local towns or in the export of grain abroad. We cannot accept *a priori* that the peasants supplied grain to the domestic market while the demesne gave grain for export, nor divide estates into those which produced for the home market and those which produced for export. The supposition that the producer sold grain wherever more attractive terms were found at a given moment seems to be more probable. The existence of a trade in grain by merchants could be an indication that peasant grain also was able to reach the foreign market (see Table 5.1).

One can thus accept that the first stimulus for the development of manorial estates aimed at a market production was supplied by an increase of demand on the domestic market. This would accord with the well-known fact that Polish towns in the fifteenth and sixteenth centuries experienced a period of strong demographic development. John Długosz, an outstanding Polish historian from the fifteenth century and author of the extremely valuable *Libri beneficiorum dioecesis Cracoviensis* (*c.* 1470), gives much information concerning the high rate of obligatory serf labour in the villages of the Cracow diocese, amounting to three to four days a week. Perhaps it was precisely the suburban location of those villages (with Cracow being at that time the state capital) that was decisive for the early demand for grain on the local market.[7] One should also add that even today we are unacquainted with the geography of the emergence of demesne agriculture, the development of serf labour or with the geographical shaping of the Gdańsk market. It is known in general that

Table 5.1. *Division of grain deliveries via Gdańsk in the years 1557–76 according to the social origin of the suppliers (in percentages)*

Years:	Mazovia		Little Poland		Russia + Volhynia	
	good	bad	good	bad	good	bad
Magnates	27	36	58	64	57	70
Rich gentry	13	15	15	16	21	12
Middle gentry	13	12	10	9	5	10
Merchants	33	24	10	10	16	8
Clergy	14	13	6	1	1	—
Total	100	100	100	100	100	100

Based on: A. Mączak, 'Export of Grain and the Problem of Distribution of National Income in the Years 1550–1650', *Acta Poloniae Historica*, 18 (1968), Table 2 on p. 82 (on the basis of unpublished calculations made by T. Chudoba).

the river routes to Gdańsk included ever newer regions of the Vistula basin and, as was mentioned before, even beyond, but we lack detailed knowledge of the chronology of this phenomenon. The development and fluctuations of rye exports according to the existing literature on the subject are presented in Table 5.2. Remaining grains did not hold an important position in exports.

The amount of rye exported from Poland (not including the Grand Duchy of Lithuania) in all directions was not much larger than the amount exported through Gdańsk. It is perhaps remarkable that export from such a vast territory did not reach larger amounts. According to the estimates made by A. Wyczański, export in the years 1571–90 averaged approximately 43,000 tons per annum, which constituted only 4.5 per cent of the total rye production in the above-mentioned four regions of the country, while its value made up 1.3 per cent of the national income.[8] This conclusion calls for further comment. The calculations were based on the average exports in a period when they were much lower than in previous and, in particular, subsequent years (Table 5.2). Already at the beginning of the seventeenth century export via Gdańsk reached a much higher level: 186,000 tons in 1618, for example, as against probably *c.* 250,000 tons in all directions. The average rye exports via Gdańsk in the first quarter of the seventeenth century could be estimated at *c.* 100,000 tons. This would mean that in this period exports embraced a larger percentage of production and in certain years perhaps even exceeded 10 per cent, despite the fact that the supplies for Gdańsk came from as far as Volhynia and Ruthenia. Grain production probably did not grow in the same proportion as exports, for the first half of the seventeenth century is generally recognised as a period of regression and even of a crisis in the rural economy.

In one way or another, the supply of grain to the Gdańsk market, with

Table 5.2. *Rye export via Gdańsk (selected years)*

Years	Lasts	(Tons)	Years	Lasts	(Tons)
1465	2,300	(5,060)	1590/4	2,800	(6,160)
1470	2,200	(4,840)	1595/9	38,685	(85,107)
1490	9,500	(20,900)	1615	32,600	(71,720)
1492	10,200	(22,440)	1618	84,805	(186,571)
1530	14,000	(30,800)	1625	19,200	(42,240)
1557	21,000	(46,200)	1631/5	31,400	(69,080)
1562/5*	42,720	(93,948)	1635/40	31,800	(69,960)
1566/9	35,350	(77,770)	1641/4	50,900	(111,980)
1574/9	19,780	(43,516)	1646/9	40,775	(89,705)
1580/4	18,908	(41,598)	1649	70,896	(155,971)
1585/9	27,380	(60,236)			

* Here and subsequently = annual averages.

Based on: M. Biskup, 'Handel wiślany w latach 1454–1466' (Trade upon the Vistula in the Years 1454–1466), *Roczniki Dziejów Społecznych i Gospodarczych*, 15 (1959), pp. 176–7; M. Bogucka, *Handel zagraniczny Gdańska w I połowie XVII w.* (Foreign Trade of Gdańsk in the early part of the 17th Century), Wrocław 1975, pp. 36–8; S. Hoszowski, 'Handel Gdański XV–XVII w.' (Gdańsk Trade in the 15th–17th Centuries), in *Prace z zakresu historii gospodarczej. Wyższa Szkoła Ekonomiczna w Krakowie. Zeszyty Naukowe No. 11*, Cracow 1960, pp. 31 ff; A. Mączak, 'Export of Grain and the Problem of Distribution of National Income in Poland 1550–1650', *Acta Poloniae Historica*, 18 (1968), pp. 75–98; R. Rybarski, *Handel i polityka handlowa Polski w XVI w.* (Poland's Trade and Trade Policy in the 16th Century), Warsaw 1958, 1, pp. 23–9; 2, pp. 17–18; H. Samsonowicz, 'La commerce maritime de Gdańsk dans la première moitié du XVIe siècle', *Studia Historiae Oeconomicae*, 9 (1974), p. 55.

Gdańsk itself constituting an important centre for consumption, did not always satisfy demand. The main reason for this can be seen in the low crop yields and frequent years of bad harvests. The commodity surplus could not have been large in comparison to the area under cultivation. We have already mentioned peasant farms. At the end of the fifteenth century a manorial demesne belonging to a member of the middle gentry, i.e., an owner of one or two villages, could supply the market with 9–10 tons of wheat and rye during the course of a good-harvest year. His productive potential was limited.[9] However, it was not this type of manor but the great latifundia which became the largest suppliers of grain to the foreign markets. They had greater opportunities for increasing production with practically unlimited land resources and labour power at their disposal. They were also able to organise long-distance transportation more cheaply and safely. The administration of great estates was better acquainted with the situation in the Gdańsk market. The social origin of grain suppliers to Gdańsk depended upon the structure of landownership in the country, and this is understandable. But attention has been drawn to the fact that the participation of the wealthy gentry and magnates was higher than the percentage of land owned by them. By way of example, the structure of grain transport to Gdańsk in the years 1557–76 according to the social affiliation of the suppliers is shown in Table 5.1. The participation of the magnates and wealthy gentry was very considerable in Mazovia (which was not a region of large properties) while in Little Poland, Ruthenia and Volhynia it dominated and exceeded their participation in landownership. It is characteristic that during the 'lean' years this participation grew, since obviously the great landowners had better opportunities for supplementing shortages with stores from previous years. One should take into consideration the fact that soon the process of land concentration was to begin, which must have increased the role of the great landowner in supplying Gdańsk.

Even the greatest landowners at times sent by river transport not very abundant amounts of grain, if one can rely on the records of the Warsaw river customs dating from the first decades of the seventeenth century, and this was, after all, the peak period for the export of Polish grain. The location of Warsaw, deep in the centre of the country, means that these registers could not have included grain transport from all the estates of a given owner. The magnates of that period owned estates mainly in Little Poland and further away on Ruthenian and Ukrainian lands. Transport from Volhynia was certainly not registered in Warsaw because it went by the River Bug which joins the Vistula past Warsaw. The greatest amount of grain was supplied in 1605 by John Zamojski, one of the richest men in Poland in that period; it amounted to 2,333 tons of various grains, not only rye. His son and heir was already able to provide only 900 tons annually; a number of magnates 1,000 to 1,600 tons each, while others 800 tons and less. Upon the basis of a general acquaintance with the crop yield and grain sales one can accept that the commodity surplus in large estates occurred within the framework of 40–50 per cent in relation to demesne harvest. If our calculations are close to reality, then the great estates which had 340–530 mansi under cultivation (including demesne and peasant land, which supplied compulsory labour) were able to provide the market with 100 tons of rye; in other words in order to produce one ton of rye for sale one had to have from 3.4 to 5.3 mansi (57–89 hectares) under cultivation. This was caused on the one hand by a system of extensive agriculture (three-field or even two-field rotation) and a low yield. A great divergence of the areas under cultivation in our calculations – hypothetical in any case – derives from the fact that fluctuations in harvests must be taken into consideration and also the different levels of commodity production on the manorial estates and the different proportions of demesne and peasant lands. The results of the calculations presented here are confirmed by concrete examples of certain great landed estates.[10]

The estimates cited here may help us to understand such phenomena as

(1) the tendency of magnates and the prosperous landowners generally to increase and expand their properties: under conditions of an extensive economy and a lack of a clear-cut progress in agriculture as well as the serf-labour organisation of production, this was actually the only way of increasing the grain supply for the market; (2) an insufficient grain supply in Gdańsk: the local merchants frequently sought grain with the help of intermediaries and made contracts 'on the spur of the moment'. The town authorities, concerned with satisfying the needs of the citizens, sought refuge in limitations and regulations. Let us also add that exports were subject to major fluctuations. Probably to a large degree this was the consequence of unsteady supplies. We have centred our attention on Gdańsk since export from Poland in other directions was slight. A separate problem is that of exports from the Grand Duchy of Lithuania via Königsberg, Memel, Labiau and Riga.

As has been mentioned, the first quarter of the seventeenth century constituted the zenith of grain exports from Poland. From 1625 the war with Sweden halted trade in the Vistula estuary and, despite the return of peace on the Baltic with the Oliwa Treaty of 1660, the grain trade did not regain its former proportions. A regression, although not a downfall, occurred. In the best years of the second half of the seventeenth century exports did not reach 150,000 tons and hence were considerably lower than at the beginning of the seventeenth century. The causes of this regression were complex: demand in the West fell and the favourable price structure for agriculture in the sixteenth century changed. This meant a downward trend in the purchasing power of Polish grain.[11] We shall not consider at this point whether the shrinking of Polish grain exports was one of the symptoms of a general crisis in the European economy and of a regression in the rural economy of Poland, or whether it was a phenomenon with causes of its own.

II

Bohemia was surrounded by countries having similar conditions of development and, let us add, with a similar economic structure: Silesia, Saxony, Lusatia, Bavaria, and the neighbouring Austrian lands as well as western Slovakia. They were situated in the interior of the European continent and did not possess a great waterway transport system which could connect them with Western Europe. The Upper Elbe could not fulfil the role that the Vistula did in Poland. Overland transportation did not create possibilities for the bulk export of agricultural products although it could satisfy the needs of domestic, local and border trade, considering the relatively small area of Bohemia as well as its compact geographical shape. Changes which occurred in the trade routes during the sixteenth century did not embrace Bohemia, which remained on the sidelines of the great trade routes, but within the radius of influence of such centres as Nuremberg, Linz, Vienna, Leipzig, Wrocław and Cracow which had an important significance for the sale of handicraft articles and directly increased the purchasing power of the non-agricultural population.

In these conditions the agrarian development of the country was dependent on the domestic market, and this was a receptive market considering the high percentage of the population employed outside agriculture in crafts, especially cloth-making and mining. In the intermediate period, between the Hussite Wars and the White Mountain (1620), there began an intensive development of private towns and townships, both in Bohemia and Moravia, which possessed trading privileges. It is also characteristic that a part of the townspeople were engaged in farming. This may indicate the attractiveness of farming and not the fact that it was difficult to earn a livelihood in urban occupations as was the case in contemporary Poland. Demand from the town markets was considerable and the prices enticing. The mountainous and highland regions created deficit districts which could not satisfy their own needs for supplies. On the other hand, we can distinguish those regions with a high grain yield such as, for example, along the Ohře and Elbe rivers in the north of the country.

The principal grain producers for the market were the peasant farms. We do not know in detail the structure of peasant ownership of land, but examples of some of the larger estates, examined by Czech historians, indicate that farms of 0.5 mansus and more were predominant. Farmsteads of this size were already able to provide a surplus of products to the markets, especially to local markets. Grain was the basis of peasant-farm production; wheat was an especially important sale item and rye in the less fertile areas. A part of the peasant-farm products went to manorial granaries in the form of dues and in general as a result of the feudal privileges of the landlord. In the revenues of the manors during the post-Hussite period, grain received from peasant farms was more significant than the production of the manors themselves. The grain yield did not differ radically from that in Poland. In Czech studies the average yield ratio is calculated as 3.3 to 1, which would correspond to a yield of approximately 400 kg a hectare, up to the middle of the eighteenth century. Only in large estates in some years could higher yields be attained owing to better organisation of work and the use of fish fertiliser. After the Thirty Years' War the grain yield began to fall because of the lack of labour power. It should be added that, just as in Poland, the manorial estates in Bohemia, as regards technical advancement, did not differ from the peasant farmsteads. In both cases extensive agriculture based on the three-field fallow system was the norm.

The increased demand of the domestic market was an incentive to the feudal classes in Bohemia. On the one hand there was a demand for agricultural products and foodstuffs in general by the non-agricultural population and on the other hand a tremendous and universal demand for beer which grew parallel to the purchasing power of the population. Hence the domestic market, unencumbered by transportation costs, provided better possibilities for the sale of country products than the more distant foreign markets. The consumer demands of the towns and townships and of the overall non-agricultural population included a whole list of farm products, not only grain and beef. All this, together with prices advantageous for the country population, created conditions for an all-round development of farmsteads far removed from the grain monoculture. As is known, an important role was played by fish farms, animal husbandry and breweries in the Bohemian rural economy of the demesnes.

The demesne was a common phenomenon in Bohemia, at least from the fourteenth century. For a long time its aim was to satisfy the lord's need for consumer products and only afterwards to produce grain for brewing. Grain production, up to the Battle of White Mountain, played an unimportant part. It continued to be the domain of peasant farming. Perhaps that may be the very reason why we can say less about the quantity of grain production in Bohemia than in Poland because peasants did not keep accounts.

Czech historians emphasise a full reversal in the development of the demesne economy beginning from the years 1530–50. It was precisely the brewing of beer which gave the impulse in the sixteenth century when the demesne economy was going through the peak period of its development. And it is from this time that one can speak of a new type of demesne in Bohemia. However, one is struck by the assorted sizes of the demesne farms. According to A. Míka, the most usual size of farm in southern Bohemia at the end of the sixteenth century was from 2 to 7 mansi, but the author cites individual examples of farms that were over 20 mansi. The same pattern occurred in other parts of the country. Among the larger scattered properties of the Olomouc bishops in Moravia at the beginning of the seventeenth century there were 23 farmsteads of various sizes. This development did not occur in Poland. Czech scholars accepted the fact that at the end of the sixteenth century the relationship of demesne to peasant agriculture was 1:5, which means that the landlords farmed 20 per cent of the land and the peasants the remainder. In reality the proportion was very varied. There existed *de facto* semi-manorial properties but these were also ones in which the demesne produced more than the peasants.[12] We have seen that the proportions were different in Poland; however, this is not the only difference between the systems of the two countries. As has been mentioned, the demesnes (*popluzní dvory*) in Bohemia did not become the suppliers of grain to the markets or became so only to a minimal degree. The primary receiver of their grain and especially wheat continued to be the demesne breweries. The large role that breweries played in the Bohemian estates during the sixteenth century is testified by their place in the income structure of the lord of the manor: while the income from grain constituted from 1 per cent (*sic!*) to 30 per cent of the total income, the breweries brought in from 10 to 75 per cent.[13] Their own production was not always able to satisfy the needs of the breweries and therefore it was supplemented by grain received from the peasants in feudal dues as well as by purchases in the market. The serfs themselves were to a large extent the purchasers and consumers of manorial beer, which was sold to them as part of the manorial monopoly rights. The foundations of the typical feudal brewing industry had to lie in the rise of the purchasing power of the village population which could sell its own surplus farm products to receptive town markets. This was accompanied by a marked increase in the price of grain from the middle of the sixteenth century.

And what about exports? Bohemia and Moravia had for long had a marginal trade in agricultural products with their neighbouring countries. Its extent and structure are not too well known, but it could not have been large if only because of difficulties of transportation. We know more about this trade on the Bohemian–Saxon borderlands during the 1592–1643 period, already partially affected by the turmoil and destruction of the Thirty Years' War. The average yearly exports of grain from Bohemia in the years 1597–1621 were 1,800 tons and in 1629–43 not quite 1,300 tons. This was not much considering the fact that this grain was produced in the fertile regions on the Ohře and Elbe rivers which served as a water route.

The structure of grain-crop production was the outcome on the one hand of the need for a specific type of grain and on the other hand of the natural possibilities of production in the agrarian system of that time. Pride of place was held by wheat, the cultivation of which was 40 per cent, and often more, of the total amount of grain sown. Rye was grown in regions less fertile and hilly and was intended partly for sale to the population residing in deficient areas. Barley, like wheat, constituted raw material for the brewing of beer, while oats were used as fodder for horses.

Up to the Thirty Years' War there did not exist in Bohemia conditions for the development of serf labour in its pure form as occurred in contemporary Poland. Fish farming, beer making and in principle animal husbandry could not be based on serf labour. But even in the agricultural structure *sensu stricto* it did not become either the only or basic form of production. Besides permanent servants, seasonal workers were employed. In addition, compulsory employment of one's own serfs was universal. Strictly speaking, the borderline between compulsory employment and serf labour is not always clear, e.g., when serfs were supported by the manor. In the period under discussion general norms of serf labour established by the state did not exist, and the situation as conveyed by the registers (*urbaria*) kept by the manor could have been different in reality. In any case it is clear that serf labour in Bohemia did not reach the proportions that it did in Poland and Hungary. It is rather reminiscent of the situation which existed in Poland during the period before the development of 'weekly' serf labour. This meant that its scope was specified by the number of days a year to be worked (usually about fifteen, in rarer cases a few score) or the type of work that was to be done. At times this brings to mind the Polish *jutrzyna* as, for example, in the estates of the Olomouc bishops.

It indicates that the situation in the Bohemian peasant farmstead was better than in some of the neighbouring countries. In this respect important changes took place after the Thirty Years' War.

Because of the poor development of demesne farms in Bohemia peasants were not expelled from their holdings. Fish farms were usually located on waste land and in low-lying fields and meadows. On the other hand, fertile land for the demesnes was obtained mainly by exchange with the peasant plots, but these takeovers were far fewer than in Poland. The opposite phenomenon was known – the sale of demesne lands to the peasants, especially in the period up to the middle of the sixteenth century.

As mentioned earlier, the Thirty Years' War brought about important changes in the agrarian structure of Bohemia. The devastation of war, especially after 1631, and the loss of population resulted in a decline of village farming, especially of demesne farming, and created a reserve of waste land. The problem was the lack of farm-hands not of land. A period of agricultural revival and a rapid reconstruction of the country began after 1648. Simultaneously, the importance of demesne and serfdom grew in comparison to the former period. However, neither one nor the other achieved that degree of development which existed in Poland at the time. According to the Maria Theresa survey the nobles cultivated 12.7 per cent of the land, the peasants 85.1 per cent, the Church (parish) farms and community property over 2.2 per cent. According to some unpublished Czech collective research on a national scale these proportions should have been manors 25 per cent, peasant 75 per cent. The imperial decree of 1680 prescribed the serf-labour norm as 3 days a week. Of course reality must have been much more complicated. Undoubtedly the novelty was the designation of a number of days of serf work a week which points to the changed role of serf labour in the country's agrarian economy: it was becoming a basic element in the burden of the peasants and the peasants ceased being the main providers of agricultural foodstuffs for the market.

As is well known, confiscations and reassignments of landed properties after the Habsburg victory changed the national composition and structure of the feudal class. But besides political factors the economic ones must also have been vital in the process of concentrating landownership. This process had its beginnings in the fourteenth century, in the period of the great expansion of fish farming. The construction of an entire waterway system demanded the concentration of considerable areas, including large sections of river banks, in the hands of one owner. This concentration of landed property was achieved by large landowners buying out the estates of lesser ones. However, other factors besides fish farming must have operated since small estates were purchased even in regions where this industry was not established. An example of this was the property of the Olomouc bishops, the largest estate in Moravia, which in the mid-sixteenth century included 88 villages, 10 townships and 3

Table 5.3. *Percentages of landownership in Bohemia (1615) and Moravia (1619)*

	Royal property	Gentry	Knights	Church	Royal towns
Bohemia	11.6	45.3	31.3	4.9	6.8
Moravia	—	55.5	20.4	18.0*	6.1

* Included in this figure was the property of the Olomouc bishops of 7.5 per cent.

towns, and which in 1636 rose to 172 villages, 11 townships and 12 towns. Table 5.3 (according to J. Jirasek) indicates the large concentration of landed property in Bohemia in 1615 and in Moravia on the eve of White Mountain. Already in changed political conditions after the Thirty Years' War, all landed property in these two areas was entirely in the possession of 85 families.

It would be inappropriate to emphasise here the feudal character of Bohemian agriculture without mentioning the vigorous sale of agricultural products on the domestic market and thus the large role played by money, the great importance of hired labour on manorial estates and probably on the peasant farms. Compulsory hired labour, manorial monopolies, in brief, extra-economic compulsion, the supremacy of the manor over the village population and its legal situation, the state of the productive forces, the structure and character of landownership – all decided for many years to come the feudal character of Bohemian agriculture.

III

Hungary within its historical boundaries, including Slovakia, Croatia and Slavonia, can be considered as a separate economic sphere; we have in mind here the development of agrarian relations in those countries. This was caused by a common historical past, the influence of Turkish wars and conquests upon the local economy, a lack of natural transportation facilities for the export of grain to distant markets, the large role of animal husbandry, especially oxen, as well as vine cultivation and wine production practically everywhere. Both oxen and wine were for several centuries the main export items of the Hungarian rural economy. One should also stress the wide differences in the natural conditions for agriculture: on the one hand the fertile lowlands of Hungary and Slavonia, on the other the highlands of northern Slovakia and Croatia. The Turkish conquest in the second half of the sixteenth century of a part of Hungary and Croatia and the subjugation of Transylvania brought enormous losses, and for the next one and a half centuries it shattered both the political and economic unity of the countries belonging to the Hungarian Crown.[14]

In this area up to the end of the Middle Ages and even longer there dominated a money-rent economy. The demesne played practically no role. Z. P. Pach correctly warns against being misled by the *aratura propria* of a landowner often mentioned by source materials. These were very slight plots of land, the produce of which, as in neighbouring Bohemia and Poland, was intended for the needs of the landowner himself. They were cultivated through labour duties of the serfs which most frequently were limited to a few days annually, and were similar to the Polish *jutrzyny*.[15]

The period from the middle of the fourteenth to the beginning of the sixteenth century is considered by Hungarian historians a favourable one in their country's history: the population increased, new areas were cultivated, local commerce intensified and exchanges between town and countryside became livelier. It would be difficult at this point to decide whether the Hungarian agriculture of the period was on a lower level – in its technology also – than that of the West, and especially whether it was approaching capitalism. Upon the basis of analogy with other countries it may be suggested that the phenomena mentioned here, together with money-rent, suited the feudal system excellently. An increase of commodity exchange and the use of hired labour naturally led to a material, and subsequently social, differentiation and hence to an exploitation of the landless population (*inquilini*).[16]

The peasant farm still remained the basic factor in agrarian production. The problem of its size including the question of production abilities is rather complicated. The technological difficulties of farming, among others the need to use a harness of 4 to 10 oxen or 4 horses, were the reason for the survival of the great families which *de facto* constituted the economic communities. Research on the basis of the tithe registers has led to divergent results (since peasant farmsteads in Hungary were burdened not only with the Church tithe but also with the manorial dues, known as the *nona* since they consisted of one-ninth of the crops after subtracting the Church dues). According to the calculations made by I. Szabó (1966), pertaining to the first quarter of the sixteenth century, the majority of peasants would have obtained 4 to 5 hectolitres of grain gross (230–350 kilogrammes), which is a figure difficult to accept. Even with a very low yield ratio (from 2 to 2.5 to 1) this would work out as the harvest from approximately one hectare, or slightly more, of land under cultivation. It does not correspond to the structure of peasant ownership. A subsequent attempt, undertaken by Z. Kirilly and I. N. Kiss (1968), concerns a number of districts in Hungary and Slovakia in the second half of the sixteenth century. In the fertile district of Nitra (western Slovakia, on the lower Wah), the average harvest of a peasant farmstead amounted to as much as 44 hundredweight, while in the remaining *comitates* (counties) they were lower: Bereg 10, Zemplén 15, Borsod and Heves 22.5 each (all in north-western Hungary). The Church tithe and manorial dues together (*quinta*) took up 20 per cent of the harvest, while the planting absorbed *c.* 30 per cent. The authors estimated the consumption of the peasant family to equal only 120 kilogrammes annually per adult. This is a very low estimate, half of the one made for Poland in that period. The final calculation shows that only in the Nitra district, and of course wherever the grain production was on a similar level, was a peasant able to plan to supply the market with *c.* 20 hundredweight of various types of grain annually. The possible commodity surplus in the remaining districts under examination has to be slight. Was this situation in the Nitra district close to that of the country as a whole? The research of Z. Kirilly and I. N. Kiss leads to one more conclusion: the shrinkage of peasant production during the course of the second half of the sixteenth century, unless this was merely an illusory decline suggested by the gaps in the tithe registers.

Recently (in 1974) L. Mákkai presented the results of calculations on the production of 22,152 peasant farmsteads in four *comitates* (the author did not say which) upon the registers from 1580. The average harvest per farmstead was estimated by the author at 8.7 quintals (i.e., 870 kg), and it is his opinion that this result can also be extended to the first half of the seventeenth century. On this, perhaps insufficiently certain basis, the author estimated the total grain production of Hungary during this period, thus:

	Area in ha	Production in tons
Peasants: 950,000 farmsteads	1,150,000	827,450
Manors (demesne):	230,000	165,600
Total:	1,380,000	993,050

In this calculation one finds disturbing the exceedingly small sizes of the peasant allotments with an average of only 1.2 hectares under cultivation, which in the three-field system would mean not quite 2 hectares cultivated in any given farmstead. Is it possible to accept precisely those sizes as average? Individual examples of farmsteads examined do not confirm this. Moreover, the productivity of one hectare would be very high, because it would amount to approximately 7.25 hundredweight, i.e., a yield ratio of no less than 5 to 1. If one were to accept these calculations as being close to reality, then one would have to assume that the Hungarian peasant lived on the borderline of hunger, regardless of high crop yields. However, attention has been drawn to the great role played in the supply to the population of non-grain products such as beans, lentils, millet, broad beans, cabbage and later on maize and, naturally, wine and grapes. The cultivation of these products did not require large areas. The same was also true of animal products, whose basis of production did not necessarily have to be arable land. In those conditions, lands close to farm buildings were significant, and they were fenced in and cultivated intensively, independent of the crop rotation necessary to the three-field system.

Perhaps all this means that a different yardstick has to be used to measure the area of a peasant farmstead in Hungary from one in countries of a grain monoculture. However, one would suppose that the scarcity of rural products would make it difficult to supply the towns, especially the larger ones. Evidence of this is the purchasing of landed estates by the towns themselves in order to ensure supplies of agricultural products – Pozsony (today Bratislava) owned five villages and Košice as many as twenty-four.[17]

The research by I. N. Kiss on the stratification of about 100,000 peasant farmsteads gives more meaning to the above statistics. The author verified the existence in the second half of the sixteenth century of a group of relatively prosperous peasants; not more than 15–20 per cent of the total number of farmsteads produced for the market, but even within this group it is possible to notice a sharp economic differentiation: over 50 per cent of the goods produced (grain and wine) came from 10 per cent of the farmsteads and only 1 per cent of them produced (depending on the year) 9 to 33 per cent of grain for sale and 24 to 37 per cent of wine. Is this not already a polarisation?[18]

The movement of prices in Hungary during this period tended in the same direction as in the rest of Central Europe. A large increase in grain prices in neighbouring Austria had already occurred at the end of the fifteenth century. In those conditions the activity of the feudal class, which strove towards increasing its profits from landed estates, could go in two directions: it could either organise its own agricultural production for the market, or appropriate the surplus which came from peasant farms. In contrast to the landowners of Poland and Bohemia, those in Hungary got involved earlier in the trade of agricultural products than in their production. The access of the feudal class to economic activity constituted a very significant moment in the internal development of Hungary. Certain Hungarian historians see it as a 'deviation' from their country's previous line of development, but parallel to the development of Western Europe at the time; as a result Hungary entered upon the path of a manorial serf-labour economy.[19]

The premises for the development of a trade in agricultural products conducted by the gentry were as follows:

(1) The accumulation in the hands of the feudal class of an important part of the peasant production in the form of payments (especially the *nona*); the leasing or buying up of Church tithes could double these amounts again (*quinta*);

(2) A relative weakness of the towns of the period, which were dealt a blow by the commercial activities of the gentry;

(3) The political and social superiority as well as the trade privileges of the feudal class;

(4) An increase in the demand for agricultural products, and prices favourable for agrarian production;

(5) A large demand for food on the part of the army, especially in the period of the Habsburg–Turkish wars. Not only the grain trade but also, and perhaps above all, trade in wine and beef were important here.[20]

This was a typically feudal trade, based upon the privileges of the gentry which made it possible to carry out the compulsory purchase of peasant products as well as to create a compulsory market in their own manors. One should mention here the so-called *regalia minora*, such as sales of wine, more rarely of beer or spirits (*educilatio*), the mill and slaughter-house monopoly and the freedom from duties on articles *de propria allodiatura*. In 1550 the Hungarian gentry won the right of precedence in the purchase of agricultural products from their own serfs at market prices, which were in practice fixed unilaterally by the manor. In 1617 a royal decree endorsed the freedom of the gentry from tariffs and taxes. In 1625 county assemblies won formal rights, actually already being exercised, to regulate prices and wages.[21]

The establishment of compulsory sales on the estates of the gentry may indicate that the army and towns did not absorb the entire supply of agricultural goods. We are unable to cite the initial date of the compulsory buying of spirits from the estates but in *c.* 1570 it was already a universal phenomenon. The manorial monopoly of wine sales was in force formally from Easter (or 24 April) until St Michael's Day (29 September). But these dates could be changed at the will of the landlord (*pro arbitro domini terrestris*). Wine sales by the manor were based on demesne production only to a small degree and essentially on the peasant *nona*, *munera* (dues), the lease of the *decima*, as well as the privilege of priority in the purchase of peasant wine. The buyers of grain sold by the manor could also include the peasants themselves – such grain came from the same sources as the wine. On the other hand, the sale of oxen for slaughter was essentially for export, to Austria, Moravia, Upper Germany and Venice. Already at the end of the fifteenth century the export of oxen reached up to a hundred thousand animals annually and constituted 50–60 per cent of Hungary's exports; copper made up *c.* 20–25 per cent of the remainder. In the sixteenth century the export of oxen rose from 100,000 to 200,000 animals, depending on the year. In that period, unlike the wine and grain, the oxen came to a large extent from the gentry's own farms. The organisation of grazing was easier than growing grain and producing wine. Moreover, manorial agents bought oxen in the open market.

Simultaneously the manor supplied its serfs with such indispensable goods as salt, iron and herrings. Briefly speaking, the economic policy of the feudal classes aimed at eliminating the peasant from the town market and at the same time at transforming their own estates into 'closed markets'. However, these tendencies were not fully realised because in practice such an objective proved to be impossible. The view that peasant production for sale was hampered as late as the Fifteen Years' War (1593–1606) is justified.[22]

Hungarian historians place the first stage of manorial development in the years 1530–40 and in Slovakia as late as the middle of the sixteenth century. But, as has been mentioned, wars with the Turk and the disintegration of the Hungarian national territory limited the possibilities for manorial development to those regions which were left intact. The geography of the emergence and development of the manor in Hungary – just as in the case of Poland – has not been adequately examined. However, attention has been drawn to the fact that the development of the manor in Hungary occurred earlier along river basins and in general close to transportation routes. This could be an indication that the products of a manorial estate were not consumed in the place of their origin. The devastation of war in the 1593–1606 period put a halt to further development of the manor for a certain amount of time, but the subsequent economic reconstruction of the country went in the direction of serf labour.[23]

As in neighbouring countries, the development of the manorial economy solved three problems for the Hungarian feudal class: it ensured sales of surplus commodities, gain of demesne land and provision of a labour force for its cultivation. The *Tripartitum* – the Hungarian law code of 1514 – clearly stated 'totius terrae proprietas ad dominum terrestrem spectat et pertinet' (the whole ownership of the land belongs to the landlord). However, the former view about a mass expulsion of peasants from their land plots has been abandoned by Hungarian historians as incorrect. One cannot, on the other hand, totally rule out such expulsions. They occurred before 1526 and increased in the years 1530–40 but disappeared towards the close of the sixteenth century. As a result of large demographic losses during the 1593–1606 war, the manorial estate suffered not only from the lack of land but also from the lack of a labour force. It may be said that in general during the sixteenth century the manor in Hungary developed mainly at the cost of waste lands (woods, groves, pastureland) and only afterwards at the cost of peasant plots, both settled and unsettled.[24]

In the initial stages of the development of the manor hired labour and serf labour probably coexisted. The Diet of 1514 resolved that one day a week would constitute the normal labour due from each farmstead (in Poland an analogous decree of 1520 mentioned one day per mansus owned and not per farmstead). Hungarian legislation of a later period is proof of an increased need for serf labour. The pattern of class forces enabled the local gentry to substitute serf labour for hired labour in those branches of production where it was possible and useful. This occurred in approximately the third quarter of the sixteenth century when serf labour reached two to three days a week per farmstead. It seems that insufficient attention has been drawn to one other factor in the development of serf labour: the low productivity of human labour in the agriculture of the period could have made hired labour unprofitable by raising the financial costs of production excessively. Moreover, serf labour freed the landowner from various investments indispensable for hired labour, as well as from breeding draught animals. The final transition to serf labour occurred as early as the seventeenth century, following the Fifteen Years' War, as in Bohemia after the Thirty Years' War.[25] It is also worthwhile to recall that in Poland serf labour reached its full development long before the great wartime devastation of 1655–60 and not afterwards.

Naturally, the development of the manorial economy and the entire economic policy of the feudal class led to a degradation of the peasant farmstead. This found expression in the shrinking of the amount of peasant land under cultivation, a change in its proportion compared to manorial land and a reduction of production abilities (an increasingly greater percentage of peasants had no draught animals). As we have already pointed out, an absolute elimination of the peasant from the urban market was not possible.

In this way the transitional character of the sixteenth century in the agrarian economy of Hungary came to an end: the serf-labour manorial estate became the fundamental producer and not only the supplier of agrarian products to the market. In contrast to the situation in Poland, the foreign grain market played practically no role in Hungary during this period and manorial estates did not become grain monocultures. In both Poland and Hungary, as well as in Bohemia – although in the last analogous changes occurred later – it was a regressive phenomenon. As has been mentioned, oxen and wine became the objects of large-scale export, not only to neighbouring countries.

At the present stage of research it would be rather difficult to define quantitative relations, the proportions of manorial and peasant production, and more exactly the area under cultivation. F. Maksay (1958) estimated manorial land under cultivation at 5–10 per cent, Z. P. Pach (1965) at 25–30 per cent, L. Mákkai (1963) at 25–33 per cent for grain and 12–14 per cent for vines, while Z. Kirilly and I. N. Kiss (1968) put it at 10 per cent.[26]

The conditions and organisation of the grain market have already been mentioned. The large part played by wine sales in the manorial economy (at times 50 per cent and more), including the creation of a compulsory market by the landowner in his own estates, can be indication of a growing difficulty in selling grain when the favourable market situation of wartime disappeared in the second half of the seventeenth century. A decline in the export of oxen during this time was the result of wars with the Ottoman Empire and a general peasant uprising. Hungary became a great grain exporter from the middle of the eighteenth century and especially later on, during the wars with revolutionary and Napoleonic France when the Vienna government undertook great road-building works, planning to join Trieste and Rijeka with their Austrian and Hungarian–Croatian hinterland.[27]

Perhaps we have concentrated our attention on agrarian economy rather too one-sidedly, losing sight of other branches of the economy, especially mining and trade. But subsequently all branches of economic activity influence each other.

IV

The period chosen for study was a time of great changes in the internal development of Poland, Bohemia and Hungary. In the middle of the fourteenth century, Europe entered into a long period of economic development which lasted for over two centuries. Historians see signs of a decline in Poland in the last quarter of the sixteenth century. These were symptoms more of a regression than a crisis. In Bohemia an economic catastrophe was brought about by the defeat at the White Mountain and the start of the Thirty Years' War. It seems that the conquest of a considerable part of Hungary and the shattering of the political and economic unity of the countries of the St Stephen's Crown (1526–42) did not hamper the development of the region which found itself under the rule of the Habsburgs and which did not suffer wartime devastation. On the other hand, great destruction took place there during the Fifteen Years' War (1593–1606).

In the sixteenth century, during the internal development of Poland and Bohemia as well as of Hungary, one can observe two overlapping processes. On the one hand there was further economic growth and development based on a money economy and an increasing division of labour between the countryside and town, accompanied by internal colonisation and urban growth. On the other hand, from the end of the fifteenth century (this is naturally an approximate chronology) one can observe the beginning of new phenomena, a new period in the history of that part of Europe. A growing demand for agricultural products and in general for animal and vegetable raw materials created possibilities for the feudal class to increase the income from their landed estates. This could be achieved, as has been mentioned above, by the takeover of commodity sales, in other words by participation in trade or by the organisation of their own produce for sale. The new economic policy was facilitated by the social and political position of the feudal class, a monopoly of landed property and feudal privileges in relation to the peasant population. This led to the emergence and development of their own manorial estates producing for the market, and, to put it succinctly, towards a reconstruction of the entire agrarian system, as well as towards an obvious worsening of the situation of the peasant population and to its economic, social and legal degradation. Profits gained from an increase in demand for agricultural products and raw materials were appropriated by the feudal class. The townspeople's participation was determined by the degree to which they were able to enter into trade as intermediaries.

These processes did not take place in a uniform way in all countries in the region 'east of the Elbe' (some scholars point to the River Enns as a continuation of the Elbe). Poland, Bohemia and Hungary were an eastern area of European countries which at the time was experiencing increased demand for agricultural production and raw materials, and also a price revolution. One should at this point also mention Livonia, i.e., Estonia and Latvia, as an area farthest to the north. Countries further to the east either experienced the effects of those phenomena much later (e.g., Russia and the Ukraine) or the Turkish conquests suddenly put a stop to the direction their development had pursued up till then, e.g., a part of Hungary, Romania and the Balkan countries.

The increase in demand mentioned here created different possibilities for each of the countries under study. Poland, lying within the Baltic zone and possessing a convenient transportation route (the Vistula) as well as large areas of arable land, had at its disposal natural conditions for becoming a great producer and supplier of agricultural products to the market. Most certainly the first stimulus for the development of cereals was given by the domestic market, but in the long run it was unable to absorb the great agricultural surplus as a result of the relatively weak urbanisation of the country. Neighbouring countries could not become a permanent market because their own economic structure was similar to that of Poland. The most developed countries of Western Europe became such a market thanks to the convenient river network and the Baltic. The spread everywhere of serf labour ensured that the manorial estate would be 'profitable' from the point of view of the owner. As the financial costs of production and investment were minimal, the sums gained from sales were essentially net profit. This was bound to increase the competitiveness of Polish grain on the European markets.

The situation was different in Bohemia and Hungary. At that time neither of these countries had the conditions for becoming a great grain exporter. But Bohemia was an urbanised country with a high percentage of non-agrarian population. It was also surrounded by countries equally well developed economically. Thus there arose an absorbent domestic market both for grain and its by-products, especially beer. Equally significant was the fact that the demand of the national market also embraced a long list of foodstuffs, both of plant and animal origin. It is thus understandable that the Bohemian rural economy did not become a grain monoculture but also developed the production of such comestibles as fish, meat, fruit and vegetables. This variety of production explains the relatively high participation of hired labour and the weak development of serf labour. Bohemia entered the path of the manorial serf-labour economy as late as the second half of the seventeenth century under different economic and political conditions after the great destruction caused by the Thirty Years' War.

On the other hand, Hungary was a country much less urbanised than Bohemia and with a lower population density. We have indirect indications that the local towns had difficulties with food supplies. But in Hungary there existed premises for an early economic activisation of the feudal class, great opportunities for cheap animal husbandry as well as for wine production on a large scale. The transport of both oxen and wine over great distances was more profitable than that of grain. Both neighbouring and distant countries could become buyers of these products since the countries surrounding Hungary produced small quantities or none at all. It is well known that German towns experienced difficulties with meat supplies from the middle of the sixteenth century up to the Thirty Years' War.[28] Hungarian grain, meanwhile, basically did not make its way to foreign markets. The local grain market was neither absorbent nor stabilised since, along with the towns, its primary buyer was the army. Moreover, the development of a domestic market was not favoured by the low density of population, despite an influx of people into the Habsburg part of Hungary from regions occupied by the Turks. The Hungarian feudal class utilised its monopoly privileges and made attempts to create compulsory closed markets on its own estates. This phenomenon occurred also in Poland but considerably later and above all in those parts of the country from which shipments of grain to Gdańsk were either difficult or impossible. The main items sold to the serfs were wine in Hungary and beer and spirits in Poland. The demesne cereal cultivation in Bohemia and Hungary did not develop to the same degree as it did in Poland, perhaps because the local market did not create the strong economic stimuli of the more absorbent foreign markets.

Let us recall once again that the three-field system which dominated in Poland, Bohemia and in Hungary was a very extensive form of agrarian economy which demanded great expanses of land. It was associated with a structure of grain cultivation from which it was difficult to depart. An increase in production could not occur through intensification. One cannot see progress in agrotechnology or an increase in productivity up to the middle of the eighteenth century. As a sign of progress in Hungarian agriculture one can acknowledge the ever more widespread vine cultivation and the appearance of maize in the second half of the seventeenth century.

Of course, the stressing of the totally feudal character of the economy in the three countries of interest to us would be superfluous. It was to retain its feudal character for a long time to come, actually up to the first half of the nineteenth century. This is true of both agrarian production and of the circulation of agricultural products. However, one should underline a certain modernisation of trade which found expression in the increased circulation of mass goods such as grain.

It is worthwhile to draw attention once more to certain differences between the economic situations of each of the three countries. In Poland the export of agricultural commodities and raw materials was an economic necessity; in reality there was no comparable means of bringing money and precious metals into Poland. The situation was different in Bohemia which owned and exploited rich silver mines and in Hungary which was a great exporter of copper. The economic ties between the countries of the Baltic area to which Poland belonged and the countries to the south of the Carpathian mountains were relatively insignificant. Perhaps these circumstances help us to understand why the reconstruction of the agrarian system was not identical everywhere and did not transform earlier relations to an equal degree.

In what way did the transitional character of the period from the middle of the fourteenth century up to the middle of the seventeenth century in this part of Europe express itself? This was a transition from the money-rent system to a serf-labour economy and to a commodities production of which a considerable part became assigned to export. We have in mind Polish grain and Hungarian oxen and wine in particular. In a certain sense it defined the place and function of those countries in the European economy for centuries. Changes which have been mentioned here influenced not only economies and social structures but also political and cultural relations. Can one treat these phenomena as a symptom of an economic dualism in Europe? Or should one see in them the symptoms of a closer unification, a linking up of the East-Central European with the European economy, and perhaps even with the then emerging world economy? Countries of Central Europe were the less prosperous partners. Their development was soon hampered for a rather long period of time, practically up to the eighteenth century, while the leading countries of Western Europe still enjoyed a period of development, despite the crisis, or crises which they experienced.

6 ❧ Agricultural and livestock production: wine and oxen. The case of Hungary

ISTVÁN N. KISS

Statistical sources for the socio-economic development of the historical Kingdom of Hungary are available only from the mid-sixteenth century. These sources determined the limits of my research.

Demographic background

After the Turkish conquest of 1541 the central and southern parts of Hungary became a province of the Ottoman empire; only the western and northern territories of the country remained under the rule of the Habsburgs as Hungarian kings. The eastern part of the country, the so-called Principality of Transylvania, was an independent state in the sixteenth to seventeenth century.[1] My sources also cover a major part of territory conquered by the Turks, and these sources enabled me to establish the size of population in the total area of about 190,000 sq km (see Figure 2).

I derived the total population[2] from estimates for four periods of the sixteenth century on an area of 25–30,000 sq km, on a few thousand sq km in the seventeenth century, and on about 10,000 sq km in 1707, taking account of peasantry, nobility, clergy and the population of market towns. Thus in the sixteenth to seventeenth century 1.5 to 1.6 million people lived on the above-mentioned territory of 190,000 sq km, a population density of 8 persons per sq km. In 1707 1.7 to 1.8 million people lived on the same territory, with a population density of about 9–10 persons per sq km. At the end of the eighteenth century, in relatively quieter circumstances, natural increase and mass immigration raised the population of the Kingdom of Hungary, not including Transylvania, the Croatian–Slavonic kingdom and the Military Border, to 6.5 million.

Cereal production

Of the cereal production of the area 85–90 per cent was grain for bread, 10–15 per cent grain for fodder (barley, oats). The latter was produced as spring grain.

84

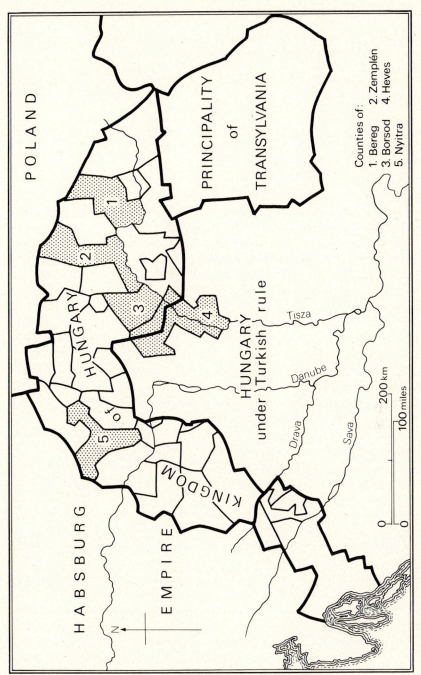

POLAND

HABSBURG

EMPIRE

PRINCIPALITY

of

TRANSYLVANIA

HUNGARY

KINGDOM of

HUNGARY under Turkish rule

Tisza

Danube

Drava

Sava

N

Counties of:
1. Bereg   2. Zemplén
3. Borsod   4. Heves
5. Nyitra

200 km

100 miles

0

0

2 Hungary in 1600

86 István N. Kiss

Table 6.1. *Quantity of grain in quintals per family*

(1 quintal = 100 kg)

1550	12.1
1570	9.6
1585	7.8
1600	7.3
1659	4.6
1664	5.1
1707	10.4
1707	23.1 (demesne farms)

An analysis was made of the yields of over 100,000 peasant farms in the sixteenth century, over 13,000 in the seventeenth century and of nearly 5,000 peasant and demesne farms in 1707.[3]

Averages, of course, obscure both the regional differences in grain production and the income stratification of the peasantry as well. The average quantity of cereals (bread grain and fodder grain) per family can be estimated as shown in Table 6.1. In comparison to the 1550s, the volume of cereals decreased rapidly in succeeding years: at about 1600 it reached only 60 per cent of the 1550s production, in the second half of the seventeenth century 38–42 per cent, but in 1707 it rose again to 86 per cent of the 1550s figure. The secular trend of corn production is therefore characterised from 1550 onwards first by a gradual, later by a quick decrease and a subsequent rise almost up to the mid-sixteenth century level. The question now to be answered is, how and in what way cereal production met the subsistence requirements of the population and what share it had in Hungarian exports.

It must be pointed out that these figures represent the total quantity of grain production divided by the total number of families; a significant number of the farms did not cultivate. The proportion of households in the sixteenth century not producing grain was 35.6 per cent, in the seventeenth century 34.9 per cent and in 1707 as high as 49.8 per cent. These consisted of different social groups: the population of certain regions of monocultural stock-breeding and viticulture, the families *sine terra* (without land) and *sine frumento* (without corn) who earned their living by craft or as labourers, and the poor population of uncertain existence. Their needs supported the internal market by absorbing large quantities of corn, partly through local markets, partly by bartering.

Let us examine to what extent the grain production of Hungary could have met the subsistence needs of the population. Hungarian bread consumption did not reach the 250 litres (i.e., 175 kg) per year, acknowledged as standard in Europe. In the Kingdom of Hungary the average requirement was about 160 litres (i.e., 112 kg), which was equivalent to the same quantity of kilograms of bread. This consumption index (112 kg) seems low, but it has been well

Table 6.2. *Estimates of bread grain availability in quintals*[4]

Year	Per sq km	Per family	Per person	Per person (seed deducted)
1550	14.6	10.1	2.24	1.68
1570	13.1	8.3	1.84	1.38
1585	8.2	7.0	1.55	1.17
1600	6.6	6.4	1.42	1.07
1659	10.3	4.1	0.91	0.69
1664	10.2	4.6	1.02	0.77
1707	18.3	9.3	2.07	1.56
1707 (nobility)	3.5	23.1	5.12	3.84
1787 (the whole country)			1.65	1.23

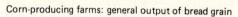

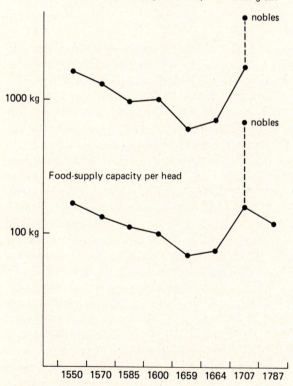

3 Supply of bread grain in Hungary from 1550 to 1787

verified. It was compensated for by a high meat consumption[5] in relation to the rest of Europe, by the inclusion of grist and millet in the diet till the end of the nineteenth century, as well as by the substitution of maize for grain in the case of the Romanian population living in Hungarian lands. Table 6.2 shows that in the second half of the sixteenth century the average consumption of 112 kg could easily be supplied from inside the country, but that it had become insufficient by 1600. In the sample years of the seventeenth century, 25–30 per cent of bread grain had to be made up by other foodstuffs, yet in 1707 the supply was abundant. One can say that the demand for bread grain in the country was amply covered by local production with the exception of some regions and certain periods of the seventeenth century (see Figure 3). The sixteenth–seventeenth-century grain surplus was absorbed by unprovided families on one hand, and on the other was consumed by armies staying in Hungary and by garrisons of castles.[6] The autarkic farming of Hungary did not produce significant quantities of grain surplus; whatever grain was bought by the market was absorbed locally. That is the reason why the country had no corn exports until the first third of the eighteenth century.

Oxen

Cattle-breeding was the most important sector of the economic life of Hungary in the tenth to the fifteenth century, as has been proved by statistical data from the sixteenth century on. When the Hungarian tribes conquered the Carpathian basin in 896, they brought with them the so-called steppe-cattle. This species was the basic stock from which the white-grey breed has developed. The climatic conditions of the Great Hungarian Plain and the care taken in the rearing of these animals developed their quantity and quality to such an extent that from the late fifteenth century they were the most wanted fattened oxen from Cologne to Venice. These white-grey cattle were of strong bony frame and of semi-nomadic breeding and were capable of reaching a market as far away as even a few thousand kilometres without great loss of weight. Ample data from the sixteenth century[7] exists concerning the number of exported oxen; according to them the basic cattle stock can be estimated at 3 million. In addition to this number, population and livestock figures of greater and lesser regions have to be taken into consideration (see Table 6.3).

The exceptionally high proportion in 1580 – (Hungary approximately) 2,000 head of cattle for 1,000 people – remained unchanged to the beginning of the eighteenth century. It was much higher in regions where grasslands dominated over agriculture. In 1787 the national ratio was only 667 head of cattle per 1,000 population, and in 1895 merely 385 (see Figure 4).

Naturally such an enormous livestock production meant an exceptionally high level of meat consumption. At the end of the sixteenth and beginning of the seventeenth century, according to data of several towns and boroughs, the

Table 6.3. *Population and cattle stock from 1580 to 1895*[8]

Territory	Year	Population	Cattle	Cattle per 1,000 population
Hungary	1580	1,520,000	3,000,000	1,974
Borough of Rimaszombat	1707	2,150	1,508	701
Kishont county	1707	5,354	6,008	1,122
Bereg county	1707	4,965	7,034	1,417
Esztergom county	1707	4,500	6,174	1,372
Komárom county	1707	5,724	12,252	2,140
Jász district	1707	6,403	21,142	3,250
servants (*famuli*)	1707	372	876	
Jász district	1710	6,274	9,206	1,467
Jász district	1713	7,264	15,000	2,065
Hungary	1787	6,460,000	4,310,000	667
Hungary	1895	15,140,000	5,830,000	385

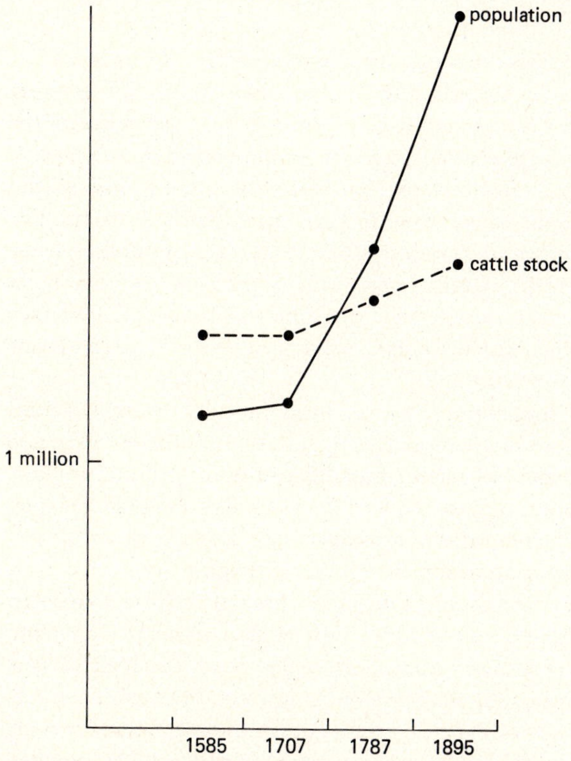

4 Population and cattle stock per million (1570–1895)

Hungarian annual beef consumption was about 63 to 69 kg per head compared with 47 kg in south-German towns and 26 kg in Carpentras in southern France.[9]

According to available data, the supply of local markets consisted of 75 per cent cows, 15 to 20 per cent calves and 5 to 10 per cent oxen. The average live weight of cows was 175–190 kg and that of oxen 400 kg.[10] The average weight of 90,000 oxen known for the years 1770–3 was 631 kg and this is a figure both for oxen intended for export and for local consumption.[11]

Because of limited space an analysis of cattle prices cannot be included; nevertheless one should mention that cattle prices differed greatly from region to region and that the price level was higher in the western parts of the country. These regional price differentials diminished during the eighteenth century.[12] Meat was sold in seigniorial butchers' shops. In some cases we can analyse the estate accounts: about 40 per cent of the net income was bought by butchers' shops. This high profit was due to special conditions. Within an estate, retailing of meat was a monopoly of the lord. It cost him nothing because drawing, slaughtering and retailing were done by peasants as their labour services. When cattle were not bought for retail sale inside the estate but earmarked for further outside sale, the profit was three times less.

From the mid-fourteenth century on, there is evidence of the exportation of Hungarian oxen to Czech, Austrian and German towns.[13] At the beginning of the sixteenth century Austria and Venice were already big markets for Hungarian cattle. About 1550 the bulk of Hungarian oxen were exported to south-German towns. Wars against the Turks in the second half of the seventeenth century brought heavy losses to Hungarian cattle breeding, but at the beginning of the eighteenth century cattle export was re-established and in 1770 it reached the 1570 level. There were significant differences in direction, however: no cattle were left for the south-German and Venetian market; from the 1750s the Austrian and Czech dominions of the Habsburgs absorbed all Hungarian exports.[14]

On average 100,000, sometimes 200,000, head of cattle were exported annually plus ten thousand or more exported duty-free by cattle-dealers as repayment of loans.[15] Export of oxen weighing less than 4.5 quintals was prohibited by Hungarian law and the bulk of oxen exported weighed between 5.0 and 6.5 quintals.[16] The majority of animals came from the monocultural regions of the Great Hungarian Plain, then under Turkish rule.

Hungarian oxen encountered competition on foreign markets: German towns imported cattle from Denmark and Poland also. Around 1580, the Danish export of oxen to Germany was about 45,000 head, the Polish about 50,000. Their joint export was less than that of Hungary and in certain periods it hardly reached half of it. Polish cattle exports in the sixteenth century were to a large extent a re-export of herds brought in from Moldavia.[17] This practice occurred in Hungary too but only in the second half of the eighteenth century.

Table 6.4. *Average prices of an ox in grams of silver from 1581 to 1590 in various areas*[18]

Western Hungary	204
Vienna	261
Brieg, Buttstädt	383
Elbe	337
Northern Germany	585
Southern Germany	394

Prices of imported oxen varied greatly. Table 6.4 compares the price of Hungarian, Polish and Danish oxen at the German wholesale markets. The market for Hungarian oxen was at Vienna; the Polish at Brieg (Lower Silesia) and Buttstädt (Saxony), the Danish at several crossing-places of the Elbe. In the 1580s the Polish ox on Silesian and Saxonian markets was one-half, the Danish ox on the German border one-third, dearer than the Hungarian ox in Vienna. These price differentials were a long-lasting phenomenon. Moreover, the Hungarian ox was at a minimum 5 quintals, i.e., 15–20 per cent heavier than the other imported oxen. In Hungary in the second half of the eighteenth century some 60 per cent of the oxen from the east – Transylvania, Moldavia and Wallachia – did not reach their destination. At this time herds consisted of 160–200 head, on average made up of 25 per cent calves, 44 per cent oxen of average size and 31 per cent heavy cattle.

From the mid-eighteenth century on, the cattle trade gained momentum. The bulk of the animal trade, both inside the country and for export, was controlled by a *societas* of five or six cattle-dealers (*quaestores boum*). Their members were well-to-do butchers and citizens who had their agents all over the country and were able to pay hundreds of thousands of florins in advance.[19] These conditions in cattle export to Austria and Bohemia continued until the beginning of the twentieth century.

Wine

There are very few Hungarian museums which lack viticultural relics from Roman times. According to some theories the continuity of viticulture was maintained through the period of the great migrations until the foundation of the Hungarian state in the tenth century. From this time on the significance of viticulture is reflected in exceptionally rich sources. The population's wine consumption was very high, especially because there was a lack of healthy drinking water. There are available from the mid-1500s customs, tax, and later also estates accounts which enable quantitative research. The region of Hegyalja (Submontanum) where the widely known Tokay wine was produced, was at that time already a land of vine monoculture. On average, in the period

1570 to 1580, 2,400 vineyard proprietors and 2,600 other families (coopers, day-labourers), the bulk of whom were interested in wine production, lived there and produced 29,000 hectolitres per year. The total population, mainly peasants, was about 25,000, but among the vineyard proprietors were nobles and burghers too. About a third of the vineyard proprietors were absentees, so they were not counted there as residents but as *extranei*. On well-cultivated vineyards in the region, one year's production could reach 20 to 22 hectolitres per ha, but the average output was much less, about 10 hectolitres. It was important that vineyards in Hungary were free possessions, *de facto* free from feudal dependency, and played an important part in money accumulation and in activating the trade balance.

The almost unlimited demand of inner markets for wine spurred production and stimulated expansion of vineyards to such an extent that vine cultivation took place even on lands unfitted for it, for example, the Carpathian valleys. High wine prices made it possible to pay transport costs, whereas in the case of grain transport was rentable only within a radius of 30–40 km. On account of its standard price, wine was used for payment in kind of soldiers' overdue pay, and as salary for civil servants.

The domain of Sárospatak was the largest estate in the region of Hegyalja. In 1570 its wine income totalled 4,226 hectolitres, 73 per cent of which was peasant wine (a tax in kind), 3.5 per cent of allodial production, 2.5 per cent from penalties and 21 per cent purchased. Wine stocks were used thus: internal consumption 11 per cent, officers' and soldiers' pay and the military supply 64 per cent, salaries 6 per cent, and market sale 19 per cent. In 1568, when Sárospatak was not burdened much by the military supply, the wine-sale portion was 54 per cent.[20] This proportion indicates that the demesne itself produced only an insignificant amount of wine but received its stocks from the peasants as tax, and had to buy wine as well.

The 'provisor' responsible for distribution had to supply the army, provide for a large internal consumption (470 hl), and pay the soldiers; the rest of the wine was taken to markets where a part was purchased by Polish merchants. According to accounts for 1634–42 of another large estate in the same region, the demesne of Tarcal, 25 per cent of its average of wine income of 1,154 hectolitres was its own production (*vinum allodiale*), 58 per cent was taken as the tax-wine from the peasants (*vinum taxale*) and 17 per cent was purchased by the demesne from its own peasants (*vinum emptum*). Most of that wine was earmarked for sale: 25 per cent was sent abroad, 40 per cent was sold in domanial wine shops, 19 per cent was given as presents by the landlord to high state and military officials, 6 per cent was for internal consumption and 10 per cent remained as a reserve.

Two-thirds of the stocks were consumed by internal and foreign markets, and, if the wine given as presents for political purposes is added, the proportion for sale comes near to 85 per cent.[21] In the second half of the sixteenth century,

Sopron (western Hungary), the centre for wine export to the West, had 43 per cent of its production sold on foreign markets.[22] The exports of the country as a whole were a much smaller proportion; wine stocks of Tarcal, Sárospatak and Sopron were of exceptional quality. Only 10–15 per cent of Hungarian wine went abroad. Export markets for western Hungary were Bohemia, Silesia and western Poland while the eastern regions of the country exported to Little Poland. There is abundant information for 1550–1650 about the volume of wine exports: exports to the west were at a rough guess 60,000 hl, to the north 50,000 hl.[23] This quantity of about 100,000 hl as an export average means a total production of 0.75 to 1.10 million hl.

Wine prices in Hungary differed a great deal depending on quality, regional conditions and transport costs. Nevertheless, the more-or-less standard relative value is that one hectolitre of export-quality wine was equal in value to one fattened ox. In Sopron in 1570, 1 hectolitre of wine cost 9.5 florins, in 1640 it cost 19–20 florins; in the region of Hegyalja in the same two periods wine prices were respectively 6 and 15–16 florins.[24]

It is hard to give a reliable estimate of incomes from viticulture, however. For Ferenc Rákóczi's state a qualitative classification and valuation of different wines and their regions has already been made. The accounts of 1707 were done on 75 per cent of the territory of Hungary. As Sopron was under Habsburg rule, the only first-class vine region of the Rákóczi state was Hegyalja. A further 23 vine regions were described as second, 9 third and 15 as fourth class. The basic unit for taxable property was the so-called *dica*, equal to two oxen, an equivalent of 30 florins. The *dica* was used as standard value for wines of different qualities. In the first class 2.6 hl of wine were equal to one *dica* while, in the fourth, one *dica* equalled 13 hl. Classifications for the 1708 tax became more precise. There were 5 classes and within the first and second class further sub-groups. First-class wine's *dica* was 2 hl. The difference between the best and the lowest grade wines was 26 times the value of the latter: one *dica* was equal to 2 hl first-class or to 52 hl fifth-class wine![25]

Balance of foreign trade

We might now try to suggest some relationships between the population, agricultural production and export capacity of Hungary. Agricultural and livestock production per head of population in 1580 may be estimated as follows: 2 oxen (small and big animals mixed), 0.5 hectolitres of wine and 1.68 quintals of bread cereals. Of the cattle, 2.5–5 per cent were exported and 10–15 per cent of the wine. Grain export was occasional and totally insignificant. These proportions of wine and oxen were to change only in the 1770s.

And now the question might be asked, How far and in what way does the distribution of income and production at that time support the above statements? (Cf. Fügedi contribution above, Chap. 4.) In the census of 1707,

Table 6.5. *Sources of income of farms in 1707 (in percentages)*[26]

Territory	Animal breed-ing	Corn pro-duction	Wine pro-duction	Handi-crafts	Cash income	Trade	Total
Komárom county	82.8	16.2	0.1	0·9	—	—	100.0
Esztergom county	76.2	16.9	4.9	2.0	—	—	100.0
Kishont county	77.1	7.8	0.1	14.2	0.8	—	100.0
Borough of Rimaszombat	30.5	4.8	3.8	19.2	26.5	15.2	100.0

Table 6.6. *Sources of income of noblemen's and Church farms in 1707 (in percentages)*

Territory	Animal breed-ing	Corn pro-duction	Wine pro-duction	Handi-crafts	Cash income	Trade	Total
Komárom county	63.5	29.3	—	6.6	0.4	0.2	100.00
Esztergom county	62.7	17.9	5.1	5.9	8.4	—	100.00
Kishont county	42.7	12.6	—	26.4	18.3	—	100.00
Borough of Rimaszombat	31.8	13.9	0.7	6.1	37.0	10.5	100.00

farm incomes in 3 counties and one borough were calculated based on 4,086 peasant and burgher, 296 noble and ecclesiastical farms (see Tables 6.5 and 6.6).

The insignificance of viticulture was due mainly to climatic conditions. The basic area of production of nobility and peasantry alike was stock-breeding. It made up three-quarters to four-fifths of the income of the peasantry and up to two-thirds of that of the nobility. In more populous market-towns where handicrafts, trade and moneylending were of great importance, the income from animal-breeding decreased to about 30 per cent. Nobles differed from peasants first of all in laying more stress on grain production and, in market-towns, being very involved in moneylending. Of 4,382 farms, 6.7 per cent belonged to noblemen and ecclesiastical institutions but their part in the total income was as much as 24 per cent. Summing up our research in the above-mentioned territories in 1707, we can conclude that 75 per cent of the income of all farms and production came from animal husbandry, and that four-fifths of that were from cattle-breeding.[27]

It is necessary to point out some more facts. Firstly, commodities for export – oxen, wine – were produced by the peasantry, especially by rich peasants (who owned about 20 per cent of peasant farms).[28] A grain surplus was

Table 6.7. *Role of oxen in Hungarian exports*[29]

Periods	Head of Oxen (yearly averages)	Thalers (millions)	Percentage of value of exports
1550–1600	100,000	1.36	75
1600–50	60,000	0.87	45
1650–1700	?	?	?
1700–50	60,000	1.16	41
1777–86	81,000	3.00	20
1787–1800	85,000	3.10	20
1802	158,600	5.74	24

produced only by noblemen's farms but it was without significance for export. Secondly, the nobility, or rather the high nobility, had a great share in the internal trade and in exports as wholesalers. Grain sold by them came from rents in kind, confiscations and from purchases. Wine production on their farms was much limited and their cattle-breeding was of no significance at all.[30] Thirdly, between 1550 and 1800 the absolute majority of Hungarian exports, sometimes more than 90 per cent, was of an agrarian character and the country's foreign trade balance was distinctly favourable all the time.[31] Foreign trade was impressive in comparison to the country's production. In 1580 the value of oxen and wine exports was 2 million thalers.[32] The state revenue of Hungary at the same time, including coinage revenue, was less than half a million thalers. But in 1640 only two-thirds of the former quantity of cattle exports and the same volume of wine exports made 2.66 million thalers.[33] This structure of exports, or rather this absolute predominance of oxen and wine exports, was slowly transformed by negative factors: war damage, the contraction of foreign markets, internal struggles for monopoly of the cattle trade, etc. (see Table 6.7). Though the volume of cattle exports reached its mid-sixteenth century level in the late eighteenth century and its value in silver thalers also increased, nevertheless its relative role decreased. The main reasons were rapid population growth, which expanded internal markets, and the increase of exports of various other products and raw materials. These changes are clearly reflected in the foreign trade balance calculated for 1770. The estimates based on assessed duty-value[34] were for exports 9.8 and for imports 8.4 million florins; export surplus was 16.7 per cent. Oxen were responsible for 26 per cent of export value, wine 7.7 and corn 15.3 per cent. These three together came to 49 per cent of the export value: the other half was due to wool (11.5 per cent), minerals and other raw materials. Imports consisted mostly of textiles, other industrial products and various Levantine goods. There are characteristic changes at the end of the eighteenth century: the classic export goods, oxen and wine, were losing their significance and new goods such as grain and wool appeared on foreign markets. Nevertheless, Hungarian exports retained their agrarian character.[35]

This structure of foreign trade characterised the Hungarian economy for three hundred years, notwithstanding economic and political crises. The foreign-trade figures may be related to the population. The country's economy was capable of sending abroad for every three families (i.e., 15 persons) the value of 1 fattened ox and 1 hl of first-class wine a year. Until the end of the eighteenth century Hungary had an active foreign-trade balance and a rich food supply.

7 ✈ The towns of East-Central Europe from the fourteenth to the seventeenth century

MARIA BOGUCKA

Historians who study the specific features of the development of East-Central Europe in the late Middle Ages and in modern times usually concentrate on the transformations which took place in the countryside. For it is easy to assume that these are precisely the kind of studies that are of fundamental value to largely agrarian countries where the gentry were predominant in social, political and even cultural life. Only the past thirty years have brought increased interest in the history of towns in those areas, and this trend is particularly clear in Polish and Hungarian historiography. Since the special role of towns in the development of civilisation in the broadest meaning of the term has been acknowledged,[1] it follows that the analysis of their functioning is an important, even indispensable element in the attempts at elucidating the historical processes occurring in East-Central Europe. Here I shall discuss the fourteenth to the seventeenth centuries and, more particularly, the late fifteenth to early seventeenth century as a time of rapid changes in Europe. I shall concentrate mainly on Poland, with Bohemia and Hungary as a comparison, for their development shows considerable analogies alongside certain characteristic differences.

The urbanisation processes which in East-Central Europe began as early as the ninth to tenth centuries, proceeded at an increased pace during the fourteenth to fifteenth centuries. It is assumed that, as a result, by the end of the fifteenth century there were more than 600 towns in Poland (without Lithuania). Only five or six of them approached the figure of 10,000 inhabitants or exceeded it, this figure being considered, in accordance with medieval European standards, the threshold between a medium and large town. They were Gdańsk (30 thousand), Cracow (nearly 18 thousand), Lvov, Toruń, Elbląg (some 8 thousand each), Poznań and Lublin (some 6–7 thousand) and Warsaw (some 5–6 thousand). Nearly 80 towns numbered 2–3 thousand inhabitants, the rest were boroughs with 500 to 1,500 inhabitants. Thus, even if the density of the urban network on the Polish lands was considerable (one town for some 210 sq km), they were mostly small centres

97

and placed much lower on the scale than the small towns of the West European type. The share of townsfolk in the population structure was also modest, amounting probably to some 15 per cent.[2] Urbanisation in Bohemia was similar at the time, with Prague (30 thousand inhabitants) occupying the first place; the other centres were much smaller (Brno some 8 thousand, Cheb and Kutná Hora some 5 thousand, České Budějovice, Hradec Kralové, Chrudim 3–4 thousand each).[3] Hungary's urban network was made up of even smaller centres. Only Buda's population amounted in the fifteenth century to 8 thousand; the rest had 4–5 thousand each (Bratislava, Sopron, Košice and Cluj; of mining towns, Banská Bystřica and Banská Štiavnica), or some 3 thousand (Pest, Szeged, Székesfehérvár, Trnava, Prešov, Bardějov, Levoča, Brašov and Sibiu; of mining towns Gelnica and Kremnica). Altogether it is assumed that in the late Middle Ages there were in Hungary some 30–35 towns, all small by European standards, whose population was estimated at around 3 per cent of the country's total population.[4] But next to them there existed some 800 boroughs (*oppida*) without full legal and political municipal status, subordinated to feudal jurisdiction, the economy of which rested on farming and breeding, but which functioned in part as towns in the field of trade and production and even social life (parishes, schools, hospitals).[5] Their rapid development was one of the characteristic features of urbanisation in Hungary at the time. These boroughs numbered 500–1,000 inhabitants on average.[6]

The process of urbanisation in East-Central Europe in the sixteenth to seventeenth century is a controversial subject. The slowing down of that process and the crisis of towns in that area have been variously dated, which is partly due to the specific features of particular regions. It seems that the earliest urban crisis occurred in Hungary, namely as early as the mid-fifteenth century (according to L. Mákkai and J. Szücs), perhaps in the early sixteenth (A. Kubinyi). In Bohemia, the first symptoms of a crisis appeared in the sixteenth century, and mostly in its later half (J. Janáček). Polish historians have shifted the beginning of the urban crisis to the late sixteenth century, some even to the later half of the seventeenth. Indeed, there is no doubt that throughout the sixteenth century, and partly also in the seventeenth, a colonisation was carried out on the Polish lands (according to A. Wyrobisz's calculations, 25 per cent of Polish towns were then established); in many existing towns the population increased considerably up to the mid-seventeenth century. At the end of the sixteenth century, the urban population amounted probably to some 20 per cent of Poland's inhabitants (Lithuania not included).[7] Some historians have raised this estimate to 22.5 per cent. Naturally, the degree of urbanisation in different parts of the country was not the same. Next to highly urbanised regions where the townspeople amounted to more than 30 per cent (Royal Prussia), or over 20 per cent of the total population (Great Poland, Little Poland, Silesia which in the fourteenth century belonged to the Kingdom of Bohemia), there were areas where the urban population constituted only upwards of 10 (Mazovia) or just a few per cent (the eastern borderlands).[8] Worth recalling, by way of comparison, is the fact that according to K. J. Beloch's calculations the inhabitants of towns at that time in some parts of northern Italy constituted over 50 per cent of the total population.[9] During the sixteenth century, the urban population in Holland increased from 46 per cent (1514) to 54 per cent (1622). The level of Poland's economic development, measured in terms of urbanisation, was thus much lower than in Western Europe, particularly in its leading regions. Although the urban network became denser in the Polish lands during the sixteenth century and by its end numbered more than 700 centres (without Lithuania and Silesia), yet only eight of them exceeded 10,000 inhabitants: Gdańsk (50 thousand by the end of the sixteenth century and probably some 70 thousand in the first half of the seventeenth), Warsaw (probably around 30 thousand in the early seventeenth century), Cracow (28 thousand), Poznań (some 20 thousand), Toruń, Elbląg, Lublin and Lvov (some 10 thousand). In the Grand Duchy of Lithuania, Vilna was quite an important town (15 thousand inhabitants by the end of the sixteenth century, 20 thousand in the mid-seventeenth). Towns with 4–5 thousand were considered medium size (Sandomierz, Kazimierz Dolny, Gniezno, etc.), but the majority consisted of townships with a population of 500–2,000[10] with farming as the predominant occupation, which invested them with a half-rural character.

At the time, Silesia, which as mentioned earlier did not then form part of the Polish state but was closely connected with it economically, had attained a high degree of urbanisation. Wrocław, which by the end of the fourteenth century numbered 20 thousand inhabitants, exceeded 30 thousand in the early seventeenth century. In the sixteenth century, Świdnica had over 11 thousand, Głogów some 10 thousand, Nysa 7–8 thousand; of the other Silesian towns, Lwówek had around 4 thousand, Bolesławiec, Jawor, Jelenia Góra and Strzegom 3 thousand each, while the rest (38 centres) had from a few hundred to 2 thousand inhabitants. Strangely enough, in the second half of the sixteenth century a certain decline in the proportion of townspeople in the population of Silesia as compared with the fourteenth century has been noted.

Wars drastically influenced the development of the urbanisation processes. In Silesia, the Thirty Years' War and the accompanying epidemics caused the Wrocław population to fall in 1640 to under 20 thousand; these losses were made good in the seventies of that century, but only in the eighteenth century did the population increase significantly. Other Silesian towns also suffered painful losses in population which were only very slowly made good. Apart from sporadic exceptions, no new towns were being chartered. Consequently, at the end of the seventeenth century, the percentage of the urban population in the demographic make-up of Silesia fell to 17; at the same time, the importance of agricultural occupations in towns increased. In Poland, similar results followed the devastation caused by the Swedish invasion in the mid-seventeenth century. Sixty per cent of the architectural substance in many towns was destroyed (the figure for Great Poland was 62.5 per cent); the losses in the demographic substance have been estimated on a similar scale, especially as they occurred as a consequence both of the hostilities and of plagues. The revival was very slow and so the share of the townsfolk in Poland's population in the eighteenth century has been estimated at barely 16 per cent. Thus the end of the seventeenth century was something of a return to the situation obtaining in the late Middle Ages. Another factor in the decline of Poland's urbanisation, a factor difficult to measure, was the extremely rapid growth of rural occupations in towns, where an estimated two-thirds of the population were employed in this way.

In Bohemia, as in Poland, the urban network became denser in the sixteenth century, but there, too, small and very small centres predominated. The only big town on the European scale was the capital city of Prague which had 50 thousand inhabitants in the second half of the sixteenth century, and even 60–70 thousand at the beginning of the seventeenth century, according to some scholars. The other Bohemian towns did not exceed 10 thousand (Cheb 7–8 thousand, Olomouc 5–7 thousand, Brno 4–5 thousand, České Budějovice, Hradec Kralové, Kutná Hora, Plzeň 3.5–4 thousand each) most of them numbering less than three thousand. There were cases of rapid growth in towns connected with a temporary development of, for example, mining: here a classic example is that of Jáchymov, whose inhabitants grew from one thousand in 1516 to 14 thousand by 1526. But these were short-lived growths. Altogether, the inhabitants of Czech towns at the end of the sixteenth century probably constituted over 20 per cent of the country's population.[11] The Thirty Years' War was responsible there, too, for considerable population losses; Prague fell to 30 thousand, and it was only in the early eighteenth century that it reached the figure of 40 thousand. In the sixteenth to seventeenth century the number of townsfolk engaged in farming also rose, although it seems that there this phenomenon did not reach the proportions noted in Poland and Hungary.

In Hungary, noticeable disturbances in her urban development appeared as early as the beginning of the sixteenth century, especially after the defeat at Mohács in 1526 and the division of the country into three parts, of which one remained under Turkish rule for 150 years; the rapidly depopulating towns of that zone (e.g. Buda and Pest) declined to the level of garrison towns. The situation was worsened by the military operations of 1591–1604 and conflicts with the Habsburgs in the seventeenth century. In the sixteenth to seventeenth century the population of the majority of Hungarian towns did not exceed the fifteenth-century level.[12] Some development was noticeable in a few trading centres (due, amongst other things, to the influx of fugitives from Buda and Pest), such as Pozsony and Trnava and in mining centres such as Banská Štiavnica. But in most towns the population declined so that they numbered barely 2–3 thousand inhabitants.[13] At the same time, the rank of agricultural occupations rose in towns.[14] The development of half-urban boroughs (*oppida*) was also characteristic of the time; besides cattle-breeding, vineyard cultivation and corn growing, trade and crafts were concentrated there; the urban functions of such boroughs expanded and their size grew, e.g., Debrecen numbered 7–8 thousand inhabitants in the mid-sixteenth century.[15] The urbanisation of Hungary in the sixteenth to seventeenth century rested mainly on the network of such boroughs.

This very brief survey suggests that a characteristic feature of East-Central Europe in the fourteenth to seventeenth century was its fairly dense urban network, made up of very small centres, often half-rural. As a matter of fact, only five towns in this region can be reckoned well-developed medium, perhaps even large, centres: Gdańsk, Prague, Warsaw, Wrocław and Cracow. The rise of the so-called second serfdom hindered the influx of peasants as early as the late fifteenth century in Poland, and later on in Bohemia and Hungary, and this in turn had an extremely adverse impact on the growth of towns in that zone. If the fourteenth to fifteenth century was a period of rapid urban development, the next period, sixteenth to seventeenth century, brought a reverse trend. At that time, urbanisation in East-Central Europe consisted mainly of the multiplication and development of small, half-rural centres, whereas in Western Europe this period saw the growth of big towns, numbering over 100,000 inhabitants (there were only five in the early sixteenth century, but twelve in the late seventeenth).[16] Consequently, both as regards quantity (the proportion of town-dwellers in the total population) and quality (the prevailing demographic type, the role of farming occupations) the urban backwardness of East-Central Europe as compared with the West was increasing.

In the opinion of the majority of historians, this backwardness should not be linked with the military events mentioned earlier. They played a significant but not decisive role in the history of the towns of Poland, Bohemia and Hungary. According to the latest studies, a much more important factor was the specific nature of the trade linking East-Central with Western Europe which emerged in the fifteenth century and continued to grow in the sixteenth to seventeenth century. It consisted of a broad range of imports of industrial and luxury goods and exports of raw materials, agricultural and forest produce (Poland exported grain and forest produce; Bohemia grain, wine, cattle and metals; Hungary wine, cattle and metals).[17] Such a structure of trade slowed down the development of these countries' own industrial production which was deprived of opportunities to sell its goods not only to the great nobles and the gentry but also to the townsfolk and the better-off among the peasants who, according to many studies of Poland and Hungary, would buy foreign commodities to the detriment of the local producer.[18] Hungarian (E. Fügedi, A. Kubinyi, L. Mákkai, J. Szücs), Polish (M. Małowist, A. Mączak, H. Samsonowicz, B. Zientara) and Czech historians (J. Janáček, A. Míka, J. Petráň,

J. Zemlička) have emphasised the weakness of urban artisans, caused by such a situation, and their petrification in guilds in the sixteenth and seventeenth centuries. Characteristically, the number of guilds rose in that period, sometimes reaching the figure of 50–60, and there developed fierce demarcation disputes among them, their backwardness in techniques and organisation increasing all the time. It is interesting to note that the idea of suppressing guilds, entertained by the gentry in Poland, and by the gentry and the rulers (Charles IV in Bohemia and later also the Habsburgs) in Bohemia and Hungary, was not carried out in practice, so that the guild system survived in East-Central Europe at a time when in the West it was gradually disintegrating. The guild system was too weak here to offer effective opposition to the competition of foreign goods; yet it was strong enough to monopolise production in the hands of a small number of privileged masters, limit the possibilities of enlarging particular workshops and oppose technical innovations.

The urban artisans were also adversely affected by the competition from craftsmen often supported by the gentry or even organised by them not only in the countryside but also in the property owned by the gentry in towns; the question of the so-called *a parte* or non-guild craftsmen became acute in the sixteenth to seventeenth century, because, among other things, of the restrictive policy of the guilds. In Poland such crafts were centred in an increasing number of houses and even whole town quarters belonging to the gentry (called *iurisdictiones*) and remaining outside the municipal law.[19] The situation was similar in Silesia and some Czech towns. In Hungary there was a rapid development of an artisan class in the half-agrarian *oppida*.[20] Yet production remained essentially small-scale, all the more so as at the turn of the sixteenth century the worsening economic conditions in the countryside and the shrinking purchasing power of the peasantry restricted demand. Consequently, in East-Central Europe very few big manufacturing centres emerged which would supply both the immediate neighbourhood and also the more outlying areas. The few exceptions only confirmed the rule. Among them was Gdańsk, which at the turn of the sixteenth century expanded into a large manufacturing centre with 3 thousand workshops supplying various commodities (textiles, furniture, arms, metal products, glassware, pottery, tools, toys, etc.) to customers throughout Poland and exporting to Scandinavia. Next came Wrocław (with 1,200–1,400 workshops at the turn of the sixteenth century). But in general East-Central European towns did not develop their own crafts (except, perhaps, the food industry) to a degree sufficient even to meet the local demand. Characteristic examples are those of the big residential centres at the end of the sixteenth century such as Warsaw and Prague, where the number of local workshops was very small and the demand for industrial products was met by foreign imports. Particularly 'stunted' was the development of crafts in Hungary where the share of artisans in the professional make-up of the towns was strikingly low (20–30 per cent).[21] The situation in Bohemia was different, with craftsmen making up 40–50 per cent of the population in many towns; it is there that in the late Middle Ages several regions emerged making textiles for large-scale export abroad (to Austria, Poland and Hungary). This flourishing of Bohemian and Moravian cloth-making did not last long; it declined in the last quarter of the sixteenth century. Also short-lived was the development of textile-manufacturing regions of some strength in Poland (Sieradz and Łęczyca voivodships in the sixteenth century, Great Poland and Royal Prussia in the seventeenth).

The organisation of production in the areas of interest to us did not undergo any large-scale transformations so characteristic of Western Europe, particularly towards the end of the Middle Ages. Even in the sixteenth to seventeenth century the small workshop with a slight output capacity, the master working personally with the help of 2–3 journeymen and apprentices, was typical of Poland, Bohemia and Hungary. The guilds fiercely resisted all attempts at increasing the size of workshops and all technical innovations. The example of Gdańsk, where in the sixteenth to seventeenth century a crisis of the guild organisation occurred and biggish manufacturing units developed fairly strongly, is an exception. Bohemian, Moravian and Polish textile-exporting townships worked on the basis of a putting-out system: attempts at organising centralised manufactories did not really appear in East-Central Europe until the second half of the seventeenth century (Bohemia), and still more in the eighteenth century (Poland).[22] This was related to the weakness of early capitalism. Indeed, the development of such manufactories can only be linked with some branches of production: mining, especially Bohemian and Hungarian,[23] production of iron and glass, and shipbuilding (Gdańsk, Elbląg). The development of various forms of the putting-out system, mostly organised by merchants, only increased the backwardness of East-Central European crafts. Numerous Polish, Czech and Hungarian scholars have emphasised that the craftsmen in those regions were poor and that they achieved prosperity by engaging in other occupations rather than plying their crafts. In the market conditions prevailing in these parts, productive activity did not allow of any accumulation of capital on a larger scale. Doubtless, a significant role was played by the prices policy extorted by the gentry. In Poland, after attempts made in the fifteenth century (1423, 1454, 1465, 1496), the regulation of prices for industrial products was entrusted to the palatines in 1565. Somewhat later, at the turn of the sixteenth century, such price lists were issued by the gentry in Bohemia and Hungary.[24] The crafts, poor and weak, became a prey to large-scale expansion of usurers and merchants, often foreigners; good examples of this can be seen in the activity of south-German merchants, as well as of the English and Dutch in Bohemia and Silesia.[25] Foreign capital also exploited Hungarian and Bohemian mining.[26] Another characteristic feature was the increased involvement of the gentry and magnates in the sphere of mining as is evident in Poland (Olkusz and the salt mines of Wieliczka and Bochnia) and

Bohemia (Jáchymov). Capital expenditure in mining was limited and it exhibited a tendency towards a wasteful exploitation which resulted in declining production.

The movement of foreign capital to the territories of East-Central Europe was particularly forceful in the field of credit and big trade. Gdańsk's overseas trade, which developed in the fourteenth to fifteenth century, turned in the next two centuries into a passive intermediary in its own port between the gentry and foreign skippers. It is assumed that at the end of the sixteenth century some 80 per cent of the Baltic trade was in the hands of the Dutch, who earned enormous profits from it.[27] Dutch merchants tried also to control the trade between Gdańsk and its hinterland by way of credits and the dependence of Gdańsk firms on their capital. A similar activity was carried out by south-German merchants in Hungary and Bohemia (direct organisation of imports and exports or the control of local merchants through credits).[28] It can safely be asserted that the development of trade in East-Central Europe was considerably weaker than in the West. Capital accumulation proceeded on a much more modest scale; truly big banker and merchant fortunes were rare and emerged only in the more developed centres of the region. The banking house of the Loitz family in Pomerania in the sixteenth century dealt in hundreds of thousands of thalers; its activity (loans to rulers, mining projects, big commerce) brings to mind the dealings of the famous Fuggers: even the bankruptcy of both the Loitz family and the Fuggers was to a large extent caused by the same factors.[29] But there are not many such analogies. At the close of the fifteenth century, the fortunes of the big merchants in Gdańsk amounted to from 14 to 30 thousand marks, that is, from 230 to 280 kg of pure silver. In the first half of the seventeenth century, there were in Gdańsk some merchants whose property amounted to 300–600 thousand Polish florins, that is the equivalent of some 2,500–4,500 kg of pure silver.[30] Yet in Warsaw the fortune of the biggest merchant in the late sixteenth century, Sigismund Erkemberger, amounted to barely 50–60 thousand Polish florins (i.e., the equivalent of only 1,000–1,200 kg of pure silver). On the Gdańsk level were the fortunes of the wealthiest Prague merchants in the first half of the seventeenth century: Eustachius Betengel's estimated at some 312,500 Rhine guldens, and Lorenz Stark's estimated at some 212,500 Rhine guldens; the Jewish banker of Prague, Markus Maisel, left half-a-million Rhine guldens in ready money. But the rest of the Prague merchants ranked far below those three, only a dozen or so having reached the figure of 37,500 Rhine guldens. In Hungary a few thousand guldens were thought to be quite a fortune for a merchant.[31] For the sake of comparison it is worth recalling that the Fuggers' legendary riches ran into millions of guldens (in 1527 their firm's assets totalled three million guldens, in 1557 two million guldens).[32] In the first half of the seventeenth century, the accumulated capital of the Netherlands firm of De Groote-Hureau-van Colen amounted to 500,000 Flemish pounds or more than

30,000 kg of pure silver.[33] Moreover, such a fortune was nothing extraordinary in Western Europe.

Besides the competition on the part of strong foreign merchants, the East-Central European middle class also felt keenly the competition of the gentry which, particularly in the sixteenth and seventeenth centuries, organised its own sales of agricultural crops and the purchase of foreign goods, by-passing the local burghers. This happened particularly in Poland where the gentry, having obtained exemption from customs duties in 1496, almost monopolised the transport of grain down the Vistula to Gdańsk where, in turn, they bought various industrial products. In the early seventeenth century, the share of the gentry in the trade with Gdańsk amounted to some 70 per cent, that of the townsfolk only 20 per cent. Similar trends developed in Bohemia, where throughout the sixteenth century the gentry vied with the towns for economic rights.[34] In Hungary not only the gentry but also the wealthy peasants competed with the burghers by attempting to monopolise the cattle, wine and corn trade.[35] During the sixteenth century, both the Bohemian and Hungarian gentry obtained exemption from paying customs duties and tolls which the townspeople were obliged to pay.[36]

A feature characteristic of the development of East-Central Europe, and one with far-reaching consequences, was the rapid outflow of merchant capital from the towns. The purchase of landed estates occurred as early as the fourteenth to fifteenth century, but in the following centuries it became the chief means of spending money earned from commerce (besides hoarding, luxury consumption and artistic and building patronage). Both entire towns (among particularly big landowners were Gdańsk and Prague)[37] and single merchants owned villages and landed estates. In Poland this was a procedure formally legalised in the sixteenth to seventeenth century only in respect of the inhabitants of towns granted 'noble rights' (Cracow, Vilna, Lvov), and to towns in Royal Prussia (Gdańsk, Elbląg, Toruń), but in practice it was quite common and was followed by inhabitants of all the major urban centres.[38] The situation in Silesia was similar,[39] as well as in many Bohemian and Hungarian towns.[40] Of course, investing capital in land was not exclusive to those areas. In the sixteenth and seventeenth centuries, the wealthy English, French, German and Dutch townspeople also invested considerable sums in landed estates; R. Mandrou has even considered this tendency a permanent feature, a mental structure characteristic of the early modern era, and emerging almost all over Europe.[41] But the point is that, in the territories covered by this survey, the outflow of capital from the towns caused by this tendency was not, as in the West, made good by increased economic activity in other fields, primarily in production and trade; it created gaps which weakened the economic potential of towns in a permanent way. This led to a so-called 'feudalisation' of the East-Central European burghers and their merging into the gentry. A complete break with urban occupations and a move to the countryside would often occur as early as the second generation.[42] Even those people who stayed in towns tried to imitate the gentry's life-style and took over its cultural patterns and ideals.[43] This subordination of the urban culture to the nobles was particularly strong in the seventeenth century in Poland and Hungary; after the wiping out of the Bohemian gentry in the battle of the White Mountain (1620) and the emigration which followed, the development of culture in Bohemian towns proceeded along different paths.

The outward movement of the rich townspeople and their capital went parallel to an opposite movement, that of the influx of the gentry into towns. In the fourteenth and fifteenth centuries, the right to own property in town was enjoyed in principle exclusively by its burghers, although there were exceptions to this rule.[44] It was the constitution of 1550 which opened the doors wide to the development of gentry property in Polish towns; it allowed the gentry to own property in towns provided the municipal taxes were paid.[45] This condition was not fulfilled and the urban real estate belonging to the clergy, gentry and magnates increased at a quick pace, in some centres such as Warsaw and Cracow reaching over 50 per cent of all property.[46] Similar processes took place in Bohemian towns, the most glaring instance being Prague which, like Warsaw, became in the seventeenth century a large agglomeration of mansions of the gentry and palaces belonging to magnates. In Hungary the influx of the gentry into towns in the sixteenth and seventeenth centuries was magnified by the fear of the Turks.[47] The Diets of 1553 and 1563 ordered the towns to accept the gentry provided they did not free themselves from municipal taxes; ultimately in 1647, the Hungarian gentry was definitively allowed to settle in towns and exempted, their servants included, from all municipal burdens and jurisdictions.[48]

The dwindling of burghers' property in towns meant the defeat of that estate, all the more painful as it was suffered on their own territory, in that stronghold which (both in reality and in the social feeling) was constituted in the Middle Ages by an area encircled with walls and reserved for the burghers alone, to whom had been granted numerous monopolistic rights and privileges relating to its surroundings. Strongly connected with this is the problem of the development of the estate consciousness of the burghers in East-Central Europe as well as of the political role played by towns in the fourteenth to fifteenth century, and which was later, in the sixteenth to seventeenth century, linked with the question of the towns' autonomy and rights.

Not all the towns in East-Central Europe had the autonomy and legal freedom characteristic of West European cities as early as the twelfth to thirteenth century; they were enjoyed only by the free royal towns. In central Poland (not including the Ruthenian lands) there were 264 of them by the close of the seventeenth century out of the total of 741 urban centres. In Bohemia, the proportions were very similar, whereas in Hungary the number of royal towns did not exceed 30 to 35. The other towns were the private property of feudal lords: their burdens were very much like those of the rural villein services (including rent in kind and sometimes even labour services); they were subjected to feudal jurisdiction and had a more-or-less restricted self-government. The number of private towns increased rapidly in the sixteenth to seventeenth century in Poland, Bohemia and Hungary, and they became typical of that part of Europe. Their development strengthened neither the burghers nor the ruler but the rich noblemen, that is, the feudal elements in the socio-political structure. Moreover, during the sixteenth to seventeenth century, the royal towns became enfeebled and the range of their self-government and legal freedoms shrank visibly. In Poland, the royal towns came under the burdensome control of royal officials. A similar subordination developed in Bohemia, where the years between the Hussite revolution and the late fifteenth century are considered the peak of the self-government and judicial autonomy of the royal towns. The famous Diet of 1547 put the Bohemian royal towns under the control of special royal officials, as had been the case in Poland. The Hungarian royal towns also went through a flourishing period of self-government and legal freedom in the later half of the fifteenth century.[49]

As regards the political rights of towns, there was greater differentiation. The situation was worst in the Polish towns. Only in the fourteenth and fifteenth centuries did they take part in important political events, such as elections of kings, approval of international treaties, etc. The second half of the fifteenth century brought a considerable weakening of such activity and, consequently, the exclusion of the towns from the just emerging Polish Diet. The Bohemian and Hungarian towns were politically extremely active throughout the fifteenth century. In the early sixteenth century (1517) the representatives of Bohemian towns obtained, despite the gentry's opposition, the confirmation of their right to what was called the third voice in the national Diet. In 1547 this right was taken away, yet a limited representation of the towns in the Diet was maintained. The Hungarian towns also retained – albeit with difficulty – their participation in the Diet up to the late seventeenth century.[50]

The politically inferior situation of the Polish townsfolk was certainly bound up with their less-developed estate awareness. One of the criteria of such awareness is the capacity to cooperate with other towns and to set up unions for the promotion of interests covering more than a single town. According to the scheme proposed by E. Lousse, three levels should be distinguished: (1) the capacity to establish *ad hoc* defensive coalitions; (2) the capacity to establish permanent unions in the defence of common interests; (3) the capacity to force the granting of estate privileges.[51] The Polish townsfolk attained the first level in the fourteenth and first half of the fifteenth century (urban confederations in 1349, 1350, accession to the gentry confederations in 1464 for the last time). From the second half of the fifteenth century, the Polish towns did not have it in them to undertake any broader solidary action even of an occasional defensive type. The Bohemian and Hungarian towns, on the other hand, exhibited a strong activity in forming unions (according to the second level of Lousse's scheme) not only in the fifteenth century but throughout the sixteenth and well into the seventeenth century. It was due to their active role in the great social and national movements such as the Hussite revolution and later the Reformation as well as to their participation (in alliance with the gentry) in the opposition against the Habsburgs in the sixteenth and seventeenth century. Although the townspeople suffered repression after the defeats inflicted on this opposition, their participation alongside the gentry awakened their estate consciousness. In this regard, they were nearer to the conscious and politically active Dutch and English town dwellers – who in the sixteenth to seventeenth century were slowly getting ready for a bourgeois revolution – than were the inhabitants of the Polish towns, politically immature and incapable of forming any ideology of their own.[52] These are matters very little studied so far and they certainly require broad comparative studies, particularly from the national and ethnic aspect. The undertaking of such studies would also mean examining, in a broader way than heretofore, the specific features of the development of burgher culture in East-Central Europe and its obvious slowing down precisely at a time when it reached its peak in the West (the Netherlands and Italy).

The considerations here have, of necessity, been stated with extreme brevity, and only the most important questions relating to the development of East-Central European towns have been touched upon. But even such a summary review reveals the specificity of the urban processes in the areas of interest to us. This specificity was doubtless one of the important elements in the different paths of the general development followed by East-Central Europe in the fourteenth to seventeenth century.

8 ❧ Comments on the circulation of capital in East-Central Europe

MARIAN MAŁOWIST

In this article I would like to present the problem of the circulation of capital in southern Poland (Little Poland), Bohemia and northern Hungary (Slovakia) from the fourteenth to the seventeenth century. These were territories which, in the period under discussion, were characterised by a high level of development in mining and which, against this background, were interconnected by close economic ties.

Little Poland had at its disposal from the middle of the thirteenth century considerable resources of rock salt; these deposits, reaching into south-western Ruthenia, were to be included in the following century within the borders of the Polish state. This salt not only satisfied the needs of the southern regions of Poland but had already in the fourteenth century become an important export – to Silesia, Bohemia and Hungary. Another extremely important element in the economic life of the region under discussion was lead ore, mined from the thirteenth and fourteenth century in the Cracow region, above all in Olkusz, Trzebnica and other localities of Little Poland; this was an ore of high quality although it contained but a slight percentage of silver. The latter was separated from lead only from the sixteenth century since earlier this was unprofitable. Lead not only completely met Polish demand but a large part of it was exported. It was indispensable for the mining industry of Hungarian Slovakia where from the thirteenth to the fourteenth century exploitation of copper, silver and also, to a lesser degree, of gold developed. Main mining centres such as Kremnica, Banská Štiavnica, Gelnica and many others constantly imported lead from Little Poland and from Silesia, in exchange for copper and silver needed by the Polish mints as well as gold from Slovakia and Transylvania. The export of Hungarian metals was intended not only for the neighbouring countries but also played a large role in the Baltic countries, in Flanders and in Novgorod. Bohemia, rich in silver, iron and tin, imported salt, Polish and Silesian lead as well as Hungarian copper and gold. In the period up to the sixteenth century when the natural wealth of Little Poland and Silesia had only inter-regional significance, the resources of Bohemia and Hungary

109

played a very important role in the developing European economy. This became possible from the thirteenth and fourteenth century when the region under discussion entered into a phase of accelerated economic development, analogous to the phenomena characteristic of Western Europe from about the middle of the eleventh century.[1] In this period in Bohemia, Poland and Hungary there was a considerable development of agriculture as well as of rural and urban settlements. In Bohemia and Silesia, and slightly later in Little Poland and Hungary, there began, in villages and towns, a development of a mercantile and monetary economy on a scale much larger than before. At this time exploitation of natural resources was increasing and a new network of trade routes developing. They linked the Baltic Sea with Hungary and the Black Sea area, with Italy and south-western Germany (by way of Bohemia and Hungary), with Poland, southern Russia and the Black Sea centres of Levantine trade, Tana and Caffa. This phenomenon was closely connected with the economic growth of East-Central Europe since its resources of copper, silver and tin ores, as well as supply of furs, wax, a particular red dyestuff and, later on, cattle had a significant attraction for foreign merchants, miners and artisans.

These trade routes together with the development of agriculture accelerated general economic growth. I have in another work drawn attention to the relatively small population density of East-Central Europe in the Middle Ages in comparison to the West.[2] There is no doubt that the East lacked trading capital as well, and that generally speaking the above-mentioned areas also had a lower technological level. The rulers and both lay and ecclesiastical magnates, if they wished to keep up with the times and to increase their incomes, had to look for new methods of running their estates: hence their support and even energetic encouragement for foreign rural and urban settlers, initially from Flanders, the Walloon country and even from France, and later Germans, who became the most numerous of them. They were granted the so-called Teutonic Law, modelled on the system already existing in central and eastern Germany, which ensured them favourable conditions. With the course of time this law was also granted to the majority of the local population, especially in Bohemia and Poland and to a large degree in Hungary. It constituted an important stimulus for general economic growth and at the same time it increased the incomes not only of peasants and burghers but also of their overlords, including the monarchs. It should be stressed that in this situation migrations were closely connected with the transfer of material resources. Great lay and ecclesiastical lords, active in the reorganisation of economic life, did not as a rule possess the necessary capital which had very often to be imported together with the people who had it at their disposal. In Little Poland as in Silesia, Bohemia and Hungary natural resources were the property of the rulers (*regale*) but a precondition of their exploitation was the immigration of foreign miners who possessed the necessary resources, skills and experience. The need for non-ferrous and precious metals was very great in medieval Europe and, from the thirteenth or fourteenth century, all the regions in question became an immigration area for miners from Germany where mining was developed early and extensively. There also emerged a technology which made possible the exploitation of at least shallow deposits and there came into being a mining law regulating the conditions of this branch of production. This emigration began in Silesia and Bohemia in the twelfth and thirteenth centuries and gradually spread east and south-eastwards to Hungary, Transylvania and subsequently also a part of the Balkans. The local population rapidly learned the new and essentially simple mining skills but nevertheless the German immigrants did not cease to play a very significant role. Miners, craftsmen and merchants of German origin as well as other German settlers swelled the populations of the already existing towns of Poland, Bohemia and Hungary or founded new urban centres. While in Brandenburg, Prussia and Livonia this settlement occurred under the patronage of secular and ecclesiastical rulers, in the entire remaining area of East-Central Europe German colonisation won the support of the local authorities and aristocracy. New towns developed most rapidly in regions favourably located as regards trade routes and natural resources. Colonisation played a great role in Bohemia where in the course of the fourteenth century Prague's population increased from 30,000 to 40,000 and that of the miners' town of Kutná Hora up to 18,000. These were particularly outstanding cases, however. Jihlava, Nemecký Brod, Štribro and other mining towns in Bohemia were much smaller and numbered a few thousand inhabitants each. The situation was similar in Silesia which in the fourteenth century was lost by Poland to Bohemia. In Slovakia one does not find large towns in the mining regions, although Kremnica, Banská Bistřica, Banská Štiavnica, Gelnica as well as the non-mining Košice reached a high level of prosperity, similar to the main towns of Transylvania, the trade and crafts of which had a solid material base thanks to local animal husbandry and the mining of copper, iron, gold and silver ores. As far as Little Poland and Ruthenia were concerned, the incentive to immigration and stimulus to the development of towns was both lead and salt mining as well as a very favourable network of trade routes which I have mentioned above. This network also had a beneficial influence upon northern Hungary, Silesia and even Bohemia although, it seems, to a lesser degree.

Let us now examine the situation of the particular countries which made up the geographical region under discussion from the thirteenth to the fifteenth centuries. Bohemia was undoubtedly in the forefront as regards economic and political life. Beginning in the twelfth century there occurred a strong and dynamic growth of the economy. A very considerable influx of German settlers certainly hastened these changes. In the towns there appeared a large number of German merchants and artisans. An outstanding role in the Bohemian economy was played by the mining of silver, tin and iron ores, the first peak period being reached in the years 1290–1350. Kutná Hora dominated in silver mining in the fourteenth century with an annual production reaching approximately 20 metric tons a year at the beginning of the century, while in Český Las considerable amounts of tin were mined. Thanks to their silver resources, the rulers of Bohemia were able, at the end of the thirteenth century, to issue a highly valuable silver currency – the grossus. Prague, above all, together with Brno, Plzeň and other towns became centres of trade in precious metals, even more so because large amounts of gold florins from neighbouring Hungary made their way there.[3] Owing to this fact wealthy merchants of Prague, Brno, Cheb and Plzeň, and to a lesser degree other towns, became rich on export–import trade, selling to merchants from Regensburg, Cologne and from the fourteenth century mainly from Nuremberg valuable Czech and Hungarian metals (in the form of currency) and other scarce products, buying in return, above all, Western cloths, metal goods and spices.[4] This was a very important element in the accumulation of capital by wealthy merchants. Rich mining entrepreneurs withdrew from production, as did those in neighbouring countries. At the present stage of research it is difficult to say to what extent merchants engaged in mining directly, i.e., whether they bought many shares in the mines and exploited them using a hired labour force, or whether they preferred a system of concessions and bought the metal from the producers for cash. This problem calls for further research but it may be supposed that both methods were used, as in the neighbouring countries. One should add that a part of the capital accumulated by wealthy merchants was invested in landed property.

The balance of Czech foreign trade during the thirteenth and fourteenth century was undoubtedly unfavourable. Large imports of cloths and metal goods from the Netherlands, England and Italy, wine from the south-west, and furs, hides and herrings from the area of Hanseatic trade called for considerable exports from Bohemia. Czech products, or even Hungarian ones which partially followed transit routes through Bohemia, did not suffice. The export of tin, which was frequently a successful rival to metal of English origin on the Flemish and German markets did not cover these costs either. It was essential to balance imports with ready cash. Czech silver grossi reached Bruges as early as the end of the thirteenth century and large amounts flowed into Nuremberg, Regensburg and other towns of Upper Germany which had connections with Bohemia in the thirteenth and fourteenth centuries, as well as Florence and Venice, especially in the fourteenth century in the times of King John and the Emperor Charles IV. All this was of great importance for the economy of Western Europe and Italy where, following the great monetary reforms of the thirteenth century, prices for precious metals grew. Large amounts of Czech currency were also to be found in neighbouring countries and especially in Poland, Silesia and Saxony. This had a very strong influence upon the shaping of a new monetary system in Poland in the fourteenth century and even in the fifteenth, although Prague grossi lost much of their value as a result of depreciation. One may assume that the influence of abundant silver (as well as tin, considered at the time to be practically a precious metal) had a great impact upon the socio-economic and political structures of Bohemia. Without these resources the power and very active foreign policy of the last Přemyslids as well as of the Luxembourg kings – John and his son Charles – would be unimaginable. The Luxembourg dynasty played a large part in bringing an increased flow of silver to Italy, where both the above-mentioned rulers were politically involved.

Great accumulations of silver currency facilitated monetary circulation. In rural life as early as the thirteenth century, tenants' rents in kind were to a large degree replaced by money-rent, and this phenomenon occurred in Poland on a large scale in the fifteenth century and in Hungary rather later. In a situation of a gradual depreciation of money this change could to a certain degree have improved the situation of the peasants, although this is an area which needs more research. How did this change affect the incomes of the Czech clergy and nobility? This too is a question which calls for more thorough research. It is probable, however, that in the thirteenth and fourteenth centuries the Church and magnates benefited from the development of mining, since they received a part of their incomes from mines located in their estates. The incomes of the more prosperous merchants undoubtedly increased thanks to the involvement of this group in international trade and, directly or indirectly, in mining.

A gradual decline in the productivity of silver mines occurred after 1350 and lasted for about a century. It cannot be ascribed to the effects of the Black Death, as was assumed by John U. Nef,[5] since this epidemic affected East-Central Europe to a much smaller degree than the West, the Black Sea regions or Russia. One should accept the opinion of J. Kořan that from the middle of the fourteenth century there occurred an exhaustion of shallow ore deposits while the reaching of deposits more difficult to mine demanded new technology and considerable investments. These circumstances, and not just the Hussite revolution and the emigration of Germans, explain the long-lasting crisis in mining.

Did the decrease of silver mining and to a certain extent also of tin rapidly cause a general decline of the situation and a social and religious ferment which found expression in the Hussite revolution in the first half of the fifteenth century? This is a problem which as yet has not been explored. I believe that the growing differences between wealthier and poorer social groups, which were connected with national differences, led towards sharp antagonisms between Czechs and Germans and favoured the Hussite movement. In the course of the first half of the fifteenth century, Bohemia was a country of heated religious and social struggles, and it found itself in an unending conflict with its German neighbours. In this tempestuous period Bohemia was cut off from its main economic partners. All this combined with the crisis in Bohemian mining, which was resolved only at the end of the fifteenth century by the discovery of till then unknown ore deposits and the use of new and expensive technologies which made it possible to reach ores below the water level. We shall return to this problem.

The Slovakian areas of medieval Hungary played a very important role in the production of precious metals and copper on a European scale. Local mining probably went back to the third century AD, and in any case existed in the Roman period and was revived after an interval during the great migrations. Primitive technology enabled the exploitation only of surface deposits. A fundamental technological breakthrough came about in the thirteenth century when Bavarian and Saxon miners, very numerous among the incoming German settlers, introduced into Slovakia more advanced methods of exploitation of metal ores.[6] This made it possible for them to acquire larger material resources than the Slovak population. Already in the eleventh century under Stephen I, King of Hungary, there functioned a mint in Banská Štiavnica which used local metal. Shortly after 1200 a mining settlement already existed there.[7] The Mongol invasion in 1241–2 hampered the development of mining only for a short time.

Just after the middle of the thirteenth century this development showed considerable growth. It was at this time that important mining towns, such as Banská Bistřica, Banská Bela and many others, mainly in the Hron and Vag river valleys, were given charters.[8] In 1328 Kremnica was founded which later became the most important centre for silver and gold mining in Slovakia and the centre of the royal mint and of the administration of the mining region. At this time many other mining towns were also established. Analogous phenomena occurred from the twelfth and thirteenth centuries in Transylvania in the eastern region of Hungary. Thanks to all these circumstances, Hungary became the largest owner of gold and copper in medieval Europe, while Bohemia retained its predominance as the producer of silver.

The earliest data concerning the export of precious metals and copper from Hungary are to be found in the customs tariff of Hainsburg which lay on the main trade route linking Hungary with Vienna.[9] In the next century this export increased enormously. Hungarian copper not only reached neighbouring countries but also the Baltic regions and Flanders, as well as Italy. The import of Hungarian gold and silver was an important requisite for the great Italian monetary reforms in the middle of the thirteenth century.[10] Hungarian silver also made its way to southern Germany and Flanders. It should be recognised that Hungarian mining of precious metals and copper even had an indirect influence on the growth of Italian Levantine trade, which demanded, after all, a considerable export of money and copper to the Near East.

The natural resources of Hungary were extremely attractive to both local and foreign merchants. Miners whose work involved a considerable risk of failure were also threatened with greater personal risk as they reached the deeper layers of ore, and they were forced to take loans from merchants, promising to pay their debts in kind, i.e., in the metal which they were planning to mine. In connection with this, as early as the fourteenth century the system of advance loans became widespread in Slovakian mining, individual shares in mines frequently became the property of merchants, and the producers depended increasingly on their creditors.[11] Originally the wealthy citizens of mining towns were the financiers, but soon foreigners also appeared among them. When the Anjou dynasty assumed power, there arose circumstances favourable to the introduction of Italians into Hungarian mining, a fact which unfortunately has not as yet received adequate attention. It was precisely these newcomers who organised the export of gold, silver and Hungarian copper from Slovakia and Transylvania to Italy, making use of southern trade routes leading to the town of Senj in Dalmatia and from there by sea to Venice. In the first half of the fourteenth century the majority of exports intended for Germany and Italy was transported to Vienna, which for a long time was the main recipient and distributor of Hungarian products and simultaneously the most important staple for goods imported to that country. However, in the second quarter of the fourteenth century changes resulted from the energetic activities in Bohemia, Poland and Hungary of merchants from Upper Germany, and especially from Nuremberg. They were the suppliers of haberdashery, of Western textiles, Italian metal goods and of spices, while in Hungary they bought gold and silver money as well as copper. This they exported to Germany and Italy, by-passing Vienna, and as a result avoided the heavy local storage dues.[12]

At the close of the first half of the fourteenth century Nuremberg merchants became interested in mining in northern Hungary, which was a logical result of their participation in the trade in metals. It does not seem, however, that they invested capital on a large scale directly in production. On the other hand they gained very considerable successes in the trade in metals. According to W. von Strömer, two large Nuremberg companies were, at the end of the fourteenth century, very close to total domination over the Hungarian export of copper and precious metals to Upper Germany, Venice and, in the north, to the Baltic regions and from there to the Netherlands.[13]

In this way a large part of the income from Hungarian trade made its way into the hands of foreign merchants. The flow of money from Hungary to the West and especially to western and northern Germany, was even larger considering that the balance of payments in Hungary in the fifteenth and undoubtedly also at the beginning of the sixteenth century was decidedly negative. Unfortunately, there is a lack of exact data for the earlier period. On the other hand, registers of the 'thirtieth' duty kept by the customs house in Bratislava in 1457–8 indicate that the value of Hungarian export covered only one-third of the costs of import. According to E. Fügedi, in the second half of the fifteenth century and at the beginning of the sixteenth Hungary added from 100,000 to 150,000 ducats annually in order to make up the difference between its export and import of foreign products only in Bratislava itself, while the national passive balance reached the sum of at least 300,000 ducats per annum.[14] This was the result of the underdevelopment of Hungarian artisan production, which was unable to fulfil the market needs not only as regards luxury goods but also for medium- or low-quality textiles, metal articles, etc. This situation could be maintained as long as Hungarian mining made up for the deficit in foreign trade, and this was the situation in the fourteenth century and for a large part of the following century as well. However, already in the mid-fifteenth century difficulties began to emerge in ore mining in Slovakia, the struggle against water flooding the mine shafts becoming increasingly laborious.[15] The gradual exhaustion of shallow ore deposits also called for a transition to deep mining. Hungary lacked the means for realising such difficult and extremely costly investments. Foreign capitalists operating in Hungarian mining in the fourteenth and at the beginning of the fifteenth century began to withdraw. Probably during the course of the fifteenth century they were discouraged by the technological problems. One should also take into account the political upheaval both in neighbouring Bohemia and Hungary itself caused by the Hussite wars and the later conflicts between Matthias Corvinus, King of Hungary, and Poland, Bohemia and Austria. These problems created an atmosphere of uncertainty which was not favourable to the activity of capitalists in the Sudeten and Carpathian regions. Fundamental changes occurred only at the end of the fifteenth century under the influence of a new increase of demand for copper and silver on a European scale.

Little Poland, like Bohemia and Hungary, underwent a period of increased growth in agriculture, urban economy and mining in the thirteenth and fourteenth centuries. The regulation of peasant payments, the frequent exemption of settlers from all obligations for a period of many years, favourable prospects in trade, industry and mining all created stimuli for economic activity in the countryside and in towns. The extremely favourable position of Little Poland and neighbouring Ruthenia (united with Poland in the mid-fourteenth century) relative to the great trade routes meant that, from the beginning of the thirteenth century, Cracow in particular and in the next century Lvov, and to a certain extent smaller towns as well had a great attraction for foreign merchants and artisans. Hence, wealthy arrivals from Silesia and Germany frequently settled there; from the latter there also came Jews, and in Russia there appeared Armenians from the Black Sea region. As J. Ptaśnik proved, many wealthy Cracow burghers of German origin actively participated in rural and urban colonisation. Following the orders of rulers or great ecclesiastical and lay lords they organised new urban and rural settlements or took upon themselves expenses connected with the transition of the so-called German law to settlements already existing.

In the villages they assumed the functions of headmen, which ensured them income from the lower jurisdiction, the possession of large farmsteads, taverns and other material gains. In towns they became hereditary mayors, also providing considerable income. In this way, already in the thirteenth and fourteenth centuries capital which mainly originated from trade was partially invested in the rural economy of Little Poland and, as we shall see, in mining as well. There was at the time no anxiety about ensuring the safety of part of the capital against the risk of loss in trade. Its investment in the rural economy frequently guaranteed considerable income and opportunities for social advancement, i.e., penetration into the then emerging nobility and even the magnate class. This was the case in many instances in Little Poland in the fourteenth and fifteenth centuries. One should at the same time stress the fact that the burghers from Silesian Germany as well as the Jews and Armenians who came to Little Poland and to Ruthenia settled permanently, strengthening in this way the quite recently weak demographic and economic potential of the country. In the course of the fourteenth and especially the fifteenth century there occurred an increase in the number of both merchants and artisans originating from the local population. In the fifteenth and sixteenth centuries town populations in Little Poland became polonised. This occurred despite the fact that the immigration of merchant families from Germany and Italy still continued.

Undoubtedly, the flourishing of Cracow, Lvov and certain other towns of Little Poland and Red Ruthenia remained closely connected with the development of trade between Poland and the East, Hungary and also the Baltic region. One should, however, also draw attention to other circumstances. I have in mind the development of rock-salt mining in Wieliczka and Bochnia in the vicinity of Cracow as well as in Red Ruthenia and the exploitation of lead in Olkusz and other centres in Little Poland. Natural resources in Poland, as in other medieval countries, were the property of the dukes and, after the unification of the state in the fourteenth century, they belonged to the king. Polish monarchs were able to keep in their own hands the exploitation of the salt resources under the administration of their own officials, although they also willingly rented out mines with contracts for a number of years. The lease-holders administered the mining of salt and the produce itself was sold to merchants from specially privileged towns which conducted a far-reaching salt trade. The renting of mines was undoubtedly a profitable undertaking since from the thirteenth century onwards it created a lively interest among local merchants and, from the fourteenth century, among foreigners arriving in Poland. It was precisely during the course of that century and up to the middle of the fifteenth century that the salt mines in Little Poland were practically always rented out by Cracow merchants and particularly by Italians residing in Cracow. As regards local merchants, it was the wealthiest who were simultaneously involved in trade with Hungary, Flanders and the East. The appearance of Italians, more exactly Florentines, Venetians and Genoese, in

Little Poland in the thirteenth and fourteenth centuries was connected with the payment of Church dues to the Pope. These sums were sent from Wrocław or Cracow by land and sea to the great Italian bankers in Bruges with whom Popes maintained permanent financial contacts. In connection with this, the agents of the Bardi, Medici and other economic potentates carried out financial transactions in Poland. However, this activity drew the attention of the Italians to numerous other opportunities in Poland, especially after the unification of the state in the first half of the fourteenth century and the incorporation of Red Ruthenia in 1340. The Italians began to utilise Little Poland's position on important trade routes to Tana and Caffa. Although these routes never had as much importance as the sea routes linking Italy with the Black Sea regions, they were frequently used because of the growing Turkish danger in Greek waters. This was especially true in the fifteenth century but was of considerable significance earlier as well. It also became rapidly obvious that Little Poland, which was developing economically, could become a growing market for Italian woollens and silks, oriental and other goods. Here one could also be supplied with furs, hides and red dyestuff. As already mentioned, a very important area for the investment of Italian capital was the salt mines in Little Poland and Russia, and Italian merchants played a considerable part in their development. One should also draw attention to another aspect of the activity of the Italians in Little Poland and Ruthenia: the purchase of property in Cracow and Lvov and in some cases the acquisition of rural possessions, as was the practice of wealthy Italian merchants in their own country. Arrivals from Florence, Venice and especially from Genoa settled in Little Poland for a period of many years or permanently and accepted citizenship in Cracow and Lvov, at the same time maintaining contacts with their home country. This phenomenon also had important cultural aspects and to a large degree contributed to the development of the Renaissance in Poland. One should add that the arrivals from Italy involved themselves to only a minimal degree in the mining of lead in Little Poland, which was essential to the Polish economy and particularly the economy of the region under discussion. In the fourteenth and especially the fifteenth century, mining in the Olkusz region and neighbouring areas became the domain of the merchants from Polish mining towns, and especially from Cracow, who bought shares in the mines and engaged in the export of metal, much as did the merchants from Wrocław in Silesia.

The export of high-quality Polish lead, indispensable also for Hungary and Bohemia, was an important means of accumulating merchant capital in Cracow and in certain other towns of Little Poland. In this area influence was also gained by the merchants of Nuremberg. In 1365 they received from King Casimir the Great the right of free trade in Poland, and especially on the routes to Ruthenia, in return for payment of ordinary customs dues. Just as in Bohemia and Hungary, they imported into Little Poland numerous metal and textile articles from Upper Germany, the Rhineland, the Netherlands and

Italy, while a very important place was held by the products from Nuremberg itself, including haberdashery, arms, objects involving the art of casting and paintings. In Poland they bought the same goods as the Italians did, later also cattle. The Nuremberg trade was conducted not only by large firms but also by innumerable vendors who reached rural marketplaces; this aroused the anger of local artisans and merchants. In the fifteenth century the activity of the Nuremberg merchants increased with the Polish–Lithuanian union and the accompanying opening of the great land route from Leipzig through Wrocław, Poznań and Warsaw in the direction of Vilna, Smolensk and Moscow, from which were bought not only cheap squirrel furs, as once from Novgorod, but also valuable furs from the Russian Far North and from the region of Kazan.[16] This contributed to the development of trade and handicrafts in western and central Poland and influenced the growth of many towns, with Poznań, Lublin and Warsaw in the lead. Everywhere there emerged wealthy local merchants. The prosperous members of the Jewish communities in Cracow, Poznań, Lvov and Brest in Lithuania became very active. The tolerant policy of the rulers of Poland and Lithuania concerned with their financial interests was also conducive to the economic development of that ethnic and religious group. Immigrants from Germany, now not very numerous but wealthy merchants, also arrived and settled permanently in Poland. They came to Cracow, as for example the Boner family from Landau, who quickly gained high positions in the administration of state finances, bought large landed possessions and entered the ranks of the wealthy nobility. It seems that an important element in the attractiveness of Cracow was not only the royal residence but also the proximity of the Polish lead mines and the copper and silver mines in Slovakia. It was precisely the wealthy Cracow merchants who sought ways of exploiting the Slovakian mines, which in the second half of the fifteenth century underwent a severe crisis. In 1469 John Thurzo from Levoča (Slovakia), a Cracow councillor, with the technical aid of J. Kolař from Nuremberg, founded the first large copper foundry in Poland in Mogiła near Cracow. We do not know, however, whether he used new methods of separating silver from copper with the use of lead. At any rate, six years later he received from the King of Hungary a privilege allowing him to use new methods of mining. This concerned the above-mentioned perfected way of extracting silver from copper, the introduction of treadmills propelled by animal or water power both for a more effective extraction of ore from the mine and for the drainage of mines through the construction of adits drawing out the water or supplying air. All this called for very large investments and, although Thurzo was a wealthy man, this undertaking exceeded his financial potential. As a result, in 1494 he established a company together with Jacob Fugger, which in reality dominated the Slovakian mining industry and became one of the largest establishments in Europe of that day.[17] This already signified new times which brought radical changes, not only in mining.

The rapid economic development of the Sudeten–Carpathian region, beginning in the thirteenth century, was one of the important symptoms of the economic growth of East-Central Europe in the late Middle Ages, and to a large degree it also influenced the situation in Western Europe and in Italy. A very important role was played by the mining of precious and non-ferrous metals, especially of copper. Bohemian and Hungarian gold and silver increased currency circulation not only in their own countries but also in Italy and in North-Western Europe, while copper and tin facilitated the development of industrial production in Germany and the Low Countries and to a lesser degree in a number of other countries. Elsewhere I have tried to prove that already in the Middle Ages there began to emerge a specific division of functions between the East and the West of Europe, the former playing the role of the supplier of raw materials, including metals, while the West developed because, among other reasons, its artisans and merchants found markets for their products in the East. Already in this period it is also possible to observe a considerable investment of German and Italian merchant capital in many spheres of production in the European East and especially in the mining industry.

In the second half of the fifteenth century Western Europe was overcoming a long-lasting economic and social crisis which it experienced for over a century. There emerged a considerable increase of demand for foodstuffs, building materials, precious metals, copper and tin. This was influenced by population growth as well as by a renewed acceleration of urban development and industrial production. The increased use of firearms brought about a demand for copper and iron. The new era of maritime expansion resulted in an increased demand for silver, copper and brass products willingly bought in Western Africa in return for gold and slaves as well as in India and other areas. New opportunities opened up for forest and agricultural products from East-Central Europe and for its other natural resources, but their exploitation demanded a considerable influx of capital into trade and production. It also happened that in the second half of the fifteenth century in central Germany copper and silver mining were being developed in Mannsfeld county and in the Habsburg domains of Carinthia and Tyrol, and in Styria iron-ore mining. In southern Saxony (Annaberg) silver mines were opened whose production grew from a few hundred marks to 44,000 in the years 1476–83, falling later. However, in the same region there emerged new mining centres. Moreover, the silver and copper mines in Mannsfeld and Schwaz showed similar results. The fundamental trait of this stage in the development of mining consisted of technological reforms in the exploitation of ores from deeper deposits and the much more efficient drainage and ventilation of mines. All this called for the use of the treadmill propelled increasingly frequently by water power, the digging of deep adits, etc., and it could be realised only if large amounts of capital were invested. Great Augsburg and Nuremberg capitalists, such as the

Fuggers, the Welsers, the Höchstetters and others, fully exploited the new market conditions and dominated a large part of the exploitation of metals.[18] The same phenomenon as in Germany and Austria occurred in Bohemia and especially in Hungary and to a slightly lesser degree in Poland. The rebirth of Bohemian mining began in the second half of the fifteenth century in its former centres but its zenith was reached in the first half of the sixteenth century. The main centre of exploitation was Jáchymov in Krušné Hory, which lay within the domains of the Šlik family. It was they who, with the aid of prosperous Upper German entrepreneurs, financed the development of mining in Jáchymov, where miners not only from Bohemia but also from Annaberg and the declining Schneeberg in Saxony, from Tyrol, Salzburg and other places arrived on a mass scale. Mining entrepreneurs also came to Jáchymov from many neighbouring regions of Germany and even Switzerland. At the end of 1516 Jáchymov consisted of 400 houses and one foundry with four furnaces, and in 1520 a population of up to 5,000, while five years later the settlement received town rights and the population exceeded 13,000, reaching probably 20,000 in 1534. Considerable sums were invested in the Jáchymov mines by wealthy Upper German burghers. J. Majer, a student of the history of Jáchymov, mentions the Welsers, the Höchstetters, the Fuggers and a number of other well-known firms. At that time mining took over a large part of the environs of Jáchymov.

In the first years of the sixteenth century, the monopoly on the purchase of Jáchymov's products was held by two Nuremberg merchants: John Nutzel and Jacob Welser. In 1519 the Šlik family deprived them of this right and founded a mint where they produced the famous silver thalers. In the years 1520–8 they minted approximately 2,200,000 thalers apart from smaller currency, altogether worth approximately four million thalers. In 1546 Jáchymov, through confiscation, became the possession of the Habsburg crown. Majer calculates the entire production of silver in Jáchymov in 1516–1601 to be 195,000 to 200,000 kilograms. Its zenith occurred in the early 1530s. In the next decade a slackening of production occurred which became increasingly evident from the middle of the century and especially from the 1560s. Majer believes that this decline was the result of a gradual retreat of great capitalists from the Jáchymov mines after 1546. This could have been caused by increasingly high prices which resulted in greater production costs, but it seems that this change was felt mainly after 1562 when Bohemia was drawn into the orbit of the price revolution. It was at that time that there began a decrease in the value of silver in connection with its inflow from Potosí. Silver and copper exploitation in the sixteenth century in Kutná Hora and tin in the regions of Horna Slavkov and Krašno underwent similar changes. The beginning of this phase of development occurred in the first years of the sixteenth century, its peak preceded the middle of the century and then there came about a gradual decline.

The situation in Slovakia at the end of the fifteenth century shows many traits characteristic of Bohemia. The exhaustion of shallow deposits of copper and silver ore posed a problem of a transition to deep mining which could not be realised without large capital investments. These problems aroused the interests of the Cracow patricians who, until a short time before, had been gaining large profits from trade in Hungarian copper. It was precisely from this milieu that the first attempts to save the Hungarian mining were made. John Thurzo began the reconstruction of mines at Banská Bistřica and other centres of ore mining. Moreover, he made very numerous loans to miners. Since his debtors were often unable to pay and were incapable of supplying him with the promised amount of ore, a large number of mines in Slovakia became his property. However, he did not have at his disposal sufficient capital for the realisation of truly great investments. As a result Thurzo made contact with Jacob Fugger (the Rich) who had already engaged large amounts of capital in Austrian mining and was striving towards a monopoly in the production and trade of copper and silver. In 1494 Fugger and Thurzo founded a firm: Der gemeine Ungarische Handel. Vladislav, King of Hungary, leased to the company mines in central Slovakia under the condition that it would reconstruct them. The company partners were exempt from many customs dues and payments on the transportation of ore and products indispensable for mining, and cumbersome control on the part of royal officials was limited. Important control points were taken over by the Thurzos while the high cost of purchasing these offices was paid by Jacob Fugger. The history of the company is relatively well known. Undoubtedly it organised the largest production–trade establishment of the period and the Slovakian parts of Hungary became, for over half a century, the most important source of copper in Europe. In the initial period (1494–1526) Jacob Fugger invested up to 1525 the enormous sum of approximately two million Hungarian florins. In 1525 the profits of the company for a few years reached 7,500,000 florins. During this period it sold approximately 731,300 centners of copper (1 centner equalled approximately 60 kg). This ore contained a high percentage of silver thanks to which the Fuggers smelted in their foundries in 1494–1526 approximately 330,000 silver marks. The Fugger family bought out the shares of John Thurzo's heirs who became members of the Hungarian aristocracy. The main centre of the Fugger activities was Banská Bistřica; they also made dependent upon themselves the mining entrepreneurs of central Slovakia or bought out their mines. Competition with the Fuggers was impossible. They had at their disposal sufficient means to dig shafts up to 210 metres deep, thanks to which they penetrated the richest depths of ore. Their Slovakian mines attained the highest technological level in Europe. The Fuggers also attempted to take over other mining regions of Slovakia and as a rule did so successfully, although they were unable to achieve this in Transylvania where they met with competition from Venetian businessmen. The Fugger domination brought about strong protests on the part of the population in the mining towns and the Hungarian nobility. The depreciation of Hungarian currency and the rise of living costs resulted in a decline of the workers' real wages and in their discontent, which was expressed in demonstrations against the Fuggers in 1525. Despite this, the following year the Crown extended the contract for a further fifteen years, not wishing to give up the income connected with it. During the entire rental period, from 1494 to 1596, the Fugger Company in the Banská Bistřica region produced, according to J. Vlachovič, 1,194,465 centners, i.e., 74,281 tons of copper and 485,621 marks (equal to 119,024 kg) of silver. However, from 1535 on difficulties began to appear.[19]

By that time the main seams of silver-yielding ore were exhausted and ore mining in general also began to fall, as a result of which the entrepreneurs moved over to the utilisation of slag heaps. This gave positive results only for a short period of time. The situation worsened even more in the 1540s when the Turks, after overpowering central Hungary, approached the borders of Slovakia and began to molest it. In 1546 Anthony Fugger relinquished Slovakian mining. For a certain period of time the renting of mines was conducted by the Mannlich firm from Augsburg and subsequently by the Crown. The indebtedness of the treasury to foreign entrepreneurs was so large that for a long time the Fuggers and then the Mannlichs were to remain the main recipients of Slovakian copper. In the second half of the sixteenth century and at the beginning of the seventeenth century, one can see the gradual decline of copper mining in the whole of Slovakia. In 1549 the central part of the country yielded 24,000 centners of copper and 8,578 marks of silver but already in 1602 only 9,043 centners and 960 marks. This was followed by an even sharper decline. Undoubtedly the main cause of this process was the exhaustion of the deposits, but one should also draw attention to other circumstances and essentially to the sharp rise in the cost of exploitation in a period of price revolution, the under-investment in mines run by the treasury and finally to the still primitive technology. The decline in silver–copper mining was balanced to a certain degree by an increase in iron-ore mining. This was related to the needs of the Habsburg army which defended the northern regions of Hungary against the Turks. However, the competition of better quality iron imported from Styria hampered the development of local production. As a result, the more prosperous entrepreneurs withdrew their capital from mining, and the miners frequently emigrated to areas under Turkish rule where they were offered favourable living conditions and payment. The mining industry of Slovakia entered a phase of decline.[20]

The situation in Little Poland presents many analogies to the processes already known to us from Hungary and Bohemia. In Olkusz – the main centre for the exploitation of lead – the crisis occurred in the second half of the fifteenth century and lasted for practically a century, but it did not attain such catastrophic dimensions as in the neighbouring countries. Simultaneously, mining developed in lesser centres such as Chrzanów and Długoszyn. However, the deposits here were much smaller than those in Olkusz and their exploitation was, as a rule, brief. From about 1530 lead deposits were discovered, containing some silver, in Olkusz and other regions. Modern researchers evaluate the content at 0.1 per cent. This ore was destined for the Cracow mint but never fully covered its needs. The main bulk of silver had to be imported from Slovakia and Bohemia.

While Polish silver never played an important role in long-distance trade, lead presented an entirely different problem. We have already pointed to the enormous significance of its export to Hungary and Bohemia and especially of its delivery to the local foundries. The main trade centre was to be found in Cracow and so it is not strange that its citizens showed a lively interest in ore mining. During the fifteenth and in the first half of the sixteenth century the office of *supparius*, i.e., the overseer of the mine nominated by the king, was for all practical purposes always held by the wealthiest Cracow merchants. Many of them simultaneously leased royal revenue from mines or held it as a pledge safeguarding loans made by the Crown. Danuta Molenda, an expert on this problem, has pointed to the fact that this was extremely profitable for the leaseholders since as a result they possessed 10 per cent of the entire production, while the payment of debts in metal was calculated in such a way that the prices of this lead were lower than market costs. Moreover, the leaseholders (the *supparii*) were able to exert pressure on the producers forcing them to lower the sale prices. All this paved the way for merchant capital to enter into lead production, just as was happening in other countries in many spheres of ore mining.

There existed two methods which enabled prosperous merchants to subject the miners to the interests of the capital owner. The first and most important was the use of credit. Merchants gave loans to miners on the condition that the latter returned their debt in lead, at prices fixed in advance and as a rule lower than the market prices. The constant lack of capital forced the miners to accept this procedure, which in the long run resulted in a total dependence of the debtors upon the creditors. Capitalists avoided the acceptance of mining shares burdened with debts; they were transferring production costs and the risk of failure onto the producers. The latter, however, were unable to manage even with an influx of capital even at relatively favourable rates. This also points to the comparatively low productivity of mining or rather of the small mining entrepreneurs. The system we have described was universal in Polish lead mining in the fifteenth and at the beginning of the sixteenth century. Nevertheless, capitalists and especially wealthy Cracow merchants, including the Thurzo family, also established their own mines and foundries using hired labour.

In the first half of the sixteenth century in Poland the easily accessible deposits of lead began to show signs of exhaustion. It became necessary to dig shafts, since this was the only way to reach the richest ore deposits. The initiative came from King Sigismund Augustus and the first shafts were dug at the close of the 1560s. Thanks to these investments in which mining entrepreneurs from Olkusz and Cracow participated, local lead mining was considerably strengthened for a period of about 100 years. This development was favoured by an increase in the demand for firearms in Poland and abroad. At the end of the sixteenth century a few score thousand centners of lead were exported via the River Vistula to Gdańsk and from there by sea to Western Europe. The former markets, i.e., Slovakia and Bohemia, lost their significance in this field.

An essential new factor in capital investment in Polish lead mining, especially evident in the sixteenth century, was the gradual increase in the participation of the nobility.[21] This was favoured by the ultimate liquidation in 1575-6 of royal ownership rights as regards mineral deposits, although these rights had already been frequently disregarded. Polish lead mining became weaker in the second half of the seventeenth century and collapsed at the beginning of the eighteenth as a result of ore exhaustion and ruin brought about by the two Northern Wars which had devastated Poland.

The history of Little Poland and Ruthenian salt mining in the sixteenth and seventeenth centuries was much less varied. No profound changes took place at that time. The Polish kings were able to retain their possession of this entire mining industry which, as a rule, developed without any great disturbance. The highest posts in mining administration were filled by persons from the royal entourage and frequently magnates, as for example the Lubomirskis. It does not follow, however, that this in any specific way influenced the course of production. Although wealthy nobles were undertaking salt exploitation in their own estates in Little Poland and the Kujawy region of Great Poland, this competition did not have fundamental importance for royal mines.

In the sixteenth and seventeenth centuries one does not notice the former lively interest in salt mining by local and foreign merchants since the control over lead mining opened up prospects of larger profits. The bigger towns, however, including Cracow, strove energetically to retain the salt storehouses supplied by the royal mines, since the distribution of salt brought large profits for the merchants.[22]

Salt and lead mining underwent heavy losses during the Swedish invasions in 1655-6 and in the early eighteenth century. The Swedes did not destroy mines but large compulsory payments, fires and pillage pauperised the mining population and frequently forced people to abandon their homesteads. A new phase in the development of, or rather an attempt to reconstruct, salt mining in Little Poland occurred in the second half and at the close of the eighteenth century.

In this article I asked the question to what extent mining, an important item in the national economy of Bohemia, Northern Hungary and Little Poland, influenced the circulation of capital. I have already pointed out the fact that from the thirteenth to the end of the sixteenth century these regions were rather closely connected economically and that their mining industry played a particularly important role in this.

One can divide the entire period examined here, i.e., from the thirteenth to the seventeenth century, into several phases. The first phase occurred from the thirteenth to approximately the middle of the fifteenth century. It was characterised by a strong development of the exploitation of shallow ore and salt deposits. Even this, however, already called for a considerable influx of skilled labour and capital which was scarce. The striving of monarchs and great landowners towards the development of the economy of their dominions coincided with the incoming supply of miners and entrepreneurs; also wealthy merchants, while showing interest above all in trade, also invested large capital in mining (predominantly in the form of loans). All these factors resulted in Bohemia and Hungary becoming, next to Africa, the main suppliers of precious metals and also of tin and copper to Western and Southern Europe and in this export paying for a large part of the import of textiles, metal products and other industrial goods. Analogous phenomena took place in Poland, although here lead had only an inter-regional if extremely large significance for the functioning of mining in neighbouring countries. An interesting phenomenon was the widespread investment in landed property of profits gained from mining and trade. This led to a rapid social advancement of many wealthy burgher families and their transition into the ranks of the nobility.

During the course of the fifteenth century, and in Bohemia perhaps from the beginning of that century, there occurred a crisis in the mining industry caused, above all, by the exhaustion of shallow metal-ore deposits. To overcome this the use of new technology and large capital investments were necessary. This occurred in the second phase of the development of East-Central European mining, which once again took place during highly favourable market conditions, not only on a European but a world-wide scale. The growing demand for silver, gold, copper and tin was fulfilled by the activity of the Augsburg and Nuremberg entrepreneurs in Hungary and Bohemia, as well as by investments in those countries and in Poland by the local merchants and nobles which made it possible to make a transition to deeper mining. Hungary and Bohemia regained their former position in the European economy; Polish mining was also developing. Everywhere merchant-banking capital played an important role in production, although it did not transform itself entirely into industrial capital.

More or less from the middle of the sixteenth century, there began in Hungary and Bohemia the decline of the new mining industry, brought about chiefly by the exhaustion of available deposits and also by a permanent rise in the costs of mine exploitation and maintenance at a time when there was an influx of American precious metals and great price changes. This decline was visible in Hungary and Bohemia at the end of the sixteenth century. In Polish lead mining the crisis was less severe and for the time being was overcome by investments from the Crown, merchants and magnates. The new era of firearms opened up favourable conditions for Polish mining for an even longer period of time.

9 ➤ A model of East-Central European continental commerce in the sixteenth and the first half of the seventeenth century

JERZY TOPOLSKI

I

In this study I understand the territory of East-Central Europe to embrace pre-partition Poland (without Lithuania, White Russia and the Ukraine), Silesia, Bohemia, Moravia, Lusatia, Brandenburg, Hungary, Wallachia and Moldavia. It is a region which in the early modern period can be regarded from the point of view of international trade as a territorial and economic unit. East-Central Europe is treated in this way by several authors who stress the usefulness of distinguishing such regions as East-Central Europe, European Russia (i.e. Eastern Europe) and North-Eastern Europe (i.e. the coastal territories of the northern and eastern Baltic).[1]

It is known that the sixteenth and the first half of the seventeenth century witnessed in East-Central Europe a fundamental transformation of the agrarian structure, consisting in a refeudalisation, i.e. in the development of a new form of the feudal system. The nucleus of that system was a relatively large farm, run directly or indirectly by the nobles and based on the unpaid forced labour of peasants who lost their late medieval liberties and became serfs. Through such an organisation, which replaced the collection of peasant rents in money or in kind, the nobles aimed to raise their dwindling incomes, which they found increasingly inadequate for their growing needs.

The reconstruction which led to the development of demesne farms based on labour services would not have been possible without a considerable extension of the market for agricultural products because the manorial-serf economy aimed, through sales, at squeezing more money and rents in kind than before. The manors sold their products on local markets which met the growing demand of expanding towns. For some regions and types of manor, export overseas was of more importance; however, on the whole the role of export in the manorial-serf economy was marginal, contrary to what historical sources would have us believe, and what the spectacular prosperity of Gdańsk and the Dutch profit-seeking interest in Poland suggested to enthusiastic contemporary witnesses and historians.

128

In the second half of the sixteenth century, the grain export from Poland (i.e., the leading country in this trade) did not exceed 2.5 per cent of the total Polish grain production. The demesne farms (*folwarki*) produced about 25 per cent of that. They almost totally monopolised the export of grain and yet the quantities they were selling on local markets still exceeded the amount exported 4–5 times. Because of high transportation costs, export via Gdańsk was profitable only for the proprietors of large estates situated not too far from the river ports. In addition the grain exported to Western Europe (70–80 per cent of which went via Gdańsk) was able to satisfy not more than 1–2 per cent of its consumption needs or 3–6 per cent of those of the urban population. Western Europe, apart from its urbanisation and proto-industrialisation processes, was a poor agricultural territory. The reasons driving Dutch merchants to seek Baltic grain were the profits ensured by the difference between the socio-economic systems in Western and East-Central Europe. Unpaid serf labour made grain production costs so much lower that estate owners could accept the price proposed them by the Gdańsk and Dutch merchants. One also has to take into consideration the different factors which, on the one hand motivated the merchants' and, on the other, the lords' economic activity. The sixteenth-century merchant was active only where he could expect adequate profit for capital invested, while the feudal lord was satisfied with a money income which enabled him to live according to his social status. The mechanism behind the maritime grain trade in the sixteenth and in the first half of the seventeenth century sprang from a combination of these interests. The objective factors taken into consideration by both parties were the increasing demand for agricultural products brought about by the growth in population and urbanisation in Europe, the difference in the socio-economic organisation of agricultural production in Western and in East-Central Europe, as well as the good natural conditions for grain cultivation in East-Central Europe.

In my subsequent remarks I do not intend to give a detailed description of the subject. My aim is to offer an overall view of the commercial activities in a given part of Europe in a given period, and to show how and why these activities changed with time. This picture is a 'model' in the sense of a deliberately simplified reconstruction of the past. This general model of the continental trade of East-Central Europe depends on the following conditions:

  (i) a constant ratio between the cost of maritime trade and trade overland;
 (ii) an unchanging structure of production in both East-Central and Western Europe;
(iii) a lack of competition from other territories;
(iv) a relatively stable political situation.

The stability of this model depends, as one can deduce, on the development of the Western European grain production, the speed of the urbanisation process in both parts of Europe and on the grain production in East-Central Europe. An additional influence might have been some non-economic factors such as wars. In other words, transformations of the system depended mainly on the relationship between the rate of growth of Western European grain production and the growth of Western demands for grain. What in fact occurred was a steady growth in Western grain production while the refeudalisation processes in East-Central Europe, which lasted until the middle of the eighteenth century, reduced the productivity of East-Central European agriculture. These factors transformed the maritime grain trade between Western and East-Central Europe.

II

The European continental trade (in cattle, furs, skins, leather, copper, spices and industrial, mostly metal, goods) developed along quite different lines. Here the difference between socio-economic systems which influenced the Western demand for grain and the Eastern propensity to supply it played only a limited role. It is true that a decisive proportion of the cattle exported from East-Central Europe was 'produced' along with grain in the demesne farms based on coerced labour, but on the other hand the cattle-breeding on these farms was normally done by hired labour. Thus one can assume that the landowners in their calculation of the profits from stock-rearing were more aware of expenses and estimated profits in relation to invested capital.

In our opinion the whole continental trade of East-Central Europe and its main partner, Western Europe, can be considered as having been shaped by three interconnected factors:

(1) the geographically complementary character of regions;
(2) the economic and/or technological difficulties in the development of profitable production of particular goods in given regions;
(3) the differing tradition of production in different regions.

Naturally these factors acted against a general background which was, as we have already stressed, a growth of demand for some goods connected with the increase in the European population, the progress of a money economy and changes in consumption patterns. There was a particular demand for textiles, furs, skins, leather, spices and industrial (handicraft) products that rose faster than population, which, of course, determined the demand for food more closely. The analysis of these problems would go beyond the immediate scope of this study; nonetheless it should be stressed that, without taking into consideration the above-mentioned general background, it would be impossible to explain the dynamics of East-Central European trade in the early modern period. In this connection, the Turkish expansion, for example, was once regarded as a decisive factor because it destroyed the Black Sea commercial centres. The role of this general background in the process is therefore fundamental. Only growing demand could provoke certain regions to start supplying others with their products or to step up their existing supply.

The complementary character of regional economies was at the root of the fur trade. Furs of wild animals from the vast hunting grounds of White Russia, Russia and Siberia were brought by Russian, Lithuanian and White Russian merchants to Poland or eastern Germany where they were sold to Western merchants, together with skins, leather, tallow, wax, etc. The fur and skin trade was instrumental in the growth of appropriate handicrafts along the overland route to Leipzig: in Shklov in eastern White Russia as well as in Poznań in western Poland.

The complementary character of the regions similarly determined the Slovakian silver and copper trade and the Hungarian wine trade, as well as the trade in goods imported from tropical countries. In the last case, Europe as a whole was a unit in the intercontinental commercial exchange.

The trade in cattle was also inspired by technical factors. Animals were driven from the stock-rearing zones which lay beyond the principal grain-growing territories (Podole, Moldavia, Wallachia, Hungary) to Western Europe, where the animal production did not match up to the growth of population and urbanisation. It would, in fact, have been possible to increase livestock production there too, but at that time it was economically more convenient to purchase cattle from East-Central Europe. The same can be said of the skin, leather and wool trade.

The third factor, i.e., differing production traditions, can be regarded as a special case of the second factor. It might not have been possible to justify the development of a given production in a region which did not yet have it. This was the case particularly with textile production and commerce. Almost every region needed different kinds of textiles but only some of them had traditional textile-manufacturing centres which were able to export their products. Technological and economic barriers hampered the development of local production. The same can be said about various other industrial (handicraft) products, as for example haberdashery produced in Nuremberg.

In the case of commerce determined by factors (2) and (3), there is a question of comparative production (and transportation) costs. Surplus-producing centres could exist only if they, for a variety of reasons, could produce more cheaply than others. In the case of factor (1) comparison of costs began to play an important role when there was competition between similar regions (for example, between different stock-rearing centres), or between alternative products (for example different textiles of similar utility). These mechanisms were all to play an even more important role in the succeeding periods.

III

The sixteenth and first half of the seventeenth century was characterised not only by the development of overland trade and the growth in the volume of trade (as a result of the growth in demand) but also by the intensification of internal commercial bonds between neighbouring regions and territories. Thanks to the development of the division of labour and the rise of the consumption level of some social groups, goods began to circulate more intensively also within the regions. Thus we observe the intensification of trade relations not only between Western and East-Central Europe but also between different countries and regions within East-Central Europe. It was connected with the fact that some of the goods which went westward (e.g., furs and skins) were purchased in the East and distributed in the area in question. On the other hand, the East-Central textile production grew and was able not only to satisfy the principal needs of East-European markets but also to be exported eastward.

The general growth of European trade was accompanied, especially from the sixteenth century (partly as a result of the intensification of the already existing structures), by the shaping of a dense network of local, regional and international fairs. Two systems of these fairs (and routes) can be distinguished: one connected with the cattle trade and the second one used for the trade in other goods. The formation of this network of fairs, which connected up with the commercially important harbours, was one of the most characteristic features of the organisation of European overland trade in the first half of the early modern era.

A general look at the East-Central European trade in the sixteenth and first half of the seventeenth century shows that goods between Eastern, East-Central and Western Europe circulated according to the pattern given in Figure 5. We have also to take into consideration in our scheme the trade between East-Central and South-Eastern Europe (Bulgaria, Macedonia, Greece). Wine was the main commodity involved in this trade, although the quantities exported were greatly exceeded by the Hungarian wines. A certain role was played by Turkish and Persian goods which passed through Edirne or Thessalonika. Exported goods included skins, textiles, different kinds of yarn and thread, clothing, carpets, paprika and olive oil. A more local exchange – for example between Bulgaria and Romanian territories – involved also food.[2] An important role in the commerce between East and West Europe (according to D. Zografski) was played by Macedonia. Macedonian tradesmen maintained contacts with Vienna, Buda, Venice, Trieste and Leipzig. Overall, only marginal quantities of goods reached Western Europe directly from South-Eastern Europe. Much larger quantities supplied East-Central European fairs and most of them went no further. More important for East-Central Europe were its commercial relations with Russia – in the sixteenth century a country of dynamic development.

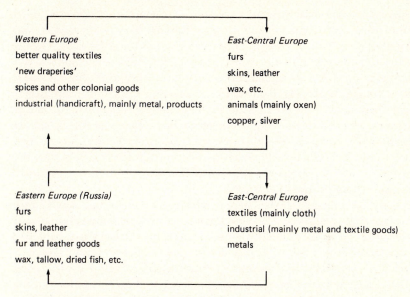

5 Circulation of goods between Eastern, East-Central and Western Europe in the sixteenth and first half of the seventeenth century (only main and characteristic commodities are given)

IV

The continental trade of Russia, White Russia, Lithuania and the Ukraine was connected with Western Europe through the already mentioned network of international fairs spread over Poland, Silesia and Bohemia (chiefly in Lublin, Poznań, Gniezno, Toruń, Cracow, Wròcław and Prague). Gdańsk also participated actively in continental trade. The most characteristic Eastern commodities sold at these fairs were furs, skins and leather. Further West the trade in Russian and other furs was concentrated at the fairs of Leipzig and Frankfurt am Main but the role of Leipzig was growing. Besides this overland route, an important role in this respect was played by the sea route through Narva, Riga, Königsberg, Gdańsk, Lübeck and, in the seventeenth century, Archangel. It is possible to estimate that quantities exported by both routes were comparable, although in the sixteenth century the land route was gaining ground. In order to shed light on the size of exports, some figures for the fairs of Gniezno at the beginning of the seventeenth century will be helpful.[3] Here about 800,000 furs (mainly grey squirrel) were sent yearly. The ready-made fur coats added to this figure gives us a total of about 1 million animals. Leon Koczy has found that in 1562–9 the export of furs via the River Narev to Riga, Königsberg and Gdańsk amounted to about 580,000 pieces a year. In the middle of the seventeenth century fur exports through Archangel can be numbered at about 500,000 pieces. The furs exported by sea were destined for

Western European markets while some furs in the.continental trade remained in the transit territories of East-Central Europe. For Polish nobles and townspeople, wearing furs was a status symbol just as it was for their Western European counterparts. I estimate that about 1 million furs per annum reached Western Europe. It was equivalent, roughly speaking, to 20,000 to 25,000 ready-made fur coats. The figure is rather impressive, when one considers it means there must have been about 1 million potential buyers (aristocracy, nobility, and rich townspeople). Assuming that on average a fur was purchased once every ten years, we conclude hypothetically that the Russian furs satisfied at least half of the total fur demand in Western Europe. Fur was thus the commodity from Eastern and East-Central Europe[4] which most completely met the Western European demand.

Russian furs and fur products were purchased by Western merchants either directly in Russia or, as was becoming common practice, at Polish international fairs from White Russian and Lithuanian middlemen (from Vilna, Mohilev, Shklov and lesser centres). Direct contacts of Western (mostly German) merchants with the Russian markets were more characteristic of the sea route.

As has already been mentioned, hand in hand with the fur trade went the skin and leather trade. The majority of skins were cattle, sheep, lamb and goat skins and the so-called Russian leather. Part of this merchandise too remained in East-Central Europe; the rest, after being partially finished, reached Western Europe via the same routes and fairs. The figures for this trade were relatively high. The overland export of skins through Poland (mainly via Cracow, Gniezno or Poznań) embraced yearly about 150,000 pieces. A certain number of skins was exported from Hungary, but in comparison with the cattle trade from this country (see section VI) the fur trade was unimportant.[5] Estimating the entire annual export of skins and leather from East-Central Europe and via East-Central Europe at 200,000 to 250,000 skins, one can assume that this was sufficient to satisfy about 20 per cent of the total Western demand. This would also mean rather considerable quantities. One has, however, to bear in mind that these were still to a large extent luxuries and that consequently the internal market, especially for furs, was rather limited. Therefore the estimates can, of necessity, only be very approximate.

V

The goods traded by Western Europe in return for furs, skins and leather (and also for cattle) were chiefly textiles (cloth, mixed stuffs, linen, silk, etc.) and to a far lesser extent ready-made textile products. Also very important in this exchange were colonial goods (mainly spices) and industrial (handicraft) products. The routes and trading-places were the same as in the fur and skin trade, i.e., the sea route and the network of overland international fairs with a fixed yearly calendar and traditional exchange and credit systems. In the textile trade, however, the situation was more complex. Western European products (Flemish, Brabant, Dutch, English, south-German, Italian) competed with larger quantities of local East-Central European textiles. At the same time a considerable proportion of Western fabrics of a more fashionable or luxury nature was sold in East-Central Europe.

In East-Central Europe there existed a large, dynamic and relatively coherent textile-manufacturing region embracing parts of Bohemia, Moravia, Silesia, Lusatia and Great Poland. Its growth reflects the progress in the European division of labour: it replaced the previous more dispersed production system, and, to a very considerable extent, home-made textiles. The East-Central European production became not only sufficient for local needs (with the exception of the more fashionable or luxury fabrics imported from Western Europe), but also provided for Russian demand and the demand of those East-Central European territories which had not developed their own textile production on an appropriate scale (Hungary, Moldavia and Wallachia). The majority of textiles traded in East-Central Europe were of local origin. As far as one can estimate, only about 20 to 30 per cent of the textiles on East-European markets were supplied by Western European centres.

This can be confirmed by several case studies. Very characteristic are purchases of the White Russian merchants at the St Adalbert fair in Gniezno in 1583. Their purchases of Moravian and Silesian cloth amounted to 80 per cent of all their cloth transactions. The remaining 20 per cent concerned chiefly German and English (or Flemish) cloth and German, Silesian and Gdańsk kersey. Western European stuffs were more broadly represented among the so-called 'new draperies' of mixed and lighter fabrics. From Flanders and south Germany were imported some better linen fabrics. The customs registers of Grodno in Lithuania from 1600 paint a similar picture. In the purchases of merchants from Mohilev, Minsk, Grodno and other Lithuanian and White Russian towns, 70 per cent was Silesian cloth mainly from Zielona Góra and Swiebodzin, 13 per cent Moravian, 7 per cent Lusatian. Linen from Cologne amounted to 15 per cent of all linen purchases. As far as absolute figures are concerned, one can estimate that at Gniezno fairs the Lithuanian and White Russian merchants purchased annually cloth sufficient for about 30,000 garments.

The structure of the Hungarian textile imports was not dissimilar. In the light of the customs books of Pozsony (Bratislava) for 1542, the value of imported textiles amounted to 70 per cent of the total import value.[6] The textiles were mostly of Bohemian, Moravian and Silesian origin. Customs books of Bártfa for 1504–7 mention materials only from these sources whilst the merchants of Kassa (Košice) imported also textiles from England, the Netherlands and south Germany (through Cracow). At Kassa, kerseys, mainly from Silesia, became increasingly popular.[7]

The same can be said of Moldavian, Wallachian and Transylvanian textile imports. In the first half of the sixteenth century Dutch, Italian and south-German textiles had played a great part but in the succeeding period dominance was acquired by textiles from Central Europe: Silesia, Moravia and Austria. Some attempts were made to organise local cloth production at Braşov and Sibiu with the assistance of Florentine craftsmen.[8]

Among goods other than textiles imported by East-Central European countries, I have mentioned spices (and other colonial goods) and industrial products (mostly metal goods). The variety of goods in this group was very rich but their value fell far below that of textiles. According to the customs register of Pozsony for 1542, metal products (mostly knives) amounted to 9 per cent, haberdashery, the so-called *nürnberger Tand*, 7 per cent, spices (mostly pepper) about 4 per cent.[9] At the Gniezno fairs, industrial goods and haberdashery again dominated. In spice imports, apart from pepper, a considerable role was played by ginger, saffron, currants, cinnamon, nutmeg along with sugar and southern (citrus) fruits. Imported industrial products also included glass, paper and dyes.

What were the quantities of imported industrial goods and spices? Purchases at Gniezno fairs amounted to 10,000 to 20,000 knives and to about 500 kg of different spices. It is clear that because there was no substitute for these commodities they satisfied the whole effective demand at existing prices. On the other hand, changing patterns of demand resulting from the rising living standards of certain social groups opened up greater possibilities in this field and raised prices. Little more can be said about demand potential and how far it was satisfied.

VI

Such goods as textiles, spices and industrial products exported from Western to East-Central Europe equalled the value of imported furs, skins, leather, wool, wax, tallow or potash; in fact there were probably surpluses. A possible deficit was levelled out with copper and cattle. Thus, in the continental trade of East-Central Europe, oxen played the same role as grain in the maritime trade, producing a strongly positive balance for East-Central Europe. Hungary, Moldavia and Wallachia based their favourable foreign-trade balance mainly on cattle exports, Bohemia, Moravia and Silesia on textiles and Poland on grain exports. In southern Poland as well, the cattle trade played an important role. According to H. Samsonowicz export surplus in Polish continental trade amounted to about 30 to 35 per cent of the value of imports.[10] He quotes in this context Mączak's estimate for the Polish maritime trade balance for 1585 of 34 per cent and also M. Bogucka's estimate for 1634 and 1640–3 of 40 per cent.[11] Furthermore, according to A. Attman, the export surplus of East-Central Europe (in which he includes Russia) in the second half of the sixteenth century fluctuated between 30 and 40 per cent.[12] It is characteristic that in the second half of the seventeenth century when East-Central Europe gradually lost its favourable trade balance, Russia maintained it or perhaps acquired it. According to the Smolensk customs registers concerning overland trade for 1673–4 and 1676–9, exported goods amounted to 63 per cent of the total value of transactions.[13]

Precious metals – among which was silver coming from Western Europe to compensate for the unfavourable balance – either went further to South Asia as payment for such commodities as silk, damask, taffeta, cottons, weapons, rice, currants, olive oil and horses, or was hoarded, re-minted or melted down for various uses. East-Central Europe's position as one of the most important producers and exporters of silver came to an end at the beginning of the sixteenth century. Silver production, which at 100 tons a year was still significant in the first quarter of the sixteenth century (though there was more from the Tyrol than from Moravia or Bohemia), came almost to a standstill under the impact of American competition.

The export of copper from Upper Hungary (Slovakia), monopolised by the south-German merchants, kept its previous level longer and even increased until the end of the sixteenth century. Until Swedish copper captured the European markets in the seventeenth century, Slovakian Banská Bystřica was one of the three European (the others were Tyrol and Thuringia) copper-mining centres. On its way to Western Europe, Slovakian copper passed through Poland and Silesia and was shipped from Gdańsk or Szczecin to Antwerp. From the end of the sixteenth century shipments went more and more from Hamburg and Lübeck to Amsterdam. A certain amount of Slovakian copper was exported to Venice and some re-exported to the Near East, India or – via Spain and Portugal – to Africa and America.[14] In the second half of the seventeenth century the production of Slovakian copper was only about a quarter of the level at the end of the sixteenth century and even that was lower than the mid-sixteenth-century level.[15]

However the sixteenth and the first half of the seventeenth century was a period of prosperity for cattle exports to Western Europe. The main factor responsible for this growth was the demand for meat in Western European towns (mainly in south and central Germany). There were two main stock-rearing zones supplying Germany, the Netherlands, Austria (especially Vienna), northern Italy (especially Venice) and the Turkish territories, where the army was the chief consumer: the northern area embracing Denmark, Skåne, Schleswig-Holstein, and the southern area with Poland, Bohemia, Hungary, the Ukraine, Moldavia and Wallachia. The southern area encompassed, as we see, almost the whole of East-Central Europe. On the borderline of these zones were Cologne and Frankfurt am Main. Cologne was supplied for the most part by the northern zone and Frankfurt by the southern one.

The values involved in this trade were very high. According to K. Glamann, the oxen exported yearly from Denmark in 1601–21 were worth about 30,000 kg of silver. At the same time the total yearly value of grain exported from the Baltic area amounted to about 55,000 kg.[16]

The cattle trade created its own particular organisation: droves and fairs. The main trading place at which the cattle going from Poland (or via Poland), Brandenburg and western Pomerania met was the small town of Buttstädt in Thuringia. For the Hungarian cattle important places of concentration were northern-Hungarian towns like Trnava, Györ and Magyaróvár. Romanian cattle were driven in large herds to Venice through Split, sometimes Vienna, through Nedelice, Pettau and Gorizia. Some of the cattle exported through Poland, via Cracow and Silesia, went to Nuremberg, Frankfurt am Main and Augsburg. Gdańsk was also an important market for cattle.[17]

The organisation of the cattle trade has already been the subject of numerous studies;[18] in our attempt at a model we are less interested in including this, from our point of view, secondary element. More important are estimates of the volume of this trade. Some estimates have been attempted on the basis of the customs records. The export of cattle from Hungary to Vienna and south Germany in the second half of the sixteenth century until the Thirty Years' War involved 50,000 to 60,000 oxen annually.[19] Export figures for Poland in this period reached the same level. If we add the cattle driven from Romanian countries to South-Western Europe – about 20,000 annually – we get a total of about 140,000 oxen exported from East-Central Europe to Western Europe and to the Turkish army.[20] The export from the northern, Danish, zone totalled about 50,000 animals a year.[21]

What do these figures mean? Hamburg in the seventeenth century needed 10–15,000 oxen a year, other important cities several thousand. Vienna purchased about 40,000 oxen annually, though some of these were for re-sale. In general, one can assume that the south-German market depended, as far as meat was concerned, on East European supplies.

VII

The circumstances necessary to the model of trade described above continued to exist, generally speaking, until the middle of the seventeenth century. The Swedish invasion of Poland in the years 1655–60 destroyed the dynamic network of international fairs. This fact only deepened the impact of the decreasing sea-transport costs and the growth of the Russian maritime contacts via Archangel. The decline of the south-German towns affected the cattle trade adversely, and in addition there was growing competition to supply them with meat from Danish sources. At the same time Western Europe had begun to produce more meat. Other products which upset the model were the North American and Canadian furs coming on to European markets. Russia found a certain compensation in directing her export of furs to China and at the same time developing her own demand for Canadian furs. The increased stock-farming in Western Europe limited the demand for skins and leather. American silver and Swedish copper contributed to the regression of the export of these metals from East-Central Europe. Furthermore, grain from Russia began to compete with Polish grain. All these, and yet other, factors contributed to the shaping of a new model of East-Central European international trade.

10 ❧ The system of power in Poland, 1370–1648

ANDRZEJ WYCZAŃSKI

Formation of the 'estates-monarchy'

When discussing the old system of the mechanics of the state and the exercise of power, one should leave out of primary consideration the so-called popular masses. Except for moments of revolt or insurrection – in principle not applicable to Poland during that period – the role of the masses was limited to obeying the decisions of the authorities, and primarily to working for those who held central or local, lay or ecclesiastical power. A long time was yet to pass before the popular masses would manifest any political aspirations.

The kings of the Piast dynasty who ruled Poland until 1370 did not have a clearly defined range of powers. What authority they did have was influenced by the distribution of power within the country, i.e., by the state of treasury resources, military potential, the ruler's personality and that of his closest collaborators on the one hand, and on the other by the families of great nobles (which emerged in the era of the country's disintegration into regional principalities), the top church hierarchy, as well as the biggest towns, e.g., Cracow. The taking over of the Piast succession by the Hungarian house of Anjou (1370), and the installation of the Lithuanian Jagiellons on the Polish throne in 1386 required some arrangements with society, primarily with the great nobles of Little Poland, who in the years 1370–1444 acquired strong political influence, and had a say in who would actually ascend the throne. Louis (Lajos) of Hungary and then Władysław Jagiełło (1385–1434) were forced to make political concessions, and some of the charters then granted were to become instrumental in the emergence of the later forms of political power. This refers to the Košice charter (1374), under which the king renounced his right to raise taxes, except for land tax limited to 2 grosze per tenant, a sum which later was not worth collecting. In 1388 the king agreed to pay the knights summoned for military service when on a foreign expedition. In 1422 to 1434, the charter of habeas corpus was issued which guaranteed to the nobility immunity of person and property. Finally, in 1454, it was established that the

140

king must not raise new taxes or call a levy without previous approval of the nobility's representatives.

These last charters or statutes bring us into the next stage of the development of political power, when certain sections of society gained some degree of participation. Up to the year 1444, we may in fact talk of the superiority of great nobles from Little Poland under the leadership, in the latter part of that period, of the Bishop of Cracow, Cardinal Zbigniew Oleśnicki. Casimir Jagiellończyk (1444–92), on the other hand, removed Oleśnicki and his followers from the position of influence, and relied on high officials, mainly magnates from Great Poland, trying at the same time if not to win over then at least to neutralise the middle ranks of the nobility, i.e., the gentry.

As a result of the earlier statutes the king was bound to allow the gentry to express their opinions as a condition of his being able to obtain additional taxes or military service. This was done through regional assemblies, so-called local diets (*sejmiki*). In fact it is hard to imagine that the gentry gathering at successive local diets could conduct a conscious policy independent of the ruler. However, in the local diets the gentry more easily yielded to pressures from the king and the local magnates. It was the future national assembly of the representatives of local diets, i.e., the General Diet, that was to allow a strengthening of the gentry's political position. In the fifteenth century, however, it suited the king to be able to steer the debates of the representatives of local diets (the deputies) as well as the King's Council at the same time and place. It is not certain precisely when the institution of the Diet (*Sejm*) established itself, yet it must have taken place in the second half of the fifteenth century, as the oldest surviving statute of the Diet is dated 1493.

The emergence of the Diet, with its Chamber of Deputies, could be interpreted as the access to power, through their representatives, of the lower ranks of nobility, the so-called knighthood (*rycerstwo*). Such a conclusion would, however, be premature, and it would be safer to assume that till the end of the fifteenth century we witness a power elite, consisting of some 100–200 families of great nobles (magnates) and rich nobility, to which the gentry is aspiring to accede, so far rather unsuccessfully.

The structure of political power at the beginning of the sixteenth century

At the end of the fifteenth century, we can observe the following distribution of influence and political power in Poland: the king held the supreme executive power, i.e., the shaping of foreign policy and internal policy of the state, command of the army, supreme jurisdiction, nomination of officials (in practice including bishops after 1512), and finally the calling of the Diet, establishing the agenda and concluding the debates. In the task of administration the king was aided by the highest officials – the chancellor and vice-chancellor, grand marshal and marshal of the royal court, treasurer, commander-in-chief and field commander. In the provinces, the main representatives of the central authority were the *starostas*. The Diet was called every 1–2 years. It consisted of the Senate, or Royal Council – bishops, local officers nominated by the king (voivods, castellans), the highest officials – and of the Chamber of Deputies, i.e., representatives of 18 local diets from Little Poland and Great Poland. In 1529, the Diet was enlarged to include the representatives of Mazovia, which had been incorporated into the kingdom, and in 1569 they were joined by those of Royal Prussia as well as Podlasie, Volhynia, the Ukraine and finally Lithuania. At the beginning of the sixteenth century the Diet had 40 to 45 deputies, 80 to 90 senators and 2 representatives of the city of Cracow. Its authority included matters connected with passing extraordinary taxation and military service as well as any changes in the common law, a principle confirmed in 1505 with the statute *Nihil Novi*.

It should be pointed out that in this period, the Polish rulers of the house of the Jagiellons were simultaneously (except for the years 1492–1501) the grand dukes of Lithuania, where they had a wider range of obedience. However, because the ruler's residence was mainly in Poland, Lithuania was administered by local magnates. The gradual introduction in Lithuania of institutions analogous to those in Poland led eventually to a convergence of the two political systems, especially after the real union concluded in Lublin in 1569.

In historical literature this period is customarily described as that of limitation of the royal power, with a permanent trend towards a shrinking of this power for the benefit of the nobility. This opinion is, however, rather superficial. As has been pointed out, the king's power in the areas of policy, jurisdiction and military matters was not curtailed. What is more, the king's right of nominations came to apply to the church hierarchy. In the area of legislature, the king was able, in a certain measure, to act independently (particular laws, edicts), while any acts of the Diet were subject to his control and endorsement. The Diet could in fact refuse to pass taxes, but it was not able to pass any law without the king's knowledge and approval, because without the king's endorsement no act could become legally binding, as was pointed out by K. Grzybowski. Moreover, the king's real power was not a passing phenomenon since in 1570 we witness its further increase. As in any political system, the significant factor was not so much the formal division of prerogatives as the actual play of power. We can appreciate this better in the times of Sigismund I (1506–48), which possess richer documentation and allow us to review the situation under various political, social and cultural conditions.

From the standpoint of participation in the exercise of power, one might conclude that the several dozen deputies represented a large proportion of the country's population, around 8–10 per cent, such being the estimated numbers of the whole nobility in old Poland. Yet this is an illusion. We must exclude the lower ranks of the nobility from conscious participation in political life, especially poor squires, whose social and cultural status corresponded to that of yeomen in England. Again, we cannot talk about a full representation of the gentry by the Diet deputies, if nearly as late as 1537 the deputies were elected at local diets partly by the gentry and partly by the senators. Under these circumstances, the gentry could achieve little in the Diet in the face of the crushing majority of the magnates and the king, and it had to content itself with making petitions (so-called *petita*), which the monarch rarely took into consideration. This left the gentry with only one opportunity to exert pressure – the occasions when thousands of armed men would gather for military service. Such opportunities were grasped during the Prussian War (1520) and during the gathering at Lvov (1537); for this reason demands were put forth, yet to no avail, for convening an assembly of mounted nobles in the Hungarian way, representing the whole of the nobility.

As has been pointed out above, among the towns merely Cracow and later Vilna were represented in the Chamber of Deputies, and their representatives had limited role and responsibilities. In 1569, Gdańsk – Poland's economic capital – refused to enter the Chamber of Deputies, claiming the right to be represented in the Senate. At any rate, the towns were not anxious to strengthen the Chamber of Deputies and neither was the clergy, satisfied with the bishops' seats in the Senate. Under the circumstances, even the most strongly critical attitude of the gentry was of no significance when a handful of their representatives faced a huge majority of king and magnates in the Diet. As a result, in the course of the 37 years of active reign by Sigismund I (from 1506 till 1543, when Queen Bona's influence prevailed), special taxes, repeatedly passed by the Diet, were in operation for 32 years, and there was military service for 3 years (1513–14, 1537); only two years (1509 and 1516) were free from those burdens.

The small size of the Chamber of Deputies and the magnates' pressure on the local diets would seem to indicate that the magnates were the main holders of power, and that the Royal Council, consisting of magnates, was a body with a decisive voice. This, however, would be an extremely simplified view of the mechanism of power in those days. Firstly, the Council expressed its opinions, while the decisions were taken by the king, who was not particularly bound by the Council's recommendations. Secondly, the king convened the Council according to his own judgement, or he requested the opinion of Council members by correspondence, writing only to those he especially trusted and esteemed. Finally, one could become a Council member, whether a layman or clergyman, only through royal nomination, and the king also decided about advancement within the Council, i.e., he himself granted a higher secular office or a richer bishopric.

The king also had other means of winning the magnates' loyalty, or even shaping their composition. Those means were afforded by the royal domain, lands which could be entrusted to magnates for administration without the obligation to account for the whole income, or leased on more or less profitable terms; finally, with the Senate's approval, these lands could be handed over for a time or as hereditary property. The *starostwa* (royal landed estates) of that period were large and profitable, consisting, for example, of several towns and a few dozen villages. If given to the *starostas* without serious obligations, they made them as rich and influential as any of the members of the traditional magnate class. A royal appointment to a bishopric could be of even greater significance since the bishoprics of Gniezno and Cracow possessed lands several times the size of the richest magnate property.

Thanks to such means of exerting influence, Sigismund I, even though he surrounded himself with magnates and sought their support rather than that of the gentry or towns, was not unduly dependent on them. What is more, he created the magnates himself in some measure. One could of course be born a magnate, as was the case with the members of the old noble families of Tęczyński, Górka, Tarnowski or Kmita, or one could become a magnate through royal nomination or donations, as happened with the families of Łaski, Szydłowiecki, Tomicki, Maciejowski, Dzierzgowski, etc. Towards the end of Sigismund I's reign, a similar policy was pursued by Queen Bona, who created a group of magnates loyal to her. They, however, were not very influential or lasting.

The way into the ranks of new magnates led most frequently through courtly service and royal offices. The office of the chancellor, the monarch's closest aide, was a major factor in the careers of the Łaskis, Szydłowieckis, Tomickis and Maciejowskis. Representatives of the old aristocracy, members of the great families of nobles, did not become chancellors. One reached the office of chancellor or vice-chancellor through the function of the king's secretary, i.e., through work at the monarch's side, or in the royal chancellery, in the diplomatic service, or possibly on home missions. A precondition for taking the office of the royal secretary, irrespective of whether one was a layman or a clergyman, a nobleman or a burgher, was a thorough and extensive liberal education and a knowledge of the world and languages. The royal secretariat of the sixteenth century was an intellectual elite *sui generis*, a group which at the same time constituted a pool for the power elite. It is enough to say that the secretaries of Sigismund I were such men as the poets and diplomats Andrew Krzycki and John Flachsbinder or Dantiscus (Dantyszek), the geographer and historian Bernard Wapowski, the lawyers Peter Tomicki and John Chojeński, the economist Hjost Dietz or Decius (Decjusz), the counter-reformation leader Stanislas Hosius, and many others. These men later often rose to high political or church offices, and their families temporarily or permanently entered the ranks of magnates.

As the above indicates, political power rested primarily in the hands of the monarch, who was surrounded by a group of for the most part talented, and always well-educated, collaborators. While the ranks of magnates did exert a significant influence on the country's politics, frequently forming powerful lobbies, predominance in these matters was still with the monarch, who did not allow the magnates an unduly large share of power, and even that share depended in some measure on the king's good will. The gentry, who formally participated in power through representation in the General Diet and local diets, could effectively influence political decisions very seldom. In the Diet and out of it, the gentry was left with the roles of petitioners or opposition; for a long time this opposition was unable to take advantage even of its main weapon, i.e., its consent to extraordinary taxation.

The gentry's way to power

A dynamic factor that upset the existing distribution of forces was the gentry. By analysing the social composition of the Diet, we find that the deputies were members of the rich gentry, hardly inferior to magnates, and of the medium bracket of this gentry. To use the contemporary measure of wealth, the politicians among the gentry were for the most part owners of one to a score of villages. In the professional sense, we would include among the activists of the gentry's party practising jurists, mainly judges, deputy judges, or court clerks, who had often studied for several years at Cracow or even at foreign universities.

The party of the gentry, later called the Executionist Party, arose gradually, together with the growth of political activity at local diets and the accumulating experience of the gentry's deputies at General Diets. This started with the presentation to the king of petitions elaborated at local diets. As years went by, these petitions changed from particular demands and individual complaints to more and more general demands concerning the political system and fiscal, juridical, military and religious matters. The starting point for these demands was the conviction that the old laws were adequate but were no longer observed, and thus it was necessary to restore their authority and application, i.e., implement them. This rule was directed primarily against endowments from the king's domain, which the magnates received not quite legally, but always to their great advantage. Another offence that the Executionists fought against was the concentration in one person's hands of several supreme offices (and maximum incomes), of which a frequent example was the combination of the office of chancellor or vice-chancellor with the bishopric of Cracow, as was the case with Peter Tomicki, John Chojeński and Samuel Maciejowski.

As the nobility became more mature politically, their party put forth further demands, for financial and military reforms, reconstruction of the juridical system, i.e., improvements of the royal court of appeals and limitation of the jurisdiction of ecclesiastical courts. Demands were also made for the conclusion of a real union with Royal Prussia and Lithuania, so far connected with Poland mainly through the person of the ruler. To these general, gradually formulated programmatic principles were added some more detailed demands, e.g., for convening the so-called Diet of Justice (1520), imposing limitations on amassment of private property by Queen Bona (1537), annulment of the 'unworthy' marriage of Sigismund Augustus with Barbara Radziwiłł (1548), etc. Such formulations appeared not only in the postulates of local diets but also in political writings, which from 1543 onwards (Nicolas Rej, Andrew Frycz-Modrzewski) attempted to shape political opinions. They were also presented in speeches in the House by the leaders of the Executionist Party, Nicholas Sienicki, Raphael Leszczyński, Hieronymus Ossoliński and others.

The most spirited activity of the gentry's party came during the reign of Sigismund Augustus (1548–72). In the first years of his reign, until 1562, the party did not score any success. Despite the mobilisation of public opinion, flourishing political literature, political maturation of the gentry and the remarkable talents of the elite in the Diet, the party could not gain predominance in the Diet and was unable to carry through the proposed reforms. But it was powerful enough to obstruct the king's policy to a significant degree, which even led the monarch to try to rule without convening the Diet (1559–62).

In the first period of his reign, Sigismund Augustus, like his father Sigismund I before him, sought support from among the magnates. The conflict provoked by his marriage with Barbara Radziwiłł which set nearly all politically significant forces, including his mother Queen Bona, against him, forced him to rely on the Crown and Lithuanian magnates (John Tarnowski, Samuel Maciejowski, the Radziwiłłs) and on the Church hierarchy. Generous donations from the royal domain from 1548 to 1550 made it possible for the king to win over more magnates, settle the dispute and have Barbara crowned. This simultaneously strengthened the king's ties with the magnates in the face of his continuing conflicts with the gentry and Queen Bona, and further reduced the income from the royal domain. Financial difficulties forced the king for years to turn to the magnates for credit on the security of the royal domain, which further increased the monarch's dependence on the magnates, and reinforced the role of the Senate.

If one were to assess the social participation in political power in the first years of Sigismund Augustus's reign, one would have to state that there was no increase in the influence of the party of the gentry, but a growing participation of the magnates in political decisions. They were, for the most part, magnates of long standing, or at any rate traditionally represented in the Senate: members of the families of Tarnowski, Tęczyński, Kmita, Firlej, Kościelecki or Górka. The king saw a remedy for his growing dependence on them in a widening of the power elite. To this end, through nominations and donations, he sought to create a new group of magnates, high officials connected with the king, who would provide a counterbalance to the great nobles with a secure footing in the Senate. In this way new faces started to appear in the king's entourage, and his closest collaborators – chancellor, vice-chancellor, treasurer – were more and more often men deriving from rich gentry or the younger magnate families. They were John Ocieski, Spytek Jordan, Spytek Tarnowski, Nicholas Sieniawski, and among the bishops Jacob Uchański and A. Noskowski, and later John Przerębski and Peter Myszkowski. They were a small circle of men, highly educated and loyal to the monarch; like the royal secretaries of the period, they knew their tasks and made skilful politicians.

This political elite consisting of magnates of old and new creation, in the absence of support from the wide ranks of the gentry, and with the towns clearly avoiding political involvement, might have provided a sufficient social basis for Sigismund Augustus at a time of the normal functioning of the state. The policy of subjecting Livonia to the Jagiellonian monarchy following the fall of the Teutonic Order there and the subsequent outbreak of the first Northern War (1563–70) called for a much greater political, financial and military effort. For Sigismund Augustus, this meant the necessity of finding a wider support for his policies, i.e., the need to make an accommodation with the party of the gentry. As a result, representatives of the gentry were admitted to the so-far narrow circle of the power elite.

The monarch's cooperation with the elite of the gentry

The agreement with the Executionist nobility, concluded towards the end of the year 1562, bore fruit in reforms passed by the Diet sessions of 1562–9. The king's cooperation with the gentry substantially increased their participation in power, and strengthened the role of the Diet in the state's overall policy. Within the Diet, it swung the balance in favour of the Chamber of Deputies, giving it a clear advantage over the Senate. However, this did not yet mean a conscious participation in power, if only through local diets, of the whole of the nobility, i.e., some 8–10 per cent of the population. We may, in practice, exclude from this participation the lesser squires, the majority of whom were illiterate, politically immature and too poor to afford a steady participation in political life. Thus, if a few hundred gentry families from which the deputies derived participated actively in the execution of power, we may perhaps be speaking, provided that we include here the local authorities and local diets, of some 2–3 per cent participation in power by contemporary society. The figure does not cover even a half of the ranks of the nobility of that period, but in terms of the sixteenth century the participation was substantial.

The question arises, however, whether this broad takeover of political decisions by the gentry and its representatives actually diminished the king's role and participation in decision making. In practice, none of the reforms then introduced limited the king's competence, and some of them even reinforced it. At the same time, the support granted by the party of the gentry enabled the king to bring the Senate under stricter control (the senator's oath became obligatory for the bishops as well). More important yet, the king managed to subjugate and take under his authority the city of Gdańsk, which until then had enjoyed a large measure of independence. In the last years of his reign (1570–2), Sigismund Augustus applied a brake to the gentry's political impetus, possibly because of differences of opinion on some concrete political problems. He may also have perceived the gentry's dynamic movement as a threat to his freedom of decision as a monarch.

Brief as this period of the king's collaboration with the gentry was, its effects were impressive. In the first place, the so-called execution of land property was implemented, i.e., the monarch's title to alienated royal domain was restored. A large-scale review of the king's domain was carried out, and its income values were assessed as a basis for subsequent rents. A fourth part of the income from the domain was used to set up a standing army, known as 'quarter troops', for protection against Tartar incursions. In 1563, a fiscal reform was introduced, with new tax bases and rates, and a redistribution of burdens; for example, taxes from peasants were reduced and partially shifted onto the Church. Payments for the benefit of Rome (St Peter's Pence, dues for vacant bishoprics) were abolished and made over to the royal treasury. Finally, the verdicts of ecclesiastical courts were no longer enforced by the *starostas*, and in this way actual religious tolerance, vital for Protestants, was ensured.

The coordinated activity of the king and the gentry also led to the conclusion, in 1569, of a real union with Lithuania (one king, a common royal election, one Diet), preceded by the incorporation of Podlasie and the south-eastern areas of the Grand Duchy of Lithuania into the Crown (i.e., Poland). At about the same time the king declared that the political distinctness of Royal Prussia had no justification, and he brought about its inclusion in the authority of the national Diet, enlarged by deputies and senators from that province.

It would be hard to enumerate here all the subsequent reforms. It is worth mentioning, however, that in the year after Sigismund Augustus's death the Executionist Party secured a legal guarantee of religious tolerance (the so-called Warsaw Confederacy), and in 1578, during the reign of Stephen Báthory, the juridical system was reformed and supreme courts of appeal were established, called the Crown and Lithuanian Tribunals.

An analysis of the political situation in the years 1563–9 and of the reforms then introduced allows us to draw conclusions of a more general nature. One, the extension of the social basis of political power with the inclusion of the politically aware and active ranks of the gentry resulted in a significant progress in the state's centralisation and a greater efficiency of administration. Two, it may be noticed that, despite the gentry's wider participation in power, the monarch's competence and actual influence often increased; this was accompanied by a corresponding erosion of the magnates' influence, also welcomed by the king. One more conclusion could be drawn from these speculations, namely that under the system then referred to as *monarchia mixta*, which we now call 'nobility's democracy', an efficient administration with active internal and foreign policies was perfectly possible. Naturally, it required political maturity and cooperation between the king and the gentry, as well as the identity of their basic goals. The effects then achieved were no worse than in the case of systems with a greater concentration of power in the hands of the monarch and his aides.

The theory and practice of the 'nobility's democracy'

Although some elements of the gentry's programme, such as religious tolerance or judicial reform, were implemented after 1572, the years 1572–1648 mark a period of a completely changed distribution of political power. The death of Sigismund Augustus in 1572, the last of the House of Jagiello, created the problem of free election, understood as a contract between society and the elected monarch. The Polish throne had been subject to election since 1386, but this had been election within the dynasty, rarely diverging from the rules of inheritance. Moreover, the previous elections had been limited to a narrow circle of electors, i.e., the Royal Council and the Diet with a clear domination by magnates. A similar type of election, with a minimum participation of the gentry, would now have been unthinkable, especially because for the time of the interregnum the gentry formed a confederacy and took security and jurisdiction into their own hands. Thus prevailed the principle of direct participation in the king's election of the full ranks of nobility, on the pattern of the previously postulated Hungarian-type assembly of the mounted nobles. The election was therefore a moment of direct democracy *sui generis*, embracing the whole of the nobility. One might, however, ask whether the participation in political decisions by the poorest and least conscious ranks of nobility enhanced the political impact of that class, or whether it simply provided a good opportunity for practising demagogy and the manipulation of crowds.

The further evolution of the political system was affected by the candidates proposed for the election. The most serious candidate was the Habsburg Archduke Ernest, a representative of the house whose anti-Protestant activities and violation of the rights and freedoms of the nobility in Germany, Bohemia and Hungary were well known in Poland. Another candidate was the Muscovite Tsar Ivan the Terrible, thought of as a remedy for the incessant conflicts between Lithuania and Moscow; he was, however, a monarch notorious for his tyranny and bloody repressions. The third, victorious, candidate was Henri Duke of Anjou, the King of France's brother, a man who had recently compromised himself by taking part in the Massacre of St Bartholomew. In the absence of stronger and more neutral candidates, it was necessary to reckon with the victory of a monarch guilty of violating the principles of the estates' participation in government and of religious tolerance. A logical yet paradoxical consequence of these circumstances was the fact that the same statesmen who had previously strengthened the royal power through rational reforms and collaboration with the throne would now have to work to opposite ends.

The election, held on 11 May 1573, was connected with the condition that the successful candidate should accept a number of obligations and take an oath to fulfil them. Some of them, the so-called *pacta conventa*, were of a temporary and personal character. The other set of conditions, known as Henry's Articles, were a short summary of the basic political principles that had to be observed in the Commonwealth from then on. They guaranteed the elective status of the throne and religious tolerance, and barred the monarch from imposing taxes or demanding military service without the Diet's approval. The Diet had to be convened at least once in two years for six-week debates. Moreover, the king's foreign policy was subjected to the Senate's supervision. It was to be a constant control, exercised by teams of four resident senators taking turns every six months. The last item of this extensive list of conditions provided that, should the king violate the laws of the country including the above articles, society was entitled to refuse obedience to him. These articles, with very slight modifications, were to remain in force till the end of the eighteenth century.

We can see that the extinction of the dynasty and the introduction of free election first led to an expansion of social participation in political decisions (confederations, elections) and then, by subjecting the king to the Senate's permanent control, transferred some political decisions from the hands of the monarch to those of a narrow circle of magnates who were at least co-deciders. It would therefore seem a turning point in the distribution of political power, a system in which the gentry willingly handed over some of its influence to magnates, whom it had been opposing, while the two groups between them deprived the king of the most significant attributes of power.

All the same, without denying the importance of the changes of 1572–3, such an interpretation would be premature. The party of the gentry did not at all renounce its programme, and in subjecting the king to the Senate's control they could well have expected that the senators would obey the Chamber of Deputies, as they had done of late. Also the limitation of the king's power should not be taken too literally. The resident senators proved to be a fiction: the high costs of their stay at the court and the limited influence they had over the king discouraged them from taking their duties seriously. Although the terms of Diets had been defined, the king was able to convene additional (extraordinary) Diets, and his impact on the debates and conclusions did not change significantly, at least from the legal point of view. In the king's hands remained the right of nomination to offices and bishoprics and of making endowments from the royal domain. He also held superior authority over the army, supreme judicial power, etc. Therefore in practice the range of the king's power would be determined by the actual play of forces, i.e., it would depend on who would lend support to the king's policy, vote for the taxes, etc. It was thus for the king to decide whether he should seek a wider social base for his power.

In this respect, however, no rapprochement took place between the king and the wider ranks of the society. Neither Stephen Báthory (1576–86) nor Sigismund III Vasa (1587–1632), and none of the latter's sons, came to rely on the gentry. This mistake was the more serious as Stephen Báthory still had to do with the old Executionist Party; in his political practice, however, he tried to weaken the Diet by appealing to local diets, and sought support among the dynamic magnate families (the Zborowskis and John Zamojski). Likewise, Sigismund III counted on new magnates of his own creation and on ecclesiastical circles, at the same time seeking support abroad, from the Habsburgs, dreaming of regaining the Swedish crown. His growing conflict with the gentry led to the rebellion of Sandomierz (1606–7). The king's military victory over the rebels did not strengthen his power. Conversely, it resulted in a permanent opposition by the gentry because of the threat to their freedom posed by the monarch's absolutist designs. The ideology of 'Golden Freedom' meant permanent opposition to the king's policies, a constant watch to prevent the growth of the king's power. A consequence of this caution was enmity towards any changes or reforms. This conviction was to become the basis for the introduction of the principle of unanimity into the Chamber of Deputies in 1652, the first *liberum veto*, designed to protect this institution against the king's pressures.

The ideology of the constant threat to 'Golden Freedom' perhaps blurred the clarity of vision of others besides the nobility. Subsequent monarchs were more prone to dream of a coup d'état with the aid of Cossacks and home or foreign troops than to seek agreement with the gentry. The alternative of cooperation with the magnates was not practicable, however, by reason of their growing independence from the king and the competition and conflicts between magnate factions. These had resulted from the growth of magnate latifundia and the rise of political clienteles, together with the monarch's shrinking capacity to create freely, or at least shape, the composition of the magnates. At any rate, the group of officials centred around the king did not gain more power, and frequently even the highest officials, e.g., the commanders-in-chief (hetmans), conducted their own policies, which were at odds with those of the monarch.

The system referred to as the Commonwealth of the Nobility of the seventeenth century was, as we can see, the result of a complicated pattern of political relations and dependencies. In theory, there continued a wide participation in power of the whole class of the nobility (about 8–10 per cent of the population), but in practice the power slipped from their hands; this was true even of the deputies to the Diet. The gentry preserved only electoral decisions and decisions on local matters, which were made during local diets. But political decisions of a more general nature rested with the king and the magnates. It was characteristic that none of the parties involved, either the king or any of the magnate factions, was able to capture full power and pass from intentions to their implementation. Remarkably missing from this system was the role of the towns. Gdańsk's behind-the-scenes influence and money did on occasion play an important part, but no burgher featured among the political elite of the country as had been the case in the sixteenth century.

Under these circumstances, the political system was increasingly based on mutual obstruction practised by the king, the magnates and the ranks of the gentry. Only in times of danger was a temporary suspension of obstruction possible. This obstruction, however, was not synonymous with a lack of conflict. It meant only that none of the parties was able to gain a sufficient majority to introduce changes and to stimulate the state structure and political life. It is therefore hard to talk of any broad political elite of the country of the type that we were able to define for the sixteenth century. At this moment of history we see a number of elites, of national and local character. These groups did not necessarily coincide with what could be defined as the intellectual elite of that epoch.

11 ❧ Borrowing and originality in the East-Central European Renaissance[1]

JAN BIAŁOSTOCKI

I

In the earlier periods of the Middle Ages, East-Central Europe was in debt to the West, having accepted, as it did, together with the Christian religion in its Roman version, the basic functions and forms of Western civilisation and artistic life; in the later Middle Ages this area not only achieved considerable cultural autonomy but, ruled by monarchs of such important dynasties as the Angevin and the Luxembourg, was able to develop extremely active creative centres of international medieval culture. This is especially true of fourteenth-century Bohemia.

As the Czech kingdom – like Germany and Italy – belonged to the empire at the time of the Luxembourg emperors, who resided in Prague or in Karlštejn, Bohemia played a central role in the art of Northern Europe. It was in Prague that Peter Parler in the mid-fourteenth century erected the spacious choir of the cathedral spanned with revolutionary vaulting discarding traditional divisions and creating in this way a unified architectural space. It was in Prague that the same master called to life a tremendous series of portrait busts full of energy and vitality, which (made by himself and his workshop in 1375–83) represented in monumental forms contemporary people of varied social standing who had in one way or another participated in the erection of the cathedral: from Charles IV and his family, to the self-portrait of the artist. For the first time a unique gallery of sculptural effigies was created in which traditional social boundaries seem to have been dissolved, as the divisions of space had been in architecture. It was also in Prague that the sweet refinement of international Gothic, developed under French and Italian influence, achieved full maturity and from there spread in all directions, which is why works in this style are to be found in the vast area extending from Austria to east Prussia.

After the splendid artistic achievement of Bohemia in the time of Charles IV, a period followed when the turbulence of the Hussite wars inhibited the artistic development of that country and then it was Buda's turn, in the early fifteenth century when the Luxembourg emperor wore the crown of St Stephen, to take artistic precedence. Close contact with the most advanced centres in the West shaped Hungarian artistic life, of which fundamental new evidence was recently discovered in the form of an incredibly rich collection of fine Gothic sculptures excavated from the soil of the Castle Hill in Buda;[2] close artistic connections with Italy also date back to that time, which laid the foundations for Hungary's unique position in the spread of the ideas and forms of the Italian Renaissance.

Humanism and the Renaissance, born and developed in Italy, came to Hungary, Bohemia and Poland from outside. In the fourteenth century there was certainly great interest in and influence from both the Italian and Northern cultures. Realistic observations used by artists trained in the Parler style, as well as the capricious, lyrical refinement of the representatives of the international Gothic, may be compared to similar phenomena in Italy. But, by the middle of the fifteenth century, a great divide developed, which was due not only to humanistic ideas, but also to the para-scientific study of nature, its detailed description as well as the discovery of its general laws, manifested in the artists' interest in the study of perspective, proportions and anatomy. This and the ever-deeper study and better knowledge of Classical antiquity meant that there could be but little in common between such contemporary works of art as Viet Stoss's flamboyant and expressive tomb of the Polish King Casimir (died 1492) in Cracow Cathedral and the classical and beautifully harmonious tomb of Andrea Vendramin by Tullio Lombardo, now in the Frari church in Venice (formerly at I Servi).

Two traditions now existed in Europe, and it was not the Northern European one that was to lead the field in the immediate future. As once before, in the early Middle Ages, East-Central Europe had to look to foreign achievements as a guide to its artistic ideals. This does not mean that humanistic interests were lacking in that region, but they were not always related to the interest in new artistic style. Cracow University was a very important centre of scholarship and humanism in the fifteenth century for the area east of Prague and north of Vienna. Contacts with Italian centres of learning were continuous and fruitful; Bylica and Regiomontanus, two outstanding astronomers of the time, were for a period active in Cracow. But with all this scholarly and scientific development no trace of interest in the art of the Renaissance as a new style may be found before the sixteenth century. It is significant that, after the death of the Italian leader of Cracow humanists, Filippo Buonaccorsi (called Callimachus), the commission for his tomb was given to the greatest artist available, to be sure, but an artist who in his works incorporated artistic ideals rather distant from those we usually connect with humanism. The commission went to Veit Stoss, who may possibly have met

Callimachus, although it is uncertain whether there would have been any contact between an Italian court humanist in exile and a late-Gothic master carver.

Stoss's design was executed in bronze by the famous Nuremberg workshop of the Vischers in about 1500, and it shows some signs of the awareness of Renaissance innovations in the ornamental border and inscription, but neither the character of the effigy itself, of the scholar in his cell, nor of its style show any direct link with Italian models and they go back rather to Eyckian and other Western inspirations.

II

The tremendous process of the absorption and adaptation of the Italian Renaissance, which fundamentally transformed the artistic character of Eastern Europe, was first initiated in Hungary which in this respect was about half a century ahead of Bohemia and Poland. Already in the early fifteenth century at the culmination of late Gothic culture, there were contacts not only with Italian humanists (Ambrogio Traversari, Francesco Filelfo and Pier Paolo Vergerio remained in Hungary for shorter or longer periods) but also with Italian artists. These contacts were prepared in the long period from 1308 to 1382 when Hungary was ruled by kings of the Angevin dynasty who claimed the throne of Naples.

From 1387 the king of Hungary was Sigismund Luxembourg, who from 1410 was also king of Germany and from 1433 emperor (died 1437). Italians were obviously present at his court in Buda and they held important positions in secular, ecclesiastical and military administration, which in consequence made Italian culture proliferate in Hungary. It was the only country in Europe to import representatives of Renaissance art as early as the first half of the century: both Masolino da Panicale, a collaborator of Masaccio in his works in the Brancacci Chapel (S. Maria del Carmine, Florence) and Manetto Ammanatini, a Florentine architect of the early Renaissance, spent some years in Hungary. Nothing remains of their activity there, but its importance is proved by the way Renaissance artistic ideas triumphed under Matthias Corvinus, who was king of Hungary from 1458 to 1490.

During his reign Hungary became the first European country outside Italy to adopt the Renaissance to any great extent, both as a trend of ideas and as an artistic style. In that period Hungary was not obliged to rely on imported Italian scholars; it already had humanists of its own, dominated by two men of different generations: János Vitéz, chancellor and primate of Hungary, and his nephew Ivan Česmički, widely known under his pen-name of Janus Pannonius, a pupil of Guarino Guarini at his famous school in Ferrara. The artistic activity of the court received a theoretical background in Italian architectural treatises: we know that both Alberti's and Filarete's treatises were copied and illustrated for Corvinus; these manuscripts have been preserved to our day.

A great number of outstanding representatives of the Italian Renaissance like Benedetto da Majano, Ercole Roberti, Giovanni Dalmata Duchnović came to Hungary. Others like Verrocchio, Mantegna, Attavante, Francia worked for Corvinus in Italy. Still others, like Botticelli and Pollaiolo, prepared designs used for textiles. Sometimes less-known artists established themselves as independent masters in Hungary, like Chimenti Carmicia. His team consisted of Baccio Cellini and four carpenters from Florence under the leadership of Dominicus Dominici. There were also several Dalmatian stone-carvers. Italians executed all the ornamental elements of architecture under the supervision of Italian *architetti* who designed them; the local craftsmen were used only for the masonry work. This system – as explained by R. Feuer Toth – is responsible for the fact that Hungarian architecture of the Renaissance, in comparison for instance with that of France, the Netherlands and Germany, is by far the most pure and that it follows Italian models in a most faithful way.

This is one of the reasons for the specific importance and quality of the Hungarian Renaissance. The other is its completeness. We have seen that it was backed by humanist education and culture, and that it was prepared by theoretical treatises imported by Matthias Corvinus; what was equally important was that the new style was penetrating all fields of artistic culture. Today it is very difficult to imagine the splendour of that art. The almost complete destruction of monumental Renaissance architecture in Hungary permits us only to reconstruct it in our imagination on the basis of extremely damaged pieces of red marble preserved in Hungarian museums and a few surviving works like Tamás Bakócs's chapel in Esztergom and that of János Lázói in Alba Julia. Useful also are the enthusiastic descriptions of chroniclers, travellers and humanists.

Fortunately, however, examples remain in the field of the decorative arts: work in gold, textiles, miniature painting, inlaid furniture. When referring to the completeness of the Hungarian Renaissance I mean all the works, in gold or silver, in silk or brocade, on parchment or in wood, which bear the imprint of the same style, of the same artistic milieu and which all point to the very place of origin of the Renaissance, to Tuscany – something which, with the exception of Poland, was elsewhere in Europe quite unusual. To France, Germany, Spain, the Netherlands and Austria went craftsmen and artists from northern Italy, mostly from the border area between Lombardy and Switzerland, and therefore the style they brought with them was far from the original pure Tuscan. In all those countries they met powerful guilds of craftsmen, defending their traditions and rights.

Even in Bohemia, when Vladislav II, already its king, received in addition the Hungarian crown and tried to introduce the Italian style from Hungary, the strong Gothic tradition there made it impossible at first to erect pure Renaissance buildings; this makes Benedict Ried's mixed style no less interesting. But, with the exception of some rare provincial initiatives like that in Tovačov as early as the 1590s, the Italian Renaissance arrived in Bohemia only in the 1630s.

III

Poland was much more eager than Bohemia to accept in its capital Italian ideas from Hungarian hands. This was due to the initiative of Sigismund I, younger brother of Vladislav II, and the results of the activity of Italian masters on the royal Wawel Hill in Cracow belong to the purest and – which makes them still more important – best-preserved examples of the early transplantation of the Renaissance to any foreign country. But the Cracow Renaissance was much more limited than that of Buda. It is true that in both cases royal patronage was involved. But, at the time that Sigismund was commissioning Franciscus Italus (or Fiorentinus) to construct the new castle and Bartolomeo Berrecci to erect and to decorate the sepulchral chapel, the Renaissance in Hungary was already spreading out: it was to be found in Visegrád, Esztergom, Oradea, Veszprém, in buildings and works of art originating from the patronage of nobles and prelates, princes and bishops, in castles and in towns. There are well-preserved fine marble tabernacles in the parish church of the Inner City in Pest, dating from about 1504–5 and a similar tabernacle, commissioned by George Szathmáry, was erected at more or less the same time in the cathedral of Pécs.

In Poland in the first quarter of the sixteenth century Renaissance art was limited to the royal castle; the only other example of patronage of the new style was that of the Gniezno archbishop Jan Łaski; and then all that remains are some stone funerary slabs commissioned for Łaski himself and for his predecessors and relatives from Joannes Fiorentinus who was working in Hungary. Poland's importance in the process of adaptation to the Renaissance increased in later periods. Sigismund I made use of Hungarian experience at just the right time, and it was really providential that the king had spent some years in the court of his brother in Buda observing, and certainly admiring, the structures erected for, and art treasures collected by, Vladislav's predecessor, Corvinus.

In 1526 the Hungarian state broke down under Turkish pressure and in 1541 Buda and Esztergom were swallowed up by the Ottoman empire, which put an end to the adaptation of the Renaissance in Hungary. In the sparse remains of the Hungarian state there was not a great deal of opportunity for art patronage, and the crown of Hungary passed into the hands of the Habsburgs who held it for centuries, which limited royal patronage in that country considerably.

At that time in Poland the inspiring spark ignited a new fire. The splendid royal chapel was finished by Bartolomeo Berrecci by 1533 and in 1536 the transformation of the Cracow castle was completed. In this way models were established, which – together with their furniture, with tombs, slabs, statues, reliefs, wall paintings, tapestries, chandeliers, altars – became objects of imitation all over the country and all through the sixteenth and early seventeenth century.

If the first initiatives in bringing the Renaissance to Poland were relatively early, the general trend of the imitation and diffusion of Italian models was rather late in that country; it started in the second quarter of the century and gathered momentum only in the second half. And then an interesting phenomenon occurred: the adaptation of the Renaissance in Poland was selective.

There were some types and specific forms which found wide acceptance: such was the case of the centrally planned chapel, whose authority relied, of course, on the fact that it was first used in Poland in the royal mausoleum; such was also the case of the niche wall tomb, originating in the same chapel, repeated in countless examples throughout the country. But there were also cases of transplantations completely rejected. Polish patrons did not accept some of the artistic types and forms which in other regions found wide recognition. Not accepted was, for instance, the free-standing tomb, so popular in France, Spain and England. There was in fact no attempt even to adapt it, whereas in Silesia, Bohemia and Transylvania it is easy to find Renaissance tombs conceived as sarcophagi in imitation of Roman ones.

Another artistic form which did not find support from Polish patrons seems to be the Renaissance wood-inlay, the *tarsia*. In woodwork the dominating tradition was Flemish or German. It is enough, however, to cross the Carpathians to be confronted with a great amount of inlay work in secular or ecclesiastical furniture in Slovakia, which – under the name of Upper Hungary – for centuries belonged to the Hungarian state. In Levoča, Bardějov and Kežmarok there are preserved excellent examples of *tarsia* work originating from the first decade of the sixteenth century. The magnificent stall from Nyírbátor signed by F.(?) Marone and dated 1511, now in the National Museum of Budapest, is a masterpiece of inlay art, displaying all the illusionist tricks – open doors, cupboards, shelves, books, vessels – found in the famous Italian inlay cabinets and *studioli*, like those in Urbino and Gubbio (now in the Metropolitan Museum, New York). Not a trace of all that seems to have penetrated into Poland. At least no such works survive.

In Poland statues are also rare, if we exclude recumbent tomb figures. In the Sigismund Chapel of Cracow cathedral there are six solemn marble statues and the same number of round reliefs. They were not imitated, although the chapel's architecture and the recumbent figures of the kings frequently served as models for artists working not only for outstanding aristocratic families but also for patrons belonging to much less prominent gentry. Only in some exceptionally rich tombs by Canavesi and Michałowicz do we find statues – figures of personifications of virtues – in the niches. Reliefs were not generally used; examples of their inclusion in the composition of tombs are rare (an enigmatic one is that in the Szydłowiecki tomb in Opatów, inspired, it seems, by the tradition of Classical *conclamatio*).

It is not always easy to tell why some of the typical features of the Renaissance style were eliminated in the process of its adaptation in Poland. It may be that the free-standing tomb recalled too much of the Gothic tradition. In Italy this type was never very popular, whereas it was most typical in Gothic art. Then, of course, the authority of the royal chapel was decisive. Had the royal tomb been conceived as a free-standing one, Polish imitation would certainly have adopted that form more often. In Hungary little sepulchral art has been preserved. The typical form, it seems, was the sepulchral slab, much less popular in Poland; in Transylvania the Roman provincial sarcophagi, quite frequent there, could have served as models.

No developed iconographic or narrative programmes are to be found in Poland outside the royal castle, where there were wall paintings illustrating *Tabula Cebetis*, The Table of Cebes (an allegorical interpretation of a painting in a Greek temple), and where carved heads in the coffers of the ceiling of the Deputies' Room (only a few of which now remain) must have had an underlying elaborate symbolic, possibly astrological, programme.[3] On the outside walls, above the windows of the upper floor, wall paintings with emperors' heads, garlands and inscriptions were executed by Master Antoni of Wrocław. In the royal chapel there were mythological reliefs, most probably with some symbolic significance which, in spite of some successful attempts, we have failed until now to decipher completely. They certainly expressed in their elegant way, *all'antica*, religious ideas of immortality of the soul and of its salvation. Nothing of all that can be traced in the numerous imitations of the chapel's architecture throughout the country.

And, finally, the Italian Renaissance was accepted in Poland only in architectural and sculptural form. Almost no painters and no pictures were imported from Italy, especially in the first half of the century and, if there were such attempts in the second half of it, the contacts were no longer with Florence but with Venice and the Veneto. The only outstanding graphic artist from Italy to work in Poland, the Mannerist Caraglio, was not employed as an engraver of prints but as a carver of precious stones.

Painters were invited to Poland from Germany, as for instance were Hans Süss von Kulmbach and Hans Dürer. In the field of decorative arts too, interest was directed to Western and Northern neighbours, namely to Nuremberg centres for metal work – as when the king ordered the silver altar for his chapel to be made by Labenwolf after Peter Flötner's models, or when he gave the commission for the bronze grille to enclose the entrance to the chapel to the workshop of the Vischers. Tapestry commissions went to the Netherlands.

Sigismund I's son Sigismund Augustus bought there and commissioned one of the most outstanding collections of figural, heraldic and animal tapestries. The *Pugnae Ferarum* series was a great achievement of landscape tapestry, in which the intimate view of woods with a relatively low horizon appears quite early, and the *Story of Noah*, designed by Coxie and Van Orley, belongs to the best ever produced by the Brussels workshops.

One has to conclude that the adaptation of the Italian Renaissance in Poland was very early compared with other countries of non-Italian Europe, that it brought to Poland artists from the main centres of the Tuscan Renaissance, but that it was limited and one-sided.

It was generally limited to architecture and tomb sculpture, while in the other fields of artistic activity German and Netherlandish production was in demand. It is true that Hans Dürer did not inaugurate in Poland any real tradition of Renaissance painting, his achievements in the royal castle being mediocre, and that excellent pictures delivered by Kulmbach to the Cracow churches remained without imitators. The best of the Northern tradition, however, may be seen not in painting but in wood sculpture: the few remaining carvings of human heads, mentioned already, in the ceiling of the Deputies' Room (of which only 30 out of the original 200 survive), represent a real originality. Maybe there were several such sets in Europe – we know about many examples of ceilings decorated with heads – but we do not know of any ensemble with such a high degree of individualisation, expressiveness, variety and mastery of execution.

Looking now not so much for what East-Central European countries borrowed from Italy, but for what they contributed to the European Renaissance as a whole, I should like to discuss three items: the splendid series of Czech and Moravian castles; the vernacular style of architecture, especially in Bohemia and Poland; the outstanding centre of international Mannerism at the court of Rudolf II in Prague about 1600. These three contributions vary in character and quality and one can perhaps object that there were also other examples of considerable achievement. It would, however, be difficult not to agree that these three are important, interesting and have considerable originality if judged against the general European background.

IV

In the eighth volume of *Propyläen Kunstgeschichte*, devoted to art and architecture of the sixteenth century, no example of Bohemian or Moravian Renaissance castles is reproduced.[4] This proves how underrated they are and how much a revaluation is needed. Nowhere in Europe is such a splendid series of Renaissance courtyards to be found. The general design of these residences is not always of the same quality – quite often they were adapted from earlier buildings – but there are several instances of masterly conception and excellent architectural execution.

After Vladislav II ordered the splendid hall (now bearing his name) to be constructed in Prague castle, in which a late Gothic interior is matched with Renaissance window frames outside (because Benedict Ried, the architect, had visited Buda's Renaissance buildings), new elements of style appeared in Bohemia in the architecture erected for the Habsburg rulers in the second quarter of the sixteenth century. The Belvedere Villa built for Queen Anne on the Hradshin between 1538 and 1563 was started by the Italian Paolo della Stella, but was continued and completed by Bonifaz Wohlmut, a German architect already working in the new style. It presents a beautiful, harmonious solution: the villa is surrounded by a light arcade on the ground floor, with Wohlmut's second floor modelled in a sculptural way, the whole looking like Bramante's *tempietto* redesigned on a rectangular plan.

Shortly after the Belvedere Villa, two castles for Florian Griespach, the secretary of the Bohemian chancellery, were started in Kaceřov and Nelahozeves. They are very individual and show some Mannerist motifs, especially in the design of the portals. Against these individual creations the group of Moravian and some Bohemian castles seems quite coherent. Typical of the group is a courtyard composed mostly of three storeys of arcades at one, two or three sides. Usually all three storeys of galleries are screened by arcades of similar character, with round arches supported by columns. But within the group there is a certain variety: in Opočno the upper storey has no arches but a straight entablature supported by columns and that storey is lower than the others; in Litomyšl and Kostelec nad Černými Lesy the ground storey has a sturdy character, being constructed in rusticated masonry modelling heavy pillars, which by contrast makes the upper arcades appear still lighter. In Litomyšl and in Jindřichův Hradec one of the arcaded walls is a curtain wall with windows and/or arcades which gives to the architecture an effect of transparent gracious refinement. All these castles were built for members of the Bohemian and Moravian nobility in the second half of the sixteenth century, before the autonomy of the Bohemian kingdom completely disappeared in 1620.

The castle in Kostelec nad Černými Lesy, built at first for the king and later for the Lords of Smiřice, was started as early as 1549. In the courtyard there are three storeys of arcades; their character has, however, been modified several times in later periods. One of the earliest castles was Moravský Krumlov, built between 1557 and 1562 by Leonardo Garda da Biseno for the Berka family of Duba and Lipé, with a fine arcaded courtyard and an open staircase in the form of another small courtyard. Between 1560 and 1567 the Gothic castle at Opočno was transformed into a charming Renaissance residence for the Trčka family. Three sides of the courtyard have arcades and the fourth is not closed; between short wings a wide space opens and broad stairs descend to the garden. The high roof has fanciful, irregularly placed chimneys. The upper storey with its straight entablature is lower, there are no arches, and columns are placed as far apart as the columns of the two lower storeys.

If in the above-named castles no valuable interiors have been preserved and the outside has no regular shape, this cannot be said of the castle in Bučovice. This was built between 1567 and 1582 by Pietro Gabri according to the design made by the imperial architect from the Como district, Pietro Forabosco, who was active in Vienna. There are several fine decorated rooms – among them the Emperor's Hall – with astrological divinities, and the regular lay-out of the whole is based on the traditional shape of a quadrangle with towers on the corners. The interior decoration was done a little later, and the towers were introduced only in the first half of the seventeenth century, so that the present appearance of the castle is not original. Furthermore, the fanciful fountain in the middle of the courtyard, by a sculptor of the Tacca circle, an excellent example of late Mannerist design, originated only in the 1630s.

The courtyard is, however, an excellent Renaissance composition. Noble arcades are composed of Ionic columns on the ground floor and of Corinthian ones on the two upper floors. Moreover, the spandrels, as well as the pedestals of the columns, are decorated with fine reliefs.

There are several other castles with similar qualities as far as sculptural decoration is concerned (reliefs on stone panels composing the balustrade at Náměst' nad Oslavou 1573–8), or architectural forms (the arcaded courtyard of Jindřichův Hradec castle with 3 storeys of arcades on one side, 1586–91, and the so-called 'Small arcade', 1590–1, on the other, both by Antonio Cometta).

V

When considering Litomyšl castle, one of the most accomplished and rich artistic achievements of the Bohemian Renaissance, we see evidence of specific stylistic trends, not merely adapting Italian models, but giving them, in this case, a Czech, in Polish castles a Polish, flavour. The castle at Litomyšl was erected by Giovanni Battista Aostalli (called Avostalis) with the collaboration of Oldřich (Ulrico) Aostalli and Hans Vlach (Italian – probably Giovanni de Statio from Massagno near Lugano) between 1568 and 1573 for an extremely rich magnate and high imperial civil servant, Vratislav of Pernštejn (for his good services awarded the Order of the Golden Fleece). In Litomyšl, as in the Polish castles at Baranów or Krasiczyn, Italian motifs are used, like arcaded courtyards and Mannerist, dramatically conceived portals, but, what is equally important, there are also specifically local features, such as sgraffiti, parapets and battlements – asymmetrical, somewhat fantastic and picturesque treatments of architectural elements.

The problem is whether what we describe in such terms is the result merely of a provincialisation of the Italian Renaissance, as occurs in Spain, France and Germany, or an original transformation of Italian ideas into a distinct

East-Central European style with its own theory and method, worthy to be considered an individual artistic style, or at least a trend within the general European Renaissance.

Also discussed by historians has been the question whether one is entitled to apply the term 'Mannerism' to those artistic phenomena which, to be sure, frequently depart from Classical models, but do not seem to be connected with any highly articulated theory of the Italian type.

Litomyšl has a courtyard with three arcaded sides, but the arcades are unlike the delicate and elegant examples in Bučovice. The ground floor has heavy rusticated pillars and the two upper floors relatively thick columns. The general character of the courtyard is determined by the lavish use of sgraffito with which the back wall of the courtyard is decorated, and the exterior by the application of picturesque gables and battlements.

The use of decorative parapets and battlements is not only popular in East-Central Europe; such architectural ornaments appear also in Germany (especially in the Weser area where a group of buildings was erected which art historians have termed the 'Weser Renaissance'), in Denmark, in Austria where they are sometimes described as 'Italian' (*welsche Giebel*), and indeed in northern Italy too (Scuola di San Marco in Venice), but they are everywhere far less numerous than in Central and Northern Europe. The popularity of parapets, battlements and gables in Silesia, Bohemia, Poland, Moravia and Upper Hungary is so great and their picturesque character so developed that they can be considered a very important element of the specific stylistic version of the Renaissance in that area. They adorn not only residences of nobles but even more frequently town halls, burgher houses, churches and military structures.

Czech art history uses the term 'Czech Renaissance', with which architecture and architectural decoration different from the classicising or Mannerist variant of the imported Renaissance are described. 'Czech Renaissance' is different from the works of Stella and Wohlmut, from the Belvedere Villa and from the Ball Court at the Hradshin, from the sophisticated castles in Kaceřov and Nelahozeves. Examples of this Czech Renaissance outside Litomyšl are very numerous: the picturesque, huge castle structures like the Lobkovic-Švarcenberk palace in the Hradshin, with its battlements, sgraffiti, a protruding cornice supported by lunettes and a rich decoration of gables; like the asymmetrical, gable-decorated Horšovský Tyń; like Jindřichův Hradec, a castle where there is an exciting combination of classical arcades, of picturesque battlements and of Italian Mannerist motifs in dramatically conceived portals, and where Antonio Cometta erected an architectural masterpiece, his round pavilion in the garden, full of current Italian motifs but of inspired originality and elegance.

In Poland there are numerous structures both secular and religious which are commonly classified as belonging to the so-called 'vernacular trend'.

Among these are, on one hand, the monumental castles in Baranów and Krasiczyn, on the other the picturesque town buildings, both secular such as the burgher houses in Kazimierz Dolny or the Chełmno town hall, and ecclesiastical like the Chapel of the Boim family at Lvov cathedral. In many respects they are close to the examples of the so-called Czech Renaissance. But there also exist differences between the two national variants of the trend.

In Poland sgraffito decoration never became popular as, in general, decoration of the outside wall was done in stucco or in relief and not in flat techniques of painting or sgraffito. In Bohemia and Moravia sgraffito work was extremely popular and determined the rather 'pictorial' type of picturesque effect. In Poland the elements which dominated were sculptural decorations of portals, windows and parapets, some of them quite elaborate, as in Kazimierz Dolny.

In Poland art was much more connected with religion than in Bohemia, which passed through the turmoil of religious conflicts from the early fifteenth century on. Attempts were made to transplant into Poland the Renaissance type of church. In Mazovia, churches in Brok, Pułtusk and Płock formed a small but significant group. It had no direct followers, but one cannot consider this transplantation as rejected. It was from such examples, at least in part, that about 1600 the Polish church type developed, in which Gothic volume acquired a picturesque gable of the vernacular trend, and the stucco decoration of vaults, inspired by rhythmically repeated medallions on the vaults of the Renaissance churches of Mazovia, added great variety, plastic richness and picturesque effect. There are countless variations of these in many churches throughout the country, from the Lublin region, where they are especially numerous, to West-Central Poland (Kalisz).

One can conclude that in the last decades of the sixteenth and first quarter of the following century, Poland, Bohemia, Moravia and, owing to the political situation of the country, Hungary (Sárospatak) to only a small extent, achieved a degree of adaptation of the Renaissance that may be said to have passed from the phase of borrowing to that of (at least relative) originality. At the same time an international artistic centre was created at the imperial court residing in Prague which constituted the last flowering of the Mannerist court culture. This was the artistic court of Rudolf II, which brought together numerous artists from many countries and turned Prague for a short time into an artistic capital of Late Mannerism, before the disaster of the White Mountain in 1620 put an end to artistic development in that area for many years.

VI

As in the time of Charles IV, Prague once more became the capital of the German empire during the reign of Rudolf II Habsburg (1576–1612) who, threatened by the Turks, did not rule from Vienna, but made his residence on the Hradshin Hill. And again, as in the Middle Ages, the artistic culture of his court was at the same time both imperial and Bohemian: it had an evident international character and did not involve Bohemian artists, but – as stressed recently by Jaromir Neumann – it obviously had a great importance for artistic life in Bohemia, because starting points were created from which in the second half of the seventeenth century, after the disasters of the Thirty Years' War, Baroque patronage could set off towards its splendid achievements in the early eighteenth century.

As an imperial art resulting from the specific interests and whims of the emperor, it was marked by the imprint of his melancholic and complicated personality. The lack of success of international political developments in keeping together an empire torn apart by religious quarrels led Rudolf II more and more towards the solitary life. He found an escape in artistic and scientific patronage of almost irrational dimensions, and concentrated both on supporting attempts at solving the mysteries of the physical world through astronomy, alchemy and anatomy, and on promoting the creation of an autonomous world of art, on which actual conflicts in religious and political life had no bearing.

Again, as at Corvinus's court in fifteenth-century Buda and Sigismund I's court in sixteenth-century Cracow, there were foreign artists who contributed to the splendid artistic flourishing in the Bohemian capital which lasted for more than thirty-five years, but this time they were not Italians. Rudolf II's patronage attracted excellent Netherlandish, Swiss and German painters, like Bartholomaeus Spranger, Hans von Aachen and Josef Heintz; Netherlandish landscape masters Roeland Savery and Pieter Stevens; sculptors and goldsmiths Adriaen de Vries and Paulus van Vianen; architectural painters Hans Vredeman de Vries and Paul de Vries; miniaturists like Joris Hoefnagel and engravers like Egidius Sadeler. The only Italian master was the arch-Mannerist Giuseppe Arcimboldo, famous for his pre-Surrealistic allegorical compositions, but many of the Flemish, Dutch and German artists had spent a long time in Italy and can be considered as representatives of an international Mannerism of Italian type. Spranger spent about ten years in Italy and Hans von Aachen more than fifteen.

In contrast to many court patronages, especially to those in East-Central Europe in preceding periods, that of Rudolf II was not for architecture or architectural decoration. The emperor's interests lay instead in collecting old and commissioning new works of art, particularly pictures. His taste and expectations were typical of Late Mannerism. Allegorical and mythological subjects with a strong stress on eroticism in both theme and sensual treatment present the dual character of Rudolfine art in which a symbolic and even mystical approach coexisted with naturalistic studies of landscape, plants and animals. Art was conceived as a way of capturing the meaning of reality, and there were two ways to be used – the ideal one, based on *concettismo*, hieroglyphics and emblematics, and the natural one leading to the most truthful portraiture of the world in its smallest aspects. The historicism, learned allusions, programmatic artificiality of Rudolfine art were qualities inherent in the Mannerist attitude. The elevated position of painting, which became the most important artistic activity at the court, was officially recognised when the emperor granted it the status of *ars liberalis* (1595). But naturalistic interests were something separate and pointed both to the Renaissance tradition (in the collecting of Dürer's and Bruegel's works) and to future development in Dutch Baroque realism.

This artistic culture, some of whose fruits are to be found in the Vienna and Prague picture galleries, approached its end when, after the emperor's abdication (1611) and death (1612), the court moved from Prague to Vienna and imperial patronage, separated now from Prague, ceased to feed artistic life in Bohemia. One had to wait until the period of High Baroque for a new, glorious chapter of artistic history in that region.

Hungary, ruled by the same Habsburg monarchs, now lacked its own court patronage, and in Poland court centres did not produce art of as high quality as in Prague because Polish kings never succeeded in bringing together important artists. Sigismund II Augustus (ruling from 1548 to 1572) and Sigismund III Vasa (ruling from 1587 to 1632) represented the Late Mannerist and Early Baroque type of patronage, but they concentrated to a much greater degree on commissions than on encouraging artists to come to court.

It was Sigismund II Augustus who succeeded in furnishing the Wawel castle in Cracow with the best-quality Flemish tapestries preserved in a great part to our own day, whereas Sigismund III Vasa bought Venetian pictures from Jacopo Palma the younger and Antonio Vasilacchi; unfortunately these works later perished in the fire at Cracow castle.

Important as these initiatives were, at that time it was not so much royal patronage as that of the nobility and the burghers which contributed to the formation of that picturesque mixture of Renaissance, Mannerism and Early Baroque which dominated the Polish artistic landscape before the High Baroque, coming from Italy (and sometimes from Holland and France) during the reign of John III Sobieski, changed the face of the country completely after the disastrous wars of the mid-seventeenth century.

12 ❧ Culture of the Baroque in Poland

JANUSZ TAZBIR

In no other period, beginning with the Middle Ages and ending with the twentieth century, has Poland created such original and different cultural forms as she did during the Baroque. The culture of the Renaissance came to the lands on the Vistula and the Dnieper belatedly; the same can be said about the Enlightenment. Only the Baroque emerged in the Commonwealth of Poland at practically the same time as in other European countries, that is at the turn of the sixteenth century. Everywhere it was marked by the weakening of superior, supranational ties which lay at the very heart of things during the preceding and following periods. In Poland it blossomed out in Sarmatism, the meaning of which term is still a matter of controversy. According to the majority of the Polish historians of culture, Sarmatism, a term derived from the Sarmatians, a tribe from which the Poles believed themselves to be descended, means a certain cultural formation amalgamating the political philosophy and the mentality of the gentry (particularly the middle-income stratum) and its life-style, its customs and likings expressed, among other things, in a community of artistic tastes.[1]

With regard to the relationship between Sarmatism and the Baroque, two opposing opinions have been propounded. The first has it that seventeenth-century Poland was the home of the Sarmatian Baroque in the same way as there existed a Spanish, Italian or English Baroque. Thus, it would be a specific branch of the Slavonic Baroque described by Angyal and Tapié.[2] Władysław Tomkiewicz, outstanding expert in seventeenth century art and history, said once: 'It should be borne in mind that despite its special features Sarmatism was an offshoot of the Baroque tree, whose roots fed it and whose branches spread over almost the whole of Europe for a century and a half.' The adherents of this theory point to the identity of artistic and Sarmatian tastes and to strong influences of the period on the gentry's life-style. This is more or less right considering that Sarmatism was the outcome of a symbiosis of the Polish gentry's political ideology with the Baroque tastes and the artistic culture moulded by them.

167

But it does not seem possible to identify the whole of the Polish gentry culture in the seventeenth century, that is Sarmatism, with the Baroque. For, on the one hand, we have a subculture limited to a certain social class, and on the other, an artistic and literary trend which penetrated to the majority of social groups and milieux. One cannot speak of the Sarmatian court of the Vasas, the dynasty which ruled in Poland for eighty years (1588–1668),[3] whereas we have countless examples of the influence of the Baroque culture there. Sarmatism only partly percolated to the cosmopolitan milieux of the great nobles who were strongly attached to Western culture; likewise, it was not very successful with the Lutherans in the towns of Royal Prussia. But the case of the dissenting gentry, Calvinist or Socinian, was different. In the Polish Commonwealth there was no separate Protestant moral culture as there was a Huguenot culture in France or a Puritan in England. The Socinians were expelled from Poland (in 1658) for their incompatibility with the Sarmatian ideology and faith (which was undoubtedly Catholic), not with the Sarmatian life-style which had its followers even among the Polish townsfolk.

The notion of the Baroque does not cover all the components of the Sarmatian culture. For what does it mean beyond the pale of literature and the arts (painting, sculpture, architecture)? The authors of writings about the socio-economic relations, the art of war, or the political ideas of the Polish gentry, can do very well without the term 'Baroque'. It would be difficult to speak about the Baroque doctrine of royal power, the relations between the lord and the serf, or the Baroque concepts of the gentry privileges. The influence of the times seems to have been felt only in the form (e.g., in a taste for rhetoric exaggeration and panegyrics) but never in the content of the political doctrine of Sarmatism.

In Western Europe the Baroque coincided with the blossoming of court culture and absolutism; Sarmatism with its followers in thousands of small manor houses professed the principle of the 'Golden Freedom'. This freedom meant the respect of the rights of an individual member of the gentry and only of the gentry. It should be noted, however, that by the end of the eighteenth century, there were in Europe three to four nobles per hundred inhabitants, while in Poland the ratio was eight to ten. Only the Polish gentry enjoyed the counterpart of the English habeas corpus (here called *neminem captivabimus*) which ruled that a member of the gentry could be imprisoned only following a valid court judgement unless he had been caught red-handed committing the crime of manslaughter, arson, theft or rape. Despite far-reaching differentiation, the whole gentry had absolute equality in law, irrespective of property and position on the social ladder. The whole class had the right to vote and to be elected to the Chamber of Deputies without the consent of which taxes could not be imposed, gentlemen called to arms, wars declared, nor laws passed concerning that class. Besides those privileges, there was also a well-developed territorial autonomy and a class representation, and all regional differences were very much respected.[4] There was also a deeply ingrained conviction that the freedom of expressing, in word and writing, one's own political, social and religious ideas was unlimited, theoretically at least. As a matter of fact, opinions on this subject differed.

William Bruce, who visited Poland at the close of the sixteenth century, wrote, visibly shocked, that 'any gentleman may speake without daunger, whatsoever he thinketh, which may cause greate stirrs, seditions, troubles, yealousyes etc.'.[5] On the other hand, the Golden Freedom, that is the Polish social system, had a considerable number of enthusiasts among the Hungarian and Silesian gentry, as well as among Russian boyars. Also many of the gentlemen in Ducal Prussia still insisted in the second half of the seventeenth century that they wanted to return to the rule of the Polish kings. The attractiveness of the system proved more important than differences in language, religion, culture or customs. The Prussian gentry, caught in the wheels of a modern administration which was building a strong state at the expense of the purses and privileges of its citizens, looked with envy across the frontier to their neighbours, where every squire was master in his own manor and a potential candidate for the throne.

Yet the Polish gentry seemed not to notice that the political system of the Commonwealth had ardent admirers in the neighbouring countries such as Bohemia, Muscovy or Hungary. Although the most famous sixteenth-century political writer, Stanisław Orzechowski, wrote that Pomerania, Mazovia, Ruthenia and, particularly, Lithuania, had united with Poland (he meant, primarily, the Lublin Union Act of 1569) because they wanted to share the same freedom, yet he had in mind only the component parts of the Commonwealth. It was generally estimated that the political structure of a state should be adapted 'to the nature of the peoples and nations'. And this was the reason why the Polish gentry, while deeming its own system perfect, did not try to impose it on its neighbours, convinced that the Golden Freedom was compatible only with the Polish national character.

Nor did the writings praising this freedom reach outside the boundaries of Poland: curiously enough, no work explaining the theoretical foundations of her system has ever gained major popularity in the West. There has been one exception: the essay by Wawrzyniec Góslicki, journalist and politician, entitled *De Optimo Senatore* (1568). Twice published in English, it became extremely popular in England; among Góslicki's readers was William Shakespeare. Góslicki, who pointed to the responsibility of the throne to the people (i.e., the gentry) and considered that power was vested in the Senate, has in a certain measure influenced English political thinking.[6] But it would be an exaggeration to maintain, as some scholars have endeavoured to do, that his role relative to the writers of the English revolution was the same as that of Jean-Jacques Rousseau relative to the writers of the French Revolution. Such suppositions are too far-fetched: yet it is worth noting that even conservative gentry opinion saw in the struggle for the independence of the United States a rebellion of free citizens against a despotic monarch who dared to infringe the privileges once granted them. It was thus an exotic, overseas version of a rebellion of the gentry against the king, well known in the history of Poland. The language of Sarmatian republicanism was particularly suited to rendering all the terms used by the leaders of the French revolution. As early as the seventeenth century, the vocabulary of the Chamber of Deputies included such notions as liberty, equality or republic, although they were applied to one estate only.

Each new event in Europe was greeted by the gentry either with fears that it might adversely affect Polish freedom, or with satisfaction that such excesses as the Massacre of St Bartholomew would not be possible in Poland, a land of free people. Suffice it to recall that one of the causes of the hatred felt for the Habsburgs by practically the whole gentry was their absolute role in Bohemia and Hungary. Jacob Sobieski (father of the future king), who travelled in France early in the seventeenth century, was horrified by the Bastille where, he wrote, the Bourbons can lock up anybody and let him rot. So the Polish Catholics condemned the Spanish and Italian inquisition, considering its judicial procedure an infringement of gentry privileges since people were imprisoned and sentenced to death following an anonymous denunciation. A pamphlet in praise of Thomas More emphasised that he defended not only the Catholic faith and the Pope but also the rights of his country and class freedoms against a tyrannical monarch.[7] It has been rightly remarked that Jan Kochanowski, an outstanding poet of the Polish Renaissance, began the dedication of one of his works (*Satires*, 1563) with words which no French poet would have penned: 'My lord (this is the grandest title among free people)'. For, though Molière and Racine were men of genius, it is worthwhile to 'compare their dedications in order to realise that as men they were not really free'.[8]

The Polish seventeenth-century gentleman saw himself primarily as a free man, and, with regard to the rest of Europe, a creditor, not a debtor. He based his attitude on three dogmatic assertions, the first of which was his conviction about the perfection of the Commonwealth's political system. The second was his assumption that Polish corn was indispensable to feed the rest of Europe; and the third, the belief that Poland was the bulwark of Christianity. This last assertion had two meanings, one temporal – we protect the safety of the continent at its south-eastern frontiers – and the other metaphysical. The fact that the Commonwealth of the gentry was surrounded by enemies of the Catholic faith was thought to stem from the will of the divine Strategist who had allotted it precisely this place on the map of the world. Hence, despite the constant fighting with neighbours during the seventeenth century, nobody ever thought of complaining about an unfavourable geographical position.

As early as the sixteenth century, the Polish intellectual elite realised its affiliation to the European cultural community, though such a notion was not, of course, in use at the time. It was determined by the influx of students to the most renowned universities (at first, only Italian, later also German, Swiss, Dutch and French), the use of Latin in learned writings, official documents or correspondence, the exchange of fictional plots and proverbs. The cultural map of Europe was not identical with the geographical one, for the Poles felt that their country was not lying at the confines of the continent but in its very centre, somewhere on the coast of the Mediterranean. Like France, Spain or Italy, Poland belonged to the same cultural circle: Western or Latin. This was linked with the belief in a common historical past in which the biblical stories constituted a kind of prehistory, and the wars waged by the ancient heroes filled all the European writers with pride. The enlightened Poles were also proud of living in a part of the world which took precedence over all others. When they wrote about Europe, they explained the achievements of its inhabitants not only by the natural resources or the climate of the continent. All the comparisons of Europe with Asia or Africa, made by Polish and other writers, extolled the gifts and industriousness of the Europeans thanks to which they had been able to outdistance the inhabitants of the rest of the world.

Both sixteenth-century poetry (Mikołaj Rej, Jan Kochanowski) and the political writings of that time (Andrzej Frycz Modrzewski) provide examples of the intellectual elite's consciousness of the Polish contribution to European culture. It was convinced that not only was its country a part of Europe but also that, as J. Pelc has recently put it, Poland had 'features of her own and a separateness which should not be shyly concealed'. In the seventeenth century the Polish cultural separation from the rest of the continent was consolidated and strengthened by Sarmatism. The Western part of Europe ceased to impress Polish travellers. The gentleman-knight, who was the defender of entire Christianity, felt superior with regard to the English and Dutch 'shopkeepers' (as some wrote). The elector of rulers, holder – thanks to the Golden Freedom – of full political rights, looked down upon the subjects of an absolute monarch; the exporter of huge quantities of grain never doubted that his corn 'fed and maintained a large part of Europe'.[9] Lastly, the civil and religious wars in France, Germany or England aroused his satisfaction that the final victory of the Catholic Church over the Reformation, and of the gentry democracy over absolutism had been won in Poland at a cost far lower than elsewhere. The power status of the Commonwealth which lasted until the mid-seventeenth century, was often opposed to the states of Western Europe plunged in terrible and cruel internal disputes.

An enlightened Pole thought that Europe ought to be grateful to his country for her role of shield and granary for the whole continent. But only the factor of the political and religious conflict was perceived in the wars with the might of Turkey or Muscovy, never the protection of European civilisation. A gentleman felt he was a knight defending Christianity, not Western culture; the term Europe was often replaced by the notion of Christian community which included, besides Catholics, also the followers of the Reformation.[10] Here it is worth noting that the term *Respública Christiana* survived the longest in countries bordering on the Muslim world, that is, besides Poland, in Spain, Austria and Hungary. At certain times they all called themselves the bulwark of Christianity.

In the seventeenth and even in the eighteenth century, none of the Polish writers ever dreamed of praising the contribution of their fellow countrymen to the development of human culture. This seems understandable: the military successes or defeats are plain to see, whereas the achievements of culture are visible only from the perspective of the following centuries. What we are boasting of now was at the time thought 'heretical' (the Socinian ideology), utopian or too radical (the conceptions contained in *De Republica Emendanda* by Andrzej Frycz Modrzewski), or else incompatible with the teachings of the Church (Nicolaus Copernicus's theory). In the seventeenth century, none of these essential achievements of the Polish religious, socio-philosophical and scientific thought were fully appreciated.

Even belles-lettres were treated with condescension by the gentry in general; they saw in them more of an intellectual game or verbal playfulness than genuine artistic achievement. Only a few compared Kochanowski to Homer; the superiority of Kochanowski to Ronsard or Petrarch was claimed only by Mikołaj Kazimierz Sarbiewski, a Polish poet of the Baroque, famous in Europe, who wrote exclusively in Latin. Anyway, the question of a writer's nationality was not important, if he was known only by his Latin works. In Poland, the Dutchman Erasmus of Rotterdam, the Scotsman George Buchanan or the Spaniard Juan Luis Vives were considered European writers, few people remembering their native countries. Outside Poland the same treatment was applied to Stanislas Hosius, Marcin Kromer or Sarbiewski who was sometimes called the Christian (not Polish!) Horace.

Nor did anybody boast of Poles playing the role of cultural links between the East and the West. Only from foreign accounts do we learn that it was through Poles that Western fashions, literature or art penetrated into Moldavia, Wallachia, Muscovy or even into Persia (figurative painting). Everywhere, the Polish writers, artisans and artists were appreciated, and the fashions and customs observed in the Commonwealth copied. The Polish theatre was very popular at the court of Muscovy, where, in the latter part of the seventeenth century, the language played a role similar to French in the entourage of Marie-Louise de Gonzague, successively queen to two Vasa kings, Władysław IV and John Casimir. Polish cultural influences contributed to the development of Russian music, painting and graphic art, and also made their mark on poetry and drama.

Lately, Soviet scholars have noted that in Russia the Baroque had played the role of the Renaissance: it served to emancipate man's personality, to secularise literature and to develop belief in the human mind and science, in the urgency of progress and socio-economic reforms. According to those scholars, a considerable part of Renaissance ideology appeared in seventeenth-century Muscovy through the mediation of Poland. For it is at that time that Russian audiences and readers got to know Polish Renaissance drama, historiography (the chronicles of Marcin and Joachim Bielski) and poetry (the works of Jan Kochanowski, among others), while Polish portrait painting had to some degree influenced the Russian *parsuny* (as portraits of exalted personages were called). But the convergence of artistic tastes does not necessarily stem from foreign influences. The emergence of similar patterns of living, of literary works with a similar climate, or ideologically convergent political writings can sometimes be explained by the similarity of class privileges or political aspirations.

Thus, if in the seventeenth century a great many similarities can be detected between the culture of the Polish gentry and that of the Hungarian, Bohemian or even Croat nobles, the reasons should be sought elsewhere than just in their geographical proximity. Suffice it to recall that on the distant Iberian peninsula our country was considered a fairy-tale land, lying somewhere between seven mountains. In spite of that, the nobles in the former exhibited great similarity to the Polish gentry, both in ideology and in life-style. Similarities between the Hungarian and Polish gentry are even easier to explain. In this case the convergence of political attitudes (the struggle against absolutism) and the geographical situation conditioned the cultural similarities. The strong element of chivalry contained in Sarmatism could all the more appeal to the Hungarians as, like their Polish counterparts, they constantly waged wars with the Turks. And as the Poles claimed their descent from the Sarmatians, so the Hungarians looked for their ancestors among the Scythians and the Huns.

The military successes paved the way for Polish cultural influences in Slavonic countries under the Turkish rule. The Croat poet and playwright, Ivan Gundulič (1583–1638), wrote a poem entitled *Osman*, which described the battle between the Poles and the Turks at Chocim (1621), and dedicated it to Prince Władysław Vasa. It was no accident that the most intense penetration of the Sarmatian culture into Southern Europe occurred at the time of the victories of John III Sobieski, when hopes were high that he would liberate all Slavs from the rule of the Sublime Porte.

Both Poland and Hungary fell equally under the influence of Eastern material culture. 'Once, the Polish men's dress was different from the Hungarian', said the Hungarian Martin Csombor, who travelled in Poland in 1616, 'but today there are only a few differences for both delight in Turkish dress' (costumes for special occasions were multi-coloured and often ornamented with fur and with diamond buttons). This trend applied not only to clothes but also to arms, rugs and even hair style (heads were shaved clean except for a tuft of hair on top). The reason for this becomes quite clear after a look at the map. Poland's geo-political situation made her particularly vulnerable to oriental culture, which in the eastern territories of Europe constituted an almost native, not merely imported civilisation. Poland's territorial expansion, on the one hand, and the expansion of the Ottoman state on the other led to direct contacts with the world of Islam.

Many Poles had spent years in Turkish or Tartar captivity. A considerable number of fugitives from justice would go to the south-eastern confines of the Commonwealth, to Zaporozhe, where, living among the Cossacks, they would adopt oriental customs and habits. Finally, the trade route linking the Baltic and the North Sea with the Black Sea led through Poland. The south-eastern Polish voivodships (counties) were the gateway through which the influences of Asian culture and art flowed into Poland; the towns which lay on that route were Brody, Kamieniec Podolski and Lvov.

Orientalisation was not peculiar to Polish culture. It came much earlier to the Spaniards who for a long time had Arabs as their neighbours on the Iberian peninsula. After the expulsion of the latter, the Moors who stayed behind exercised their influence on customs, cooking, farming and warfare.[11] In the fifteenth to seventeenth century, the peoples living in the Balkans also underwent some orientalisation, and the Hungarians came under that spell almost at the same time as the Poles. Like the Spaniards, the Poles encountered representatives of Eastern culture also on their own territory: the Armenians, Karaites or the Tartars settled in Lithuania. The popularity of oriental influences grew as the centre of gravity of the huge Polish–Lithuanian state was shifted eastwards; the geographical location of most manor houses of the Polish gentry and Ruthenian or White Russian–Lithuanian landowners brought them into direct contact with oriental culture. In the seventeenth century the language used in those borderlands strongly affected the literary Polish language.

The type of education also underwent a change. The people educated at Western universities who spent their time in the Sejm or at the courts of the members of the ruling classes were followed by a generation often brought up in Jesuit colleges only, who supplemented their education on the battlefields or in Turkish or Tartar captivity. They saw more Turks and Tartars than their ancestors living in the sixteenth century had seen Frenchmen, Dutchmen, Italians or Englishmen! No wonder then that it was the battlefields that began to dictate fashions instead of foreign courts. Dress and military equipment were not only taken from the Turks; as early as the first half of the seventeenth century, Polish writers noted that the ample and trailing furs (lined with ermine or sable) were copied from the Russians, the military coats, as well as the short and very tight-fitting jackets, from the Tartars. Even native arms would be taken to local goldsmiths in order to be ornamented in the oriental style. In the early eighteenth century, special Janissary formations and Tartar regiments were set up in the Polish army, in which served many Muslims recruited earlier from Tartars settled in Poland and Lithuania, or from Turkish prisoners-of-war.

The gentry looked askance at the people who affected French dress, suspecting that a courtier or magnate thus attired might plan the introduction into Poland of absolute rule (*absolutum dominium*), whereas the wearing of Eastern clothing (and the richer the noble the more his dress recalled that of Turkish high officials) did not at all mean a political taste for the social and political institutions of the Sublime Porte. The gap between Turkey and Poland was too big for this to carry a threat that the Polish kings wished to imitate the sultan, whereas the fear of a Polish Bourbon or Habsburg seemed quite real, all the more so as members of those dynasties often solicited the Polish crown.

Turkish dress was imitated but not Turkish customs. Nor was there any fear that the Turkish or Russian language could drive out the Polish, as was possible with the French or German tongue. It seems that Sarmatism considered its culture superior to that of the East. Another factor favourable to the adoption of oriental tastes and fashions was that no negative aspects were attached to the notion of the East, so much so that the gentry willingly traced its origins to the ancient Sarmatians[12] who, having left their settlements between the Don and the lower Volga in the first centuries of our era, conquered the territories stretching from the Dnieper to the Vistula (turning the native population into slaves). In the eyes of the Polish gentry, Asian provenance was as good as the ancestral ties with the Romans boasted by the Lithuanian gentry.

Almost throughout Europe, the Baroque brought in its wake a taste for the exotic. Whereas in the West it was inspired primarily by the newly discovered cultures of America or the Far East, in Poland it was fuelled by the well-known civilisations of the Middle East. In France, England and the Netherlands the exotic was found mostly in decorative motifs, striking for their outlandishness; in Poland, the oriental influences combined with an orientalism which constituted an integral part of the daily life. Another difference was that in English, Dutch or French collections the exotic was represented also by objects coming from Turkey, the Crimea or even Poland, while here, because of the orientalisation of tastes and the country's geo-political position, the artistic products of those countries did not, at least in the sixteenth and seventeenth centuries, qualify as collectors' pieces.

Yet at the same time, Sarmatism, like the Baroque, sought separateness and delighted in the exotic. In Poland only images made of feathers, clothes or fans originating in countries discovered by far-ranging sailing expeditions were deemed exotic. These were the objects collected by Polish connoisseurs. Thus, King Sigismund III Vasa would buy pictures made of ostrich feathers in the West Indies, in the manufacture of which the local artists attained near-perfection. The collections of great Lithuanian nobles (the Radziwiłłs of Birze in Lithuania), started in the seventeenth century, contained large numbers of 'Indian' objects imported from the territories discovered in the sixteenth century. There were exotic drinking-vessels, pieces of clothing, pictures. Similar collections were also put together by well-to-do Gdańsk burghers.

The cultural syncretism of the Polish Baroque did not only consist in its orientalisation, for Sarmatism was made up of many elements, among which Western culture still played a considerable role. In the seventeenth century, Poles continued to participate (albeit on a smaller scale) in European cultural life, reading works written in Latin (later in French), following trends in architecture and painting, etc. Yet, the Eastern and Western influences on the Polish Baroque seldom merged. The Orient influenced decorative art, dress or arms, never ideology, while the West made its mark on Polish literature, architecture and, to a certain extent, science. Neither of these two cultural systems had any essential influence on the social and political system of the Commonwealth of the gentry. Although, for instance, it would be easy to detect oriental inspiration in its art of war, there was nothing like the Golden Freedom in the Turkish, French or Spanish monarchies.

The fascination with the arts of the Orient had its negative external effects in that the wearing of oriental hair style, dress or arms created the opinion in the West that Poland was an extremely exotic country whose inhabitants revelled in oriental luxury. When the French (Jean Le Laboureur, Françoise de Motteville or Charles Ogier) likened the clothes, harness and the banquets of the Polish gentry to 'the wealth and magnificence of the ancient Persians', their opinion communicated not only astonishment but also a negative judgement. For Asia and its inhabitants were associated not only with wealth but also with barbarism. If in the Middle Ages the powerful but little-known countries of the Far East were much admired, colonial conquests prompted the Europeans to think that not only their war techniques but also they themselves were superior to Indians, Japanese, Red Indians or Negroes. The slavery of the Blacks and the extermination of the Red Indians led to the conclusion of the natural inferiority of other continents and their inhabitants. Everything outside Europe should have been – according to the French, English or Dutch – either adapted or liquidated; everything which did not conform to the general standards of European civilisation deserved contempt and disregard.

The fact that the pageants, balls and processions of the time included, next to Red Indians, Arabs, Chinese, Persians or Turks, also Poles, and replaced 'wild Americans' by people dressed 'in the Sarmatian', Hungarian or Muscovite fashion,[13] indicates a decidedly negative opinion about the fashions and artistic tastes of the Polish gentry. Mme de Motteville wrote in her account of the entry of the Polish embassy to Paris in 1645 that it showed 'the former splendour which came to the Persians from the Medes', and Charles Ogier seeing the Polish palatines praying in their national dress was reminded of 'the adoration of the Eastern kings who with great pomp and long retinue of courtiers and camels…came to the Child Jesus'.[14]

As a type of culture which was to constitute a symbiosis of Asian and European influences, it came at decidedly the wrong time, either too soon or too late, because at that point Europe, starting its struggle for hegemony over the world, did not want such a symbiosis at all. In the sixteenth to seventeenth century the majority of West European countries found themselves at a turning point in history. The development of Western Europe, often at the expense of less-developed countries of the Eastern part of the continent, went forward by great leaps, while in Poland wars, the economic crisis and political anarchy were beginning to have their adverse effects. In this situation, the orientalisation of the Sarmatian culture was, on the one hand, the result of the deepening split of our continent into its Eastern and Western parts, and on the other it consolidated this very split by enhancing and petrifying the differences which separated Poland from France, England or Holland.

Sarmatism was probably one of the few attempts in the history of Europe at cultural mediation; this role is often played by peoples inhabiting cultural borderlands or living in diaspora (e.g., the Jews). This bridge proved effective only in one direction, West to East; for the few elements of the Orient's material culture which, thanks to Poland, penetrated to Holland or France (e.g., oriental sashes) went into various collections but did not permanently affect the daily life-style.

It is a paradox of history that the final triumph of the Counter-Reformation in the lands on the Vistula and the Dnieper coincided with a demand for rugs, arms and pottery made by the followers of Muhammed. 'The bulwark of Christianity' (as the Commonwealth of the gentry was often called in the seventeenth century) turned out to be a fortification conquered by the hostile world of Islam in one respect only: the influence of the material culture. Nowhere else (except, perhaps, in Spain) had the artistic tastes of Islam had such an impact as on 'the tastes of one of the most Catholic societies, that is the Polish gentry community of the second half of the seventeenth century and the first half of the eighteenth' (Mańkowski, 1959).

A similar historical paradox from the religious point of view seems to be the fact that the triumph of Counter-Reformation in Poland coincided with a cultural flourishing of various heretical centres, on the one hand, and with the decline in the intellectual level of Catholicism on the other. Up to the mid-seventeenth century, the commonwealth of the gentry was still an asylum for all those who were persecuted for their religion in other countries of our continent. A similar role was played at the time only, it seems, by the Netherlands, though – officially at least – it did not accept anti-Trinitarians (Socinians), who could count on tolerance only in Poland and Transylvania. True, in the seventeenth century the Hungarian Unitarians did not publish any outstanding theological writings so that the burden of defending that denomination had to be borne almost exclusively by the Socinians, also called Polish Brethren. The Unitarian church in Transylvania recruited its priests and teachers from the Polish Brethren, while the catechism of the Hungarian Unitarians was marked by the strong influence of the catechism of the Polish anti-trinitarians.

Socinian works published in Poland spread throughout the continent demands for religious tolerance and a rationalist approach to religious affairs. The works of theologians such as Samuel Przypkowski, Andrzej Wiszowaty or Jonasz Szlichtyng were discussed with vivid interest in English, French or Dutch intellectual circles. Moreover, it would not be an exaggeration to say that they had a certain impact on the development of the early Enlightenment in those countries.[15] Anyway, the very fact that there was freedom to exercise one's faith publicly and propagate one's denomination, an aim of the gentry's efforts, was bound to influence other fields of public life in the future. The fight for the freedom to celebrate services and convene synods prompted the later demands for freedom of assembly; the efforts to win unfettered publication of theological works prompted the demands for the freedom of printing; the demand for the free propagation of the 'genuine God's truth' brought the demand for freedom of speech.

The Polish 'asylum for heretics' made it possible for the Bohemian Brethren, who were being progressively expelled from their own country (after 1627), to set up schools which later served as models for both Protestant and Catholic schools in many countries of Europe. Leading educational centres existed in Leszno (college of the Bohemian Brethren), Raków (Socinian academy), in Toruń and Gdańsk (Lutheran colleges). Leszno owed a great deal to the prestige and experience of Jan Amos Komenský (Comenius) who had been rector of the school from 1635. In Raków, many foreign anti-trinitarians, mostly from Germany, used to lecture and, in turn, Toruń and Gdańsk professors (including Bartholomew Keckermann) lectured at Western universities.

In the seventeenth century, at a time when the cultural achievements of Polish Catholicism were declining, the various heretical centres were at their cultural peak. The Reformation shook the Church in Poland, compelling it to an extremely fruitful reaction, from the cultural point of view, which often resulted in outdistancing the adversary. But when these sects ceased to be a genuine threat to Catholicism and no new ones appeared, such as Jansenism, libertinism or religious scepticism (all of which were unknown in Poland), the Counter-Reformation lost its former intellectual drive. When the adversary had been silenced or simply expelled (as were the Socinians in 1658), preaching, theology and denominational polemics declined, for they had been used in the first place to fight 'heresies'.

The Polish Counter-Reformation adapted itself skilfully to local conditions, tradition and culture. It followed the blooming of native culture with the Polonisation of religious culture, the demands for a national church with a further nationalisation of Catholicism, which in the hundred years since the acceptance (1577) by the clergy of the resolutions of the Council of Trent had become more indigenous than during the following several generations. For example, it spoke of the people of Israel as mirroring in their institutions the Polish gentry republic, with its hetman, Diet, and so on.[16] Polish Catholicism rested, first and foremost, on emotion and imagination. In this it was not so very different from the Spanish or Italian brand which was almost as loud and colourful; the main difference lay in that its doctrinal content practically spent itself in the constant, noisy and ostentatious demonstration of feelings, whereas the Italianisation or Hispanisation of Catholicism did not kill profound theological reflections in either the Iberian or Apennine peninsula.

However, it should be noted that the Polish religious communities, particularly the Protestants, exhibited strong ecumenical features,[17] so often appealed to by Catholic theology in the time of Vatican II. In no other European country did religious life experience such early, numerous and persistent efforts towards reciprocal ideological tolerance as in Poland. As early as the sixteenth century, the Sandomierz Accord (1570) was concluded by Calvinists, Lutherans and Bohemian Brethren, and there was also canvassing for union of all the Christian denominations. Their representatives (with the exception, however, of the Orthodox Church and the Socinians) met at religious talks (*colloquium charitativum*) called by King Władysław IV Vasa in 1645 in Toruń.[18]

It can be seen from this article that Poland, the 'bulwark' of Christianity, became a melting pot in which the alloy of various civilisations brought new cultural values. This was favoured by the territorial community, the identity of class privileges and political ideals, and, lastly, the reference to the same national myth which assumed descent from Sarmatian ancestors. The culture which emerged as a result of the action of all these elements has been properly assessed only in recent years. Its genuine achievements first attracted the attention of foreigners. German scholars and French intellectuals (including André Malraux) admired the old-Polish portrait painting; its exhibition in the Warsaw National Museum (1977) was an artistic revelation. The latest studies carried out by art historians have revealed many valuable achievements of Sarmatian art in painting and sculpture as well as in architecture, wood carving, goldsmithery, embroidery and cabinet-making. These discoveries prompted one student, T. Chrzanowski, to reflect: 'The aspects of our art which were inferior to the art of Italy, France or Germany were perceived but not the aspects which made it different.'

It was a foreign scholar, Claude Backvis, who first pointed to the independent values of Polish political culture of the sixteenth and seventeenth centuries, one of the 'most valuable and permanent aspects of which is the loftiness, subtlety and effectiveness of the political thinking engendered by it'.[19] Should we analyse the frequency of various notions in the political writings of the gentry in the sixteenth to eighteenth century, we would probably find that the most frequent was the word 'freedom', the rarest 'fear'. The latter is mostly to be found in the context which says that a king who breaks the assumed obligations (called *pacta conventa*) should fear the gentry; on the other hand, the gentry was extremely rarely threatened with royal reprisals. 'Education by fear' was a system unknown to the Polish gentry. This applied both to the political system and to religion, for the preachers, too, presented God not as an absolute ruler but as a kindly monarch whose rule was limited by His own goodness and man's free will. No wonder then that Backvis saw the fundamental feature of the old-Polish political culture as putting civil liberties above the ruler's rights.

If the Polish culture of the Baroque has, in the past twenty-five years, been judged differently from earlier assessments, this has been due to two essential factors. First, the decline of the Eurocentric assessment of world culture has led to justice being rendered to the original achievements of the Sarmatian culture which combined native traditions with Asian influences, which were earlier viewed with contempt. Secondly, in the ideology of freedom of the seventeenth century, Polish historians of the gentry have perceived the condemnation of all manner of despotism, an aspect most topical in the twentieth century which is filled to a considerable extent with struggles against different varieties of totalitarianism.

Notes

Introduction: A note on the historiography of East-Central Europe

1 Examples of this usage are the journal *East Central Europe* (founded in 1974 and published in Pittsburgh), and I. Berend and G. Ránki, *Economic Development in East Central Europe in the Nineteenth and Twentieth Centuries* (New York and London, 1974).

2 P. F. Sugar and D. W. Treadgold (eds.), *A History of East Central Europe* (Seattle, 1974).

3 *La Renaissance et la Réforme en Pologne et en Hongrie* (Budapest, 1961).

4 There is a study of him in French, J. Oberuc, *Matthieu Bel* (Strasbourg, 1936).

5 J. Lelewel, *Histoire de Pologne* (2 vols., Paris and Lille, 1848), pp. 97f. 161f, 183f. On him, M. Serejski, *Joachim Lelewel, sa vie et son oeuvre* (Warsaw, 1961); J. S. Skurnowicz, *Joachim Lelewel and the Polish National Idea* (New York, 1981). On his contribution to economic history, J. Topolski, 'Le développement des recherches d'histoire économique en Pologne', *SHO* 1, 1966.

6 F. Palacký published the first part of his major work in German in 1836 as *Geschichte von Böhmen*, and continued it in Czech as *Dějiny českeho národu* (1848). On him, R. G. Plaschka, *Von Palacký bis Pekař* (Graz and Cologne, 1955).

7 Plaschka.

8 M. Horváth. *Az ipar és kereskedelem története Magyarországban* (Budapest, 1840).

9 *Polska xvi wieku*, ed. A. Jabłonowski and A. S. Pawiński, 4 vols. (Warsaw 1883–6).

10 *Magyar Gazdaságtörténelmi Szemle*, 1894–1906. On this group, see S. B. Vardy, *Modern Hungarian Historiography* (New York, 1976), pp. 40f, 171f.

11 I. Acsády, *A magyar nemesség* (Budapest, 1890); idem., *A magyar jobbágyság története* (Budapest, 1906).

12 I. Baranowski, *Wieś i folwark* (Warsaw, 1914).

13 J. Rutkowski, *Le régime agraire en Pologne au 18e siècle* (Paris, 1927).

14 Klíma's work is assessed by R. L. Rudolph and F. Hahn in a special issue of *East Central Europe*, 9, 1982.

15 On Dománovszky and Mályusz, Vardy, pp. 41f, 166f.

16 Kula (1962). Reviewed by J. Topolski in *Ekonomista*, 1964, pp. 137–44; by A. Mączak in *Kwartalnik Historyczny*, 70, 1963, pp. 675–90; and by Z. Bauman in *Studia Socjologiczne*, 1963, pp. 219–28.

181

1. Feudalism and capitalism

1 Cf. Bergier (1963), p. 432; Małowist (1966), p. 15; Pach (1968a), p. 287; Pach (1970a); Topolski (1968), p. 3; Petráň (1973); Russell (1972), p. 15. See also Pirenne (1951), p. 415; Lütge (1963), pp. 333f; Cipolla *et al.* (1963–4), pp. 519f; Pitz (1965), pp. 347f; Kosminsky (1957), p. 569; van der Wee (1969), p. 233; Posthumus (1908), p. 45; Power (1941), pp. 33f; Hatcher (1969), pp. 208f; Pitz (1966), p. 200; Mollat *et al.* (1965), p. 902.

2 Małowist (1957).

3 Fügedi (1956); Janáček (1962); Janáček (1973), p. 245; Krekič (1961); Nef (1941); Probst (1966); Ratkoš (1971), p. 584; Pickl (1971b), p. 320.

4 Abel (1935); Russell (1958); Beloch (1900), p. 420; Bellettini (1973), p. 497; Barkan (1957); Faber *et al.* (1965), p. 97; Blaschke (1967); Utterström (1954), p. 103.

5 Unpublished research by H. Samsonowicz.

6 Bog (1971); Attman (1973); see also note 1.

7 Mols (1954–6).

8 Wallerstein (1974) pp. 301f.

9 Samsonowicz (1979), p. 191.

10 Małowist (1957); Pach (1964), p. 1.

11 Posthumus (1908), p. 45; Power (1941), pp. 33f; Hatcher (1969) pp. 208f; Pitz (1966), p. 200.

12 Mollat *et al.* (1955), p. 902.

13 Stromer (1970), p. 641.

14 Rokkan (1969); Rokkan (1975), pp. 562–600; Wallerstein (1974).

15 For surveys of Polish agriculture, see Żytkowicz (1972) and Mączak (1972); for a theoretical model, Kula (1962).

16 This hypothesis has been presented in greater detail in Mączak (1968) and Mączak (1976), pp. 98–101.

17 For Livonia, Niitema (1952), pp. 138f, 153f; Soom (1961), chaps. 3 and 4.

18 Moryson (1617), 4, p. 70.

19 See *Produzione, commercio* (1976), esp. papers by Janáček, Mączak and Samsonowicz.

20 These phenomena were discovered by J. Rutkowski in 1928. See Mączak (1974a), pp. 322–6, 340f.

21 See *Produzione, commercio* (1976), *passim*; Bog (1971), *passim*; Aubin and Kunze (1940).

22 In this respect the Vistula and (to some extent) the Dvina basin differed profoundly from that part of Eastern Europe which mainly supplied tallow, wax, furs, flax and hemp.

23 Mączak in *Produzione, commercio*, pp. 589–90.

24 Wallerstein (1980), p. 66.

25 Polišenský (1968); Hroch (1976).

26 The standard work in English is Kirchner (1954). See also Rasmussen (1973).

27 Anderson (1974), pp. 199f.

28 On the growing importance of the Baltic in European politics, see Roberts (1967) and Hroch (1976), chaps. 1 and 2.

29 There are numerous monographs on this question, in particular Wätjen (1909), and also a superb general survey by Braudel (1949), part 1, chap. 3, and part 2, chap. 3. M. Aymard, P. Jeannin and A. Manikowski are preparing an edition of reports by the Venetian envoy to Gdańsk, Marco Ottobono (1590–1).

30 Attman (1973), and Hroch (1976).

31 Romano (1978); on the year 1630, Hroch (1976), chap. 2.

32 Montesquieu, *L'esprit des lois*, book 20, chap. 23.
33 Faber (1966).
34 A. Manikowski has a book forthcoming on the Cracow merchant, Marcantonio Federici, and Polish silk imports from Italy in the late seventeenth century.

2. Economic landscapes: historical Hungary

1 Mákkai (1974b), with bibliography.
2 Górka (1916).
3 Browne (1673).
4 Pach (1964).
5 Belényesi (1957).
6 Szabó (1960).
7 Mákkai (1978a).
8 Mákkai and Zimányi (1978).
9 Kiss (1971–2); Prickler (1965).
10 Bökönyi (1961); Matolcsi (1970); Mákkai (1978b).
11 Szabó (1944).
12 Paulinyi (1965); Ratkoš (1971); Vlachovič (1971).
13 Szücs (1963).

3. Economic landscapes: Poland

1 Gieysztorowa (1958, 1968).
2 Wyrobisz (1973).
3 Małowist (1960); Mączak (1970).
4 Mączak (1970).
5 Mączak has a study of this subject forthcoming.
6 Mączak (1974b).
7 Bogucka (1977a).
8 Wyrobisz (1976).
9 Pazdur (1968).
10 According to the estimates (too low, perhaps) of Adam Miłobędzki, only 0.4 per cent of all buildings in Poland *c.* 1500 were of brick and stone. Cf. Wyrobisz (1976), p. 219.
11 On this subject, see particularly Małowist (1958, 1972).
12 Romano (1971).

4. The demographic landscape of East-Central Europe

1 Gürtler (1909).
2 Hollingsworth (1969), p. 111.
3 Gieysztorowa (1968).
4 Dávid (1977).
5 Fügedi (1969).
6 Fügedi (1969); Biraben (1975), pp. 71–85.
7 Szabó (1960).
8 Schultheiss and Tardy (1966).
9 Maur (1974).
10 Maur (1974), p. 40.
11 Maur (1974), p. 83.

12 Maur (1974), p. 82.
13 Gieysztorowa (1968), p. 11.
14 Wrigley (1973), p. 78.

5. Trends of agrarian economy in Poland, Bohemia and Hungary

 1 Topolski (1972), pp. 52f. The relevance of the term 're-feudalisation' to Poland can be called into question; after all, the feudal system in Poland was not shaken or even affected in this period.
 2 Tits-Dieuaide (1975), pp. 214–42, 257.
 3 Rusiński (1962, 1976).
 4 Rusiński (1974); Kula (1962).
 5 However, in another work on royal estates in the Sandomierz region, generally considered to be a fertile area, the same author accepted significantly lower yield ratios: 5.34 (1564), 4.83 (1569), and 4.23 (1615).
 6 We do not cite figures for Royal Prussia because of the different agrarian structure of that region, which was characterised by large peasant holdings, sometimes of 30 hectares or more.
 7 Długosz (1863), pp. 107, 198, 297–8, 415, 520–1, 579, 580, 597–8, 615.
 8 Percentages calculated by the author on the basis of Wyczański's research.
 9 Wyczański (1963).
10 Wyczański (1971a).
11 Faber (1966), pp. 118–23, 131.
12 This really concerns Moravia, and one cannot be sure that further research will not correct these estimates.
13 Calculations made by A. Míka on the basis of the registers of 20 estates in southern Bohemia at the end of the sixteenth century.
14 As a result of language difficulties, the author was only able to make use of works in Hungarian with the help of summaries in other languages.
15 Mákkai (1963); Pach (1960, 1966).
16 Mákkai (1963), pp. 29–31, 38.
17 Szabó (1966), pp. 18–19, 28, 35–7; Kirilly and Kiss (1968); Mákkai (1974b), pp. 203–5; Zimányi (1962), pp. 376–7.
18 Kiss (1978a), pp. 151–2.
19 Pach (1964), pp. 10, 30–1, 223–45. Pach's theory of a Hungarian 'deviation' has been opposed by the works of Małowist and by Sinkovics (1963), pp. 51–2. On the other hand, the attempt to perceive capitalist elements in Hungarian agriculture as early as the sixteenth century has now been abandoned.
20 Szabó (1966), pp. 1–10; Belényesi (1957), pp. 302–9.
21 Hoszowski (1961); Zimányi (1973), p. 310; Sinkovics (1963), p. 53; Pach (1964), p. 41. Similar privileges were also enjoyed by the nobility of Croatia.
22 Pach (1964), pp. 18–23, 82–3; Pach (1968b), pp. 1219–20, 1224; Mákkai (1971), p. 501; Kiss (1978a), pp. 153–5.
23 Maksay (1958), pp. 44–5, 50; Pach (1964), p. 25.
24 Werböczy (1656), article 30, paragraph 7; Maksay (1958), pp. 50–3, 58–61. A similar position was already taken by Szabó (1947), pp. 189–90.
25 Pach (1964), p. 79; Pach (1968b), p. 1226. For complaints about the unprofitability of hired labour, see Mákkai (1963), p. 40.
26 Maksay (1958), p. 46; Pach (1965), p. 225; Kirilly and Kiss (1968), pp. 1212–31; Mákkai (1963), p. 41.
27 Krajasich (1967), pp. 197–200.
28 Wiese (1966), p. 134.

6. Agricultural and livestock production: wine and oxen. The case of Hungary

1 In the sixteenth to seventeenth century, the Kingdom of Hungary was roughly 105–120,000 sq km in area, while the territories occupied by the Turks accounted for 95–110,000 sq km. We have no data for the south of the country, which suffered most from Turkish devastation (33,000 sq km). Only a part of the Croatian–Slavonic kingdom (19,000 sq km), which belonged to the Hungarian Crown, remained free from Turkish occupation. The Principality of Transylvania was 55,000 sq km.

2 Figures from a forthcoming study by the author, to be published in *Cahiers d'histoire*.

3 See the author's contribution to the forthcoming volume on *Prestations paysannes, dîmes, rente foncière et mouvement de la production agricole à l'époque préindustrielle*.

4 Figures for 1707 from the records of the conscription ordered by Prince Ferenc Rákóczi II. Figures for 1787 from Benda (1973).

5 Kiss (1978b).

6 Kirilly and Kiss (1968).

7 Ember (1971); Pickl (1973).

8 See the author's paper to the 7th International Congress of Economic History (Edinburgh, 1978), forthcoming.

9 Kiss (1978b).

10 See note 8 above.

11 Kiss (1978c).

12 See note 8 above.

13 Pickl (1973).

14 Riedl (1893); Klier (1965); and see note 8 above.

15 Prickler (1971). I should also like to thank Štefan Kazimir of Bratislava for allowing me to see his research on this topic.

16 See note 8 above.

17 Wiese and Bölts (1966); Wyczański (1971a).

18 See note 8 above.

19 Kiss (1978a).

20 Kiss (1970).

21 Kiss (1971).

22 Prickler (1971).

23 Prickler (1965, 1971).

24 Prickler (1965).

25 Kiss (1971–2).

26 See note 8 above.

27 Horse-, sheep-, and pig-breeding brought in much less than cattle-breeding, as we know from the Rákóczi conscription records.

28 Kiss (1974).

29 See note 8 above.

30 Kiss (1971).

31 Ember (1971).

32 For the price of oxen, Pribram *et al.* (1938) on Vienna; for the price of wine at Sopron, Sárospatak and Tarcal, see the studies by Prickler and Kiss already mentioned.

33 Considering the decrease in the market value of silver in the seventeenth century, this 2.66 million should be reduced to 1.7 million to give its purchasing power in 1580. See the author's forthcoming article in *JEEH*.

34 The assessment of goods for duty often differed considerably from their market price. In 1780, exports of cattle, grain, and wine were assessed at 4.8 million florins but their current market price was at least 7.46 million; Kiss (1978a).

35 In 1770 mining and industrial products accounted for only 6.2 per cent of exports, while agrarian products were over 90 per cent.

7. The towns of East-Central Europe

1 Mumford (1961), chap. 1; Sjöberg (1960), pp. 5f; Rausch (1963), pp. 9, 13f; Abrams and Wrigley (1978), pp. 215f.

2 According to H. Samsonowicz, 'Liczba i wielkość miast późnego średniowiecza Polski', *Kwartalnik Historyczny*, 86, 1979, part 4, p. 16.

3 Zemlička (1978).

4 Bonis (1974); Fügedi (1956); Granasztoi (1956); Györffy (1960); *History of Hungary* (1973), pp. 87, 103; Kubinyi (1977); Mályusz (1927); Szücs (1955, 1963).

5 *History of Hungary* (1973), p. 87; Mályusz (1953); Szabó (1960); Székely (1960, 1963).

6 *History of Hungary* (1973), p. 105.

7 Samsonowicz (1963), p. 92.

8 *ibid.*, p. 93.

9 Beloch (1961), pp. 339–85.

10 Bogucka (1976b), p. 131.

11 It is estimated that at this time the royal towns in Bohemia had about 200,000 inhabitants.

12 Szücs (1963), pp. 149–50.

13 There was decline in Košice, Bardějov, Prešov, and Levoča; Szücs (1963), pp. 149–51. Higher figures have recently been given for Košice.

14 In sixteenth-century Hungary, the proportion of the urban population involved in vine growing rose from 63 per cent to 80 per cent: Szücs (1963), p. 125.

15 Székely (1963), p. 83.

16 Cipolla (1976), p. 42; Mauersberger (1960); Mols (1954–6).

17 Bog (1971). Cf. Amber (1960); Hoszowski (1960); Mákkai (1963); Małowist (1959); Rusiński (1959).

18 Mákkai (1976); Mákkai and Zimányi (1978); Samsonowicz (1976).

19 Bogucka (1976b), pp. 140–1.

20 Szücs (1963), pp. 118f, 141f.

21 *ibid.*, pp. 100, 103.

22 It is worth emphasising the fact that in many of these industries, organised by the rich gentry, serf-labour was used. The establishments did not have a capitalist character.

23 Molenda (1976); Paulinyi (1971); Probst (1966); Vozar (1971).

24 Szücs (1963), pp. 148, 160.

25 Aubin (1942); Zimmermann (1885); Zimmerman (1956–8).

26 Ehrenberg (1896); Pölnitz (1960); Strieder (1935).

27 In a forthcoming study, the author estimates the annual profit from the exports of Baltic grain to Western Europe in the first half of the seventeenth century as the equivalent of 26–36,000 kg of pure silver.

28 Szücs (1963), pp. 111f.

29 Papritz (1957).

30 See the author's forthcoming history of Gdańsk, vol. 2.

31 Szücs (1963), pp. 110, 135.

32 Ehrenberg (1896).
33 Baetens (1976), vol. 2, pp. 82–3.
34 These rights included the organisation of fairs and the production and sale of beer as well as the cattle and grain trade.
35 Pach (1968b); *History of Hungary* (1973), p. 137.
36 Szücs (1963), pp. 128, 136, 137.
37 In the middle of the fifteenth century, Gdańsk became the owner of more than 70 villages, thanks to the privileges of King Casimir, and the figure was to be increased later by purchase. At the end of the fifteenth century the city of Prague owned about 100 villages, and more still at the beginning of the sixteenth century; all this property was confiscated in 1547. The property of Hungarian towns was more modest; at the end of the fifteenth century, for example, the city of Košice owned 24 villages (Szücs, 1963, p. 101). After attempts to take their rural property away from the towns, in 1608 the Hungarian Diet declared that only communities owning land and serfs should be regarded as towns. The point was to reduce the number of places with the rights of towns (Szücs, 1963, p. 154).
38 The Polish Diets of 1496 and 1536 forbade burghers to own land, but this rule was broken all the time: Bogucka (1976a).
39 Petry (1935), pp. 147f.
40 Szücs (1963), pp. 114–15, 118, 125, 135–7.
41 Mandrou (1969), pp. 12f.
42 In Warsaw, for example, all the old families disappear from the city in the second half of the seventeenth century.
43 Bogucka (1976a); Szücs (1963), pp. 158f; see also McCagg (1972).
44 Bogucka (1976b), p. 135.
45 *ibid.*, pp. 135–6.
46 *ibid.*, pp. 136–8.
47 Szücs (1963), p. 156.
48 *ibid.*, pp. 157–8.
49 Bonis (1974), pp. 79–92.
50 Szücs (1963), p. 158.
51 Lousse (1937).
52 Bogucka (1976a, 1980).

8. Comments on the circulation of capital in East-Central Europe

1 Małowist (1974).
2 *ibid.*
3 Bastian (1944), pp. 86, 179, 430, 632–40, etc.
4 *ibid.*
5 Nef (1941), pp. 5–6.
6 Probst (1966), pp. 23, 29.
7 *ibid.*, pp. 23–6.
8 *ibid.*, pp. 23, 28.
9 *ibid.*, p. 28.
10 *ibid.*, p. 35.
11 *ibid.*, pp. 4–5.
12 Stromer (1970), pp. 19–20, 91, 93, 99f, 104.
13 *ibid.*, pp. 113–15.
14 Fügedi (1956).
15 Probst (1966), pp. 60–2.

16 Stromer (1970), pp. 94, 131; Ammann (1970), pp. 43, 148–50.
17 Probst (1966), pp. 63–4.
18 Cf. Strieder (1935), Ehrenberg (1896), Pölnitz (1960), Nef (1941), etc.
19 Vlachovič (1971); cf. note 18.
20 Vlachovič (1971).
21 Molenda (1976).
22 The Polish gentry enjoyed the privilege of purchasing a certain amount of royal salt at a lower price.

9. A model of East-Central European continental commerce

1 This region is not distinguished by Glamann (1976), but it is a subject of special study by Pach (1970b).
2 Panova (1975).
3 The author has published a study of this topic in Polish.
4 Some of the furs came from White Russia and Lithuania.
5 Pach (1970b), p. 235.
6 *ibid.*, p. 242.
7 *ibid.*, pp. 248–9.
8 Goldenberg (1976), p. 197.
9 Pach (1970b), p. 234.
10 Samsonowicz (1970).
11 *ibid.*, p. 322.
12 Attman (1973), p. 172.
13 *ibid.*, p. 162.
14 Glamann (1976).
15 Pach (1970b), pp. 256–7.
16 Glamann (1976).
17 Goldenberg (1976), pp. 199–200.
18 Wiese and Bölts (1966); Mákkai (1971).
19 Pach (1970b), p. 252.
20 Goldenberg (1976), p. 191.
21 Wiese and Bölts (1966), p. 94.

11. Borrowing and originality in the East-Central European Renaissance

1 For a full bibliography, see Białostocki (1976) and the additions and corrections in Kaufmann (1978). Important recent publications include Balogh (1975) and Kozakiewicz (1976), on Hungary and Poland respectively. On the court of Rudolf II, see Evans (1973).
2 Zolnay and Szakál (1976).
3 Mossakowski (1975).
4 Kauffmann (1970).

12. Culture of the Baroque in Poland

1 Ulewicz (1960); Cynarski (1968); Tazbir (1968), pp. 262–6.
2 Angyal (1961); Tapié (1961), pp. 121–3.
3 Bogucka (1977b).
4 Backvis (1957).
5 Bruce (1598), pp. 106–7.

6 Filipowicz (1932).
7 Tazbir (1976).
8 Lechoń (1967), p. 124.
9 This view was expressed by the well-known seventeenth-century political writer
  Łukasz Opaliński.
10 Tazbir (1977).
11 Arnoldsson (1960), pp. 19–20, 91–2.
12 Sulimirski (1964).
13 Held (1944), p. 259, note 114.
14 Ogier (1656), p. 172.
15 Ogonowski (1977).
16 Tazbir (1973a).
17 Jørgensen (1942).
18 Jobert (1974), pp. 375f, and Tazbir (1973b), pp. 87–9 and 189.
19 Backvis (1957), p. 355.

Bibliography

This bibliography contains all the works cited in the references to chapters 1–12, whether directly concerned with East-Central Europe or not.

APH   *Acta Poloniae Historiae*
AÉSC   *Annales: Économies, Sociétés, Civilisations*
EcHR   *Economic History Review*
JEEH   *Journal of European Economic History*
P&P   *Past and Present*
SHASH   *Studia Historica Academiae Scientiarum Hungariae*
SHO   *Studia Historiae Oeconomicae*
VSWG   *Vierteljahrschift des Sozial- und Wirtschaftsgeschichte*

Abel, W. (1935) *Agrarkrisen und Agrarkonjunktur*, Berlin. Trans. *Agricultural Fluctuations in Europe*, London 1980.
    (1973) 'Hausse und Krisis der europäischen Getreidemärkte', in *Mélanges F. Braudel*, Toulouse.
Abrams, P. and Wrigley, E. A. (eds., 1978) *Towns in Societies*, Cambridge.
Amber, G. (1960) 'Zur Geschichte der Aussenhandels Ungarns im 16.Jh.', *SHASH* 44.
Ammann, H. (1970) *Die wirtschaftliche Stellung der Reichstadt Nürnberg*, Nuremberg.
Anderson, P. (1974) *Lineages of the Absolutist State*, London.
Angyal, E. (1961) *Die slawische Barockwelt*, Leipzig.
Arnoldsson, S. (1960) *La leyenda negra*, Gothenburg.
Attman, A. (1973) *The Russian and Polish Markets in International Trade*, Gothenburg.
Aubin, G. and Kunze, A. (1940) *Leinenerzeugung im östliche Mitteldeutschland*, Stuttgart.
Aubin, H. (1942) 'Die Anfänge der grossen schlesischen Leinweberei und Handlung', *VSWG* 35.
Backvis, C. (1957) 'Les thèmes majeurs de la pensée politique polonaise au 16e siècle', *Annuaire Institut Philologie Histoire Orientale Slave* 14.
Baetens, R. (1976) *De nazomer van Antwerpen welvaart*, 2 vols., Brussels.
Balogh, J. (1975) *Die Anfänge der Renaissance in Ungarn*, Graz.
Barkan, C. (1957) 'Les données des registres de recensement dans l'empire ottoman', *Journal of Economic and Social History of the Orient* 1.
Bastian, F. (1944) *Das Runtingerbuch*, Regensburg.
Belényesi, M. (1957) 'Der Ackerbau und seine Produkte in Ungarn in 14.Jh.', *Acta Ethnographica* 6.
Bellettini, A. (1973) 'La popolazione italiana', *Storia d'Italia* 5, ed. R. Romano and C. Vivanti, Turin.

190

Beloch, G. (1900) 'Die Bevölkerung Europas im Mittelalter', *Zeitschrift für Sozial-wissenschaft* 16.

Beloch, K. J. (1961) *Bevölkerungsgeschichte Italiens*, 3, Berlin.

Benda, G. (1973) 'Production et exportation des céréales en Hongrie, 1770–1870', in Köpeczi and Balázs.

Berend, I. and Ránki, G. (1974) *Economic Development in East Central Europe in the Nineteenth and Twentieth Centuries*, New York and London.

Bergier, J. F. (1963) *Genève et l'économie européenne* , Paris.

Białostocki, J. (1976) *The Art of the Renaissance in Eastern Europe*, Oxford.

Biraben, J. N. (1975) *Les hommes et la peste*, Paris and The Hague.

Blaschke, K. H. (1967) *Bevölkerungsgeschichte von Sachsen*, Weimar.

Bog, I. (ed., 1971) *Der Aussenhandel Ostmitteleuropas 1450–1650*, Cologne and Vienna.

Bogucka, M. (1976a) 'L'attrait de la culture nobiliaire', *APH* 33.
    (1976b) 'Quelques problèmes de la socio-topographie des villes de Pologne', *APH* 34.
    (1977a) 'Le sel sur le marché de Gdańsk', *SHO* 11.
    (1977b) 'The Vasa Dynasty in Poland', *Kungliga Akademiens Årsbok*.
    (1980) 'Towns in Poland and the Reformation', *APH* 40.

Bökönyi, S. (1961) 'Die Haustiere in Ungarn im Mittelalter', in *Viehzucht und Hirtenleben in Ostmitteleuropa*, Budapest.

Bonis, G. (1974) 'Die ungarischen Städte am Ausgang des Mittelalters', in Rausch.

Braudel, F. (1949) *La Méditerranée et le monde méditerranéen à l'époque de Philippe II* . Second ed. 1966. English trans. 2 vols., London 1972–3.

Browne, E. (1673) *A Brief Account of Some Travels*, London.

Bruce, W. (1598: ed. C. H. Talbot, 1965) *Relation of the State of Polonia*, Rome.

Burke, P. (ed., 1972) *Economy and Society in Early Modern Europe*, London.

Cipolla, C. (ed., 1976) *Fontana Economic History of Europe* 2, London.

Cipolla, C. (*et al.*, 1963–4) 'Economic Depression of the Renaissance', *EcHR* 16.

Cynarski, S. (1968) 'The Shape of Sarmatian Ideology in Poland', *APH* 12.

Dávid, G. (1977) 'The Age of Unmarried Children in the Tahrir Defters', *Acta Orientalia* 31.

Długosz, J. (1863) *Liber Beneficiorum Diocesis Cracoviensis*, Cracow. *Domande e consumi*, Florence 1978.

Ehrenberg, R. (1896) *Das Zeitalter der Fugger*, Leipzig. Abridged English trans. by H. M. Lucas, *Capital and Finance in the Age of the Renaissance*, London 1928.

Ember, G. (1971) 'Ungarns Ausserhandel mit dem Westen um die Mitte des 16.Jhs.', in Bog.

Evans, R. J. W. (1973) *Rudolf II and his World*, Oxford.

Faber, J. A. (1966) 'The Decline of the Baltic Grain-Trade in the Second Half of the 17th Century', *Acta Historiae Neerlandicae* 1.

Faber, J. A. (*et al.*, 1965) 'Population Changes and Economic Development in the Netherlands', *Afdeling Agrarische Gschiedenis Bijdragen* 9.

Filipowicz, T. (1932) 'The Accomplished Senator', *Proceedings of the American Society for International Law*.

Fügedi, E. (1956) 'Kaschau, eine osteuropäische Handelstadt am Ende des 15.Jh.', *Studia Slavica* 2.
    (1969) 'Pour une analyse démographique de la Hongrie médiévale', *AÉSC* 24.

Gieysztorowa, I. (1958) 'Guerre et régression en Masovie aux 16ᵉ et 17ᵉ siècles', *AÉSC* 13.
    (1968) 'Research into the Demographic History of Poland', *APH* 18.

Glamann, K. (1976) 'European Trade 1500–1750', in Cipolla.

Goldenberg, S. (1976) 'Les échanges économiques entre les pays roumains et l'occident', *Fifth International Congress of Economic History*, vol. 6, Moscow.

Görka, O. (ed., 1916) *Anonymi Descriptio Europae Orientalis*, Cracow.

Granasztoi, P. (1956). 'Particularités de l'urbanisme hongrois', *Települestudomanyi Közlemenyek.*

Gürtler, A. (1909) *Die Volkserzählungen Maria Theresas und Josephs II*, Graz.

Györffy, G. (1960) 'Einwohnerzahl und Bevölkerungsgeschichte in Ungarn bis zum Anfang des 14.Jh.', *SHASH* 42.

Hatcher, J. (1969) 'A Diversified Economy: Later Medieval Cornwall', *EcHR* 22.

Held, J. S. (1944) 'Rembrandt's Polish Rider', *Art Bulletin* 26.

History of Hungary, Budapest 1973.

Hollingsworth, T. H. (1969) *Historical Demography*, London.

Hoszowski, S. (1960) 'The Polish Baltic Trade in the 15th–18th centuries', *Poland at the Eleventh International Congress of Historical Sciences*, Warsaw.

(1961) 'L'Europe centrale devant la révolution des prix', *AÉSC* 16. English trans. in Burke.

Hroch, M. (1976) *Handel und Politik im Ostseeraum während des Dreissig-Jährigen Krieges*, Prague.

Janáček, J. (1962) 'Der böhmische Aussenhandel in der Mitte des 15.Jhts.', *Historica* 4.

(1973) 'L'argent tchèque et la Méditerranée', in *Mélanges F. Braudel*, Toulouse.

Jobert, A. (1974) *De Luther à Mohila*, Paris.

Jørgensen, K. E. J. (1942) *Okumenische Bestrebungen unter den polnischen Protestanten*, Copenhagen.

Kauffmann, G. (1970) *Die Kunst des 16.Jhts.*, Berlin.

Kaufmann, T. D. (1978) Review of Białostocki (1976), *Art Bulletin* 58.

Kirchner, W. (1954). *The Rise of the Baltic Question*, Newark (Del.)

Kirilly, Z. (*et al.*, 1965) 'Production et productivité agricoles en Hongrie', *Études Historiques* 1.

Kirilly, Z. and Kiss, I. N. (1968) 'Production des céréales et exploitations paysannes en Hongrie', *AÉSC* 23.

Kirsten, E. (ed., 1956) *Raum und Bevölkerung in der Weltgeschichte*, Würzburg.

Kiss, I. N. (1970) 'Weineinkauf für die Wiener Hofhaushalt', *Bürgenländische Heimatblätter.*

(1971) 'Die Rolle der Magnaten-Gutswirtschaft im Grosshandel Ungarns im 17.Jh.', in Bog.

(1971–2) 'Monoculture de vigne et qualité des vins dans la Hongrie des 16e–18e siècles', *Proceedings of the Hungarian Agricultural Museum.*

(1974) *Bauernwirtschaft und Warenproduktion in Ungarn*, Cologne.

(1978a) 'Der Agrarcharakter der ungarischen Exports, vom 15. bis 18.Jh.', *Jahrbuch für Wirtschaftsgeschichte.*

(1978b) 'Fleischversorgung und Fleischkonsum in Ungarn des 16.–17.Jh.', in *Festschrift Kellenbenz.*

(1978c) 'Die Krise der Fleischversorgungs von Wien 1770–3', in *Beiträge zur Handelsgeschichte*, ed. P. W. Roth, Graz.

Klier, R. (1965) 'Der schlesische und polnische Transithandel durch Böhmen', *Mitteilungen des Vereins für Geschichte der Stadt Nürnberg.*

Klíma, A. (1957) 'Industrial Development in Bohemia, 1648–1781', *P&P* 11.

(1979) 'Agrarian Class Structure and Economic Development in Preindustrial Bohemia', *P&P* 85.

Köpeczi, B. and Balázs, E. H. (eds., 1973) *Paysannerie française, paysannerie hongroise*, Budapest.

Kosminsky, E. A. (1957) 'Peut-on considérer les 14e et 15e siècles comme l'époque de la décadence européenne?', in *Studi A. Sapori*, Milan.

Kozakiewicz, H. and S. (1976) *Renesans a Polsce*, Warsaw.

Krajasich, B. (1967) *Die Militargrenze in Kroatien*, Vienna.

Krekič, B. (1961) *Dubrovnik (Ragouse) et le Levant au moyen age*, Paris.

Kubinyi, A. (1977) 'Einige Fragen zur Entwicklung des Städtenetzes Ungarns im 14.–15.Jh.', in Stoob.

Kula, W. (1962) *Economic Theory of the Feudal System*, English trans., London 1975.

La lana come materia prima, Florence 1974.

Lechoń, J. (1967) *Dzienniki*, London.

Lousse, E. (1937) *La formation des ordres dans la société médiévale*, Louvain.

Lütge, F. (1963) 'Das 14/15.Jh. in der Sozial- und Wirtschaftsgeschichte', in his *Studien*, Stuttgart.

McCagg, W. O. (1972) 'Hungary's Feudalised Bourgeoisie', *JMH* 44.

Mączak, A. (1968) 'Export of Grain and the Problem of the Distribution of National Income', *APH* 18.

   (1970) 'The Balance of Polish Sea Trade with the West, 1565–1646', *Scandinavian EcHR* 18.

   (1972) 'Agricultural and Livestock Production in Poland', *JEEH* 1.

   (1974a) 'Preise, Löhne und Lebenshaltungskosten in Europa des 16.Jh.', in *Festschrift W. Abel*, Hanover.

   (1974b) 'Wool Production and the Wool Trade in East Central Europe', in *La lana*.

   (1976) 'Money and Society in Poland and Lithuania in the 16th and 17th Centuries', *JEEH* 5.

Mákkai, L. (1963) 'Die Hauptzüge der wirtschaftlich-sozialen Entwicklung Ungarns im 15.–17.Jh.', *SHASH* 53.

   (1971) 'Der ungarische Viehhandel 1550–1650', in Bog.

   (1974a) 'Östliches Erbe und westliche Leihe in den ungarischen Landwirtschaft der 10.–13.Jh.' *Agrartörtenéti Szemle*, supplement.

   (1974b) 'La structure et la productivité de l'économie agraire de Hongrie au milieu du 17e siècle', in *Mélanges M. Małowist*, Warsaw.

   (1976) 'Commerce et consommation des draps en Hongrie', in *Produzione, commercio e consumo*.

   (1978a) 'Prestations paysannes, dîme, rente foncière', in 7th International Congress of Economic History.

   (1978b) 'Der Weg der ungarischen Mastviehzucht vom Nomadismus zum Kapitalismus', in *Wirtschaftskräfte und Wirtschaftswege* 2.

Mákkai, L. and Zimányi, V. (1978) 'Structure de production, structure de consommation, niveau de vie. Hongrie aux 16e et 17e siècles', in *Domanda e Consumi*.

Maksay, F. (1958) 'Gutswirtschaft und Bauernlegen in Ungarn im 16.Jh.' *VSWG* 45.

   (1968) *Ungarns Landwirtschaft zur Zeit der Türkenkrieg*, Budapest.

Małowist, M. (1957) 'Uber die Frage des Handelspolitik des Adels in den Ostseeländern im 15.und 16.Jh.', *Hansische Geschichtsblätter* 75.

   (1958) 'Poland, Russia and Western Trade in the 15th and 16th Centuries', *P&P* 13.

   (1959) 'The Economic and Social Development of the Baltic Countries', *EcHR* 17.

   (1960) 'L'approvisionnement des ports de la Baltique en produits forestiers pour les constructions navales', in Mollat, *Le navire*.

   (1966) 'The Problem of the Inequality of Economic Development in the Later Middle Ages', *EcHR* 19.

   (1972) *Croissance et régression en Europe*, Paris.

   (1974) 'Problems of the Growth of the National Economy of Central-Eastern Europe in the Late Middle Ages', *JEEH* 3.

194   *Bibliography*

Mályusz, E. (1927) 'Geschichte des Bürgertums in Ungarn', *VSWG*.
    (1953) *Le développement des bourgades*, Budapest.
Mandrou, R. (1969) *Les Fugger, propriétaires fonciers en Souabe*, Paris.
Mańkowski, T. (1959) *Orient w Polskiej Kulturze Artystycznej*, Wrocław and Kraków.
Matolcsi, J. (1970) 'Historische Erforschung der Körpergrösse des Rindes', *Zeitschrift für Tierzüchtung*.
Mauersberger, H. (1960) *Wirtschafts- und Sozialgeschichte zentraleuropäischer Städte*, Göttingen.
Maur, E. (1974) 'La structure démographique de la Bohème après la guerre de trente ans', *Historička Demografie* 6.
Molenda, D. (1976) 'Mining Towns in Central Eastern Europe', *APH* 34.
Mollat, M. (1960) *Le navire et l'économie maritime du nord de l'Europe du moyen age au XVIII siècle*, Paris.
Mollat, M. (*et al.*, 1955) 'L'économie européenne aux deux derniers siècles du Moyen-Age', in *Relazioni X Congresso Scienze Storiche*, Rome.
Mols, R. (1954–6) *Introduction à la démographie historique des villes d'Europe*, 3 vols, Louvain.
Moryson, F. (1617) *An Itinerary*. Reprint, Glasgow 1907–8.
Mossakowski, S. (1975) 'La non più esistente decorazione astrologica nel castello reale di Cracovia', in *Magia, astrologia e religione nel Rinascimento*, Wrocław.
Mumford, L. (1961) *The City in History*, London.
Nef, J. U. (1941) 'Silver Production in Central Europe 1450–1618', *Journal of Political Economy* 49.
Niitema, V. (1952) *Der Binnenhandel in der Politik der livländische Städte im Mittelalter*, Helsinki.
Ogier, C. (1656) *Ephemerides*, Paris; new ed. Gdańsk 1982.
Ogonowski, Z. (1977) 'Der Sozianismus und die Aufklärung', in *Reformation und Aufklärung in Polen*, Göttingen.
Pach, Z. P. (1960) 'Das Entwicklungsniveau der feudalen Agrarverhältnisse in Ungarn', *Études Historiques* 1.
    (1964) *Die ungarische Agrarentwicklung im 16.–17.Jh.*, Budapest.
    (1965) 'Über einige Probleme der Gutswirtschaft in Ungarn in der ersten Halfte des 17.Jh.', *Deuxième Conférence Internationale d'Histoire Économique*, 2, Paris.
    (1966) 'The Development of Feudal Rent in Hungary in the 15th Century', *EcHR* 19.
    (1968a) 'The Shifting of International Trade Routes', *Acta Historica Academiae Scientiarum Hungariae* 14.
    (1968b) 'En Hongrie au 16e siècle', *AÉSC* 23. English trans. in Burke.
    (1970a) 'Osteuropa und die Anfangsperiode der Entstehung des modernen internationalen Handels im 15.Jh', *International Congress of Economic History*, Moscow.
    (1970b) 'The role of East-Central Europe in International Trade', *Études Historiques*.
Panova, S. (1975) 'Zur Frage der Handelsbeziehungen zwischen den bulgarischen und den rumänischen Landen im 17.Jh.', *Études Balkaniques* 1.
Papritz, J. (1957) 'Das Handelshaus der Loitz zu Stettin', *Baltische Studien* 44.
Paulinyi, O. (1965) 'Die Edelmetallproduktion der niederungarischen Bergstädte', *Nouvelles Études Historiques*.
    (1971) 'Eigentum und Gesellschaft in den niederungarischen Bergstädten', in Bog.
Pazdur, J. (1968) 'Production du soufre en Pologne', *Kwartalnik Historiczny Kultury Materialnej*.
Petráň, (1973) 'Die Mitteleuropäische Landwirtschaft und Handel im 16.Jh.', *Historica*, 18.
Petry, L. (1935) *Die Popplau*, Wrocław.

Pickl, O. (1971a) 'Der Handel Wiens mit Böhmen und Ungarn in der ersten Hälfte des 16.Jhs', in Bog.

(ed. 1971b) *Die wirtschaftlichen Auswirkungen der Türkenkriege*, Graz.

(1973) 'Routen, Umfang und Organisation des innereuropäischen Handels mit Schlachtvieh', in *Festschrift H. Wiesflecker*, Graz.

Pirenne, H. (1951) 'Les nouvelles tendances économiques des 15e et 16e siècles', *Histoire Économique de l'Occident Médiéval*, Paris.

Pitz, E. (1965) 'Die Wirtschaftskriege des Spätmittelalter', *VSWG* 52.

(1966) 'Wirtschaftliche und soziale Probleme der gewerblichen Entwicklung im 15./16.Jh.', *Jahrbücher für Nationalökonomie und Statistik* 179.

Pölnitz, G. von. (1960) *Die Fugger*, Frankfurt.

Polišenský, J. (1968) 'The Thirty Years' War', *P&P* 39.

Posthumus, N. (1908) *De geschiedenis van de leidsche laken-industrie*, 1, The Hague.

Power, E. (1941) *The Wool Trade in English Medieval History*, Oxford.

Pribram, A. F. (*et al.*, 1938) *Materialien zur Geschichte der Preise und Löhne in Osterreich*, Vienna.

Prickler, H. (1965) 'Zur Geschichte des bürgenländisch-westungarischen Weinhandels', *Zeitschrift für Ostforschung*.

(1971) 'Das Volumen des westlichen-ungarischen Aussenhandels', in Pickl (1971b).

Probst, G. von (1966) *Die niederungarischen Bergstädte*, Munich.

Produzione, commercio e consumo dei panni di lana, Florence 1976.

Rasmussen, K. (1973) *Die livländische Krise 1554–61*, Copenhagen.

Ratkoš, R. (1971) 'Das Kupferwesen in der Slowakei', in Bog.

Rausch, W. ed. (1963) *Die Städte Mitteleuropas im 12. und 13.Jh.*, Linz.

(1974) *Die Stadt am Ausgang des Mittelalters*, Linz.

La Renaissance et la Réforme en Pologne et en Hongrie (1961) ed. I. Fügedi and G. Székely, Budapest.

Riedl, R. (1893) 'Der Wiener Schlachtviehhandel', *Jahrbuch für Gesetzgechichte*.

Roberts, M. (1967) 'Cromwell and the Baltic', in his *Essays in Swedish History*, London.

Rokkan, S. (1969) 'Models and Methods in the Comparative Study of Nation-Building', *Acta Sociologica* 12.

(1975) 'Dimensions of State Formation', in *The Formation of National States in Western Europe*, ed. C. Tilly, Princeton.

Romano, R. (1971) *Tra due crisi: l'Italia del Rinascimento*, Turin.

(1978) 'The Economic Crisis of 1619–22', trans. in G. Parker and L. Smith (eds.), *The General Crisis of the 17th Century*, London 1978.

Rusiński, W. (1959) 'The Role of Polish Territories in European Trade in the 16th–18th centuries', *SHO* 3.

(1962) 'Wüstungen', *APH* 5.

(1974) 'Über die Entwicklungstappen der Fronwirtschaft in Mittel- und Osteuropa', *SHO* 9.

(1976) 'Das Bauernlegen im Mitteleuropa', *SHO* 11.

Russell, J. C. (1958) *Late Ancient and Medieval Population*, Philadelphia.

(1972) *Medieval Regions and their Cities*, Newton Abbot.

Samsonowicz, H. (1963) 'Das polnische Bürgertum in der Renaissancezeit', in Székely and Fügedi.

(1970) 'Uber Fragen des Landeshandels Polens mit West-europa in 15./16.Jh.', *Neue Hansische Studien*.

(1976) 'Le commerce de drap aux foires de Pologne', in *Produzione, commercio e consumo*.

(1979) 'Soziale und wirtschaftliche Funktionen der Kleinstädte in Polen des 15.Jhs.', *Jahrbüch für Geschichte des Feudalismus*, 2.

Schremmer, E. (1972) 'Die südostdeutsche Hofmark – eine Wirtschafts-herrschaft?', *Zeitschrift für Agrargeschichte*.

Schultheiss, E. and Tardy, L. (1966), 'A Short History of Epidemics in Hungary', *Centaurus* 11.

Sinkovics, I. (1963) 'Le servage héréditaire en Hongrie', in Székely and Fügedi.

Sjöberg, G. (1960) *The Preindustrial City*, Glencoe.

Soom, A. (1961) *Der baltische Getreidehandel im 17.Jh.*, Stockholm.

Stoob, H. (1977, ed.) *Die Mittelalterliche Städtebildung im Südöstliche Europa*, Cologne.

Strieder, J. (1935) *Zur Genesis des modernen Kapitalismus*, Munich.

Stromer, W. von (1970) *Oberdeutsche Hochfinanz 1350–1450*, Wiesbaden.

Sulimirski, T. (1964) 'Sarmatians in the Polish Past', *Polish Review* 9.

Szabó, I. (1947) 'Les grands domaines en Hongrie au début des temps modernes', Revue d'Histoire Comparée 5.

   (1960) 'La répartition de la population de Hongrie', *SHASH* 49.

   (1966) 'Ungarns Landwirtschaft von der Mitte des 14.Jhs. bis zu den 1530-er Jahren', *Agrartörteneti Szemle*, Supplement.

Szabó, S. (1944) *Ungarisches Volk*, Budapest and Leipzig.

Székely, G. (1960) 'Landwirtschaft und Gewerbe in der ungarischen ländlichen Gesellschaft um 1500', *SHASH* 48.

   (1963) 'Le développement des bourgs hongrois', *Annales Universitatis Scientiarum Budapestensis, Sectio Historica*, 5.

Székely, G. and Fügedi, E. (eds., 1963) *La renaissance et la réforme en Hongrie et en Pologne*, Budapest.

Szücs, J. (1955) *Les villes et l'artisanat dans la Hongrie du 15ᵉ siècle*, Budapest.

   (1963) 'Das Städtewesen in Ungarn im 15.–17.Jh.', *SHASH* 53.

Tapié, V. L. (1961) *Le baroque*, Paris.

   (1969) *Monarchie et peuples du Danube*, Paris. English trans. as *The Rise and Fall of the Habsburg Monarchy*, London 1971.

Tazbir, J. (1968) 'The Sarmatian Baroque', in *History of Poland*, ed. A. Gieysztor, Warsaw.

   (1973a) 'La polonisation du Catholicisme après le concile de Trente', *Memorie Domenicane* 4.

   (1973b) *A State without Stakes*, Warsaw.

   (1976) 'Thomas More et la Pologne', *Moreana* 13.

   (1977) 'Poland and the Concept of Europe in the 16th–18th Centuries', *European Studies Review* 7.

Tits-Dieuaide, M. J. (1975) *La formation des prix céréalières en Brabant et en Flandre au 15ᵉ siècle*, Brussels.

Topolski, J. (1968) 'Causes of Dualism in the Economic Development of Modern Europe', *SHO* 3.

   (1972) 'La rééféodalisation dans l'économie des grands domaines en Europe centrale et orientale', *SHO* 6.

   (1974) 'Commerce des denrées agricoles et croissance économique de la zone baltique', *AÉSC* 29.

Ulewicz, T. (1960) 'Il problema del sarmatismo', *Ricerche Slavistiche* 8.

Utterström, G. (1954) 'Some Population Problems in Preindustrial Sweden', *Scandinavian EcHR* 2.

Valentinisch, H. (1973) 'Der ungarische und innerösterreichische Viehhandel nach Venedig', *Carinthia*.

Vlachovič, J. (1971) 'Produktion und Handel mit ungarischem Kupfer', in Bog.

Vogt, J. (1974) 'Die Zufuhr ungarischen und polnischer Ochsen nach Strassburg', in *Festschrift W. Abel*, Hanover.

Vozar, J. (1971) 'Die sozialen Folgen des Bergbaus für die Bevölkerung des mittel-slovakischen Bergreviers', in Bog.

Wätjen, H. (1909) *Die Niederländer im Mittelmeergebiet*, Berlin.

Wallerstein, I. (1974) *The Modern World-System*, 1, New York.

(1980) *The Modern World-System*, 2, New York.

Wee, H. van der (1969) 'Een dynamisch model voor de seculaire ontwikkeling van de wereldhandel en de welvaard (12–18 eeuw)', *Tijdschrift voor Geschiedenis*, 82.

Werböczy, I. (1656) *Opus tripartitum*, Trnava.

Westermann, E. (1975) 'Zur Erforschung des nordmitteleuropäischen Ochsenhandels', *Zeitschrift für Agrargeschichte*.

Wiese, H. (1966) 'Die Fleischversorgung der nordwesteuropäischen Grossstädte', *Jahrbücher für Nationalökonomie*, 179.

Wiese, H. and Bölts, J. (1966) *Rinderhandel und Rinderhaltung*, Stuttgart.

Wrigley, E. A. (1973) *Population and History*, London.

Wyczański, A. (1963) 'En Pologne: l'économie du domaine nobiliaire moyen, 1500 – 80', *AÉSC* 19.

(1971a) 'La base intérieure de l'exportation polonaise des céréales dans la seconde moitié du 16ᵉ siècle', in Bog.

(1971b) 'Le revenu national en Pologne au 16ᵉ siècle', *AÉSC* 21.

Wyrobisz, A. (1973) 'La crise du combustible dans l'industrie polonaise au tournant du 16ᵉ et 17ᵉ siècle', *SHO* 8.

(1976) 'Mining in Medieval and Modern Poland', *JEEH* 5.

Zemlička, J. (1978) 'Formation of the Town Network in Bohemia', *Hospodářské Dějiny* 2.

Zimányi, V. (1962) *Der Bauernstand des Herrschaft Gussing im 16. und 17. Jh.*, Eisenstadt.

(1973) 'Mouvement des prix hongrois, 16–18ᵉ siècles', *Acta Historica* 19.

Zimmermann, A. (1885) *Blüthe und Verfall des Leinengewerbes in Schlesien*, Oldenburg.

Zimmermann, E. (1956–8) 'Der schlesische Garn- und Leinenhandel mit Holland', *Economisch–Historisch Jaarboek*, 26–7.

Zolnay, L. and Szakál, E. (1976) *Der gotische Skulpturenfund in der Burg von Buda*, Budapest.

Żytkowicz, L. (1972) 'The Peasants' Farm and the Landlords' Farm in Poland from the 16th Century to the Middle of the 18th', *JEEH* 1.

Glossary

Alba Julia (Hungarian, *Gyulafehérvár*) – town in Transylvania

Banská Bystřica (Hungarian, *Besztercebánya*; German, *Neusohl*) – town in western Slovakia

Banská Štiavnica (Hungarian, *Selmecbánya*) – town in Slovakia

Bardějov (Hungarian, *Bártfa*) – town in Slovakia

Belorussia – area east of Poland and north of the Ukraine (White Russia)

Bethlen Gábor – seventeenth-century ruler of Transylvania (Bethlen is his surname)

Bohemia – the province of Bohemia (*Čechy*) in modern Czechoslovakia; should be distinguished from the Kingdom of Bohemia, which also included the provinces of Moravia, Silesia and Lusatia

Braşov (Hungarian, *Brassó*; German, *Kronstadt*) – town in Transylvania

Bratislava (Hungarian, *Pozsony*; German, *Pressburg*) – principal town in Slovakia

Breslau – see Wrocław

Brno (German, *Brünn*) – principal town in Moravia

Brzeg (German, *Brieg*) – town in Silesia

Cameralism ('*Kameralwissenschaft*') – a term used to describe the economic social and political thought of a group of German officials and academics in the seventeenth and eighteenth centuries

Carinthia (German, *Kärnten*) – mountain province of Austria, around Klagenfurt

Chmielnicki (or *Khmelnitsky*), *Bohdan* – leader of a Cossack revolt in the middle of the seventeenth century

Cluj (Hungarian, *Kolozsvár*; German, *Clausenburg*) – town in Transylvania

'*comitates*' – 'counties', administrative divisions of Hungary attributed to St Stephen, their eleventh-century king

Dalmatia – the Adriatic seaboard of modern Jugoslavia

Danzig – see Gdańsk

Diet – see Sejm

Dubrovnik (formerly *Ragusa*) – town in Dalmatia, which in medieval and early modern times was an independent city-state

Elbląg (German, *Elbing*) – town in Poland

Eperjes – see Prešov

Estates Monarchy ('*Ständestaat*') – a regime in which the monarch ruled with the advice of a representative assembly of the estates of the realm

Esztergom (German, *Gran*) – town in western Hungary

folwark – the Polish term for a manor

Gelnica (Hungarian, *Gölnicbánya*) – town in Slovakia

198

Greater Poland (' *Wielkopolska*') – region which centres on Poznań

Gyulafehérvár – see Alba Julia

hectare – 10,000 sq metres

hetman – commander in chief

Hungary – 'historic Hungary' is considerably larger than modern Hungary and corresponds to the kingdom which was divided into three after the Turkish victory at Mohács in 1526 (see Figure 2): Turkish Hungary, Royal Hungary, and Transylvania

Jáchymov (German, *Joachimstal*) – mining town in Czechoslovakia

Jagiello (Lithuanian, *Jogaila*), *c.* 1351–1434 – Lithuanian prince. He married a Polish princess and his descendants ruled both kingdoms

'*jobbagy*' – Hungarian term for serf

jutrzyna, jutrzyny – serf labour

Königsberg – town in East Prussia, now Kaliningrad in the USSR

Košice (Hungarian, *Kassa*; German, *Kassau*; Polish, *Koszyce*) – town in eastern Slovakia

Kremnica (Hungarian, *Körmöcbánya*; German, *Kremnitz*) – town in Slovakia

Kurland (*Courland*) – province in eastern Poland

Labiau – town near Königsberg

Ladislaus (Hungarian, *Lászlo*; Czech, *Vladislav*; Polish, *Władysław*), Leslie

last – about 2 metric tons

Levoča (Hungarian, *Löcsa*) – town in Slovakia

Lithuania – in early modern times a kingdom united with Poland, now a socialist soviet republic within the USSR

Little Poland (' *Małopolska*') – region which centres on Cracow

Livonia (German, *Livland*; Polish, *Inflanty*) – a region on the gulf of Riga, now the Estonian and Latvian socialist soviet republics within the USSR

Lusatia (German, *Lausitz*) – formerly part of the Kingdom of Bohemia, now part of East Germany

Lvov (Polish, *Lwów*; German, *Lemberg*) – principal town of Red Ruthenia

'*magnaty*' – 'magnates', contemporary Polish term for the Polish aristocracy

Malbork (German, *Marienburg*) – fortress of the Teutonic Knights in Prussia

mansus – *c.* 16.8 hectares

Mazovia (Polish, *Mazowsze*) – duchy centring on Warsaw

Mecklenburg – province on the Baltic coast; main towns Rostock and Wismar

Military Border – an area of defence against the Turks set up by the Habsburgs in Croatia and elsewhere

Moldavia – province now partly in northeast Romania and partly in the USSR, under Ottoman rule in the early modern period

Moravia – area around Brno, now in Czechoslovakia, part of the Kingdom of Bohemia in early modern times

Nagyszeben – see Sibiu

Nagyszombat – see Trnava

Nagyvarad – see Oradea

Neusohl – see Banská Bystřica

Oder (Polish, *Odra*) – river running through Wrocław, Frankfurt and Szczecin

Olomouc (German, *Olmütz*) – town in Moravia

Oradea (Hungarian, *Nagyvarad*) – town in Transylvania

Palatinus – high Hungarian official

Pécs (German, *Fünfkirchen*) – town in southern Hungary

Plzeň (German, *Pilsen*) – town in western Bohemia

Podlasie – province in eastern Poland

Podolia – province in south-eastern Poland

Pomerania (Polish, *Pomorze*; German, *Pommern*) – Baltic province centring on Gdańsk and Szczecin

'*popluzní dvor*' – Czech term for manor

Poznań (German, *Posen*) – town in western Poland

Pozsony – see Bratislava

Prešov (Hungarian, *Eperjes*) – town in Slovakia

Ragusa – see Dubrovnik

Riga – port in Livonia, now capital of the Latvian soviet socialist republic

Rijeka (Italian, *Fiume*) – town in Slovenia (now part of Jugoslavia)

Ruthenia (Polish, *Ruś*) – sub-Carpathian Russia. It is divided into Red Ruthenia, which centres on Lvov, and White Ruthenia, otherwise known as White Russia or Belorussia

'*rycerz*' – Polish term for knight (cf. German *Ritter*)

Samogitia – part of Lithuania

Sarmatia – the Sarmatians were a tribe which, in classical times, inhabited the region now called Poland. In early modern times, much was made of Poland's Sarmatian origins (cf. the cult of the Huns in Hungary, the Goths in Sweden, etc)

Sava – an affluent of the Danube which flows through what is now Jugoslavia

'*Sejm*' – the Polish parliament or 'Diet' (cf. Czech *Snem*)

'*sejmiki*' – local assemblies or 'dietines' in Poland

Selmecbanya – see Banská Štiavnica

Senj (Italian, *Segna*) – town on coast of Dalmatia

Shklov – town in Belorussia

Sibiu (Hungarian, *Nagyszeben*; German, *Hermannstadt*) – town in Transylvania

Silesia (Polish, *Śląsk*; German, *Schlesien*) – province centring on Wrocław, now in Poland; in early modern times, part of the Kingdom of Bohemia

Slovakia – province centring on Bratislava, now part of Czechoslovakia; in early modern times it was ruled by Hungary under the name of Upper Hungary

Split (Italian, *Spalato*) – town on the coast of Dalmatia

'*starosta*' (literally 'elder') – high Polish official

Styria (German, *Steiermark*) – province of Austria, centring on Graz

Szczecin (German, *Stettin*) – town in Pomerania

szekely ('*szeklers*') – Hungarian free peasants in Transylvania

'*szlachta*' – Polish term for nobility (cf. German *Geschlecht*, 'family')

Tisza (German, *Theiss*) – tributary of the Danube, running through Hungary

Toruń (German, *Thorn*) – town in Pomerania

Transylvania – now part of Romania, this region (settled by speakers of Hungarian, Romanian and German) formed a semi-independent principality paying tribute to Istanbul

Trnava (Hungarian, *Nagyszombat*; German, *Tyrnau*) – town in Slovakia

Vilna (Polish, *Wilno*; Lithuanian, *Vilnius*) – capital of Lithuania

voivod (Polish, '*wojewoda*') – high military or civil official

Volhynia (Polish, *Wołyń*) – rural province in eastern Poland

Wallachia – province of Romania, under Turkish rule in early modern times

Wrocław (German, *Breslau*; Czech, *Vratislav*) – the main city in Silesia

Zielona Góra (German, *Grunberg*) – in early modern times a town in Eastern Germany, now in Poland

Index

East-Central Europe(an) is abbreviated to E.-C. Eur. Diacriticals in foreign words are ignored for the purposes of alphabetisation. *passim* is used to indicate scattered references to the subject.

Past and Present Publications

General Editor: T. H. ASTON, *Corpus Christi College, Oxford*

* Also issued as a paperback
† Co-published with the Maison des Sciences de l'Homme, Paris.